5/04

The Living Art of Greek Tragedy

The Living Art of Greek Tragedy

Marianne McDonald

INDIANA
University Press
Bloomington & Indianapolis

This book is a publication of

Indiana University Press
601 North Morton Street
Bloomington, IN 47404-3797 USA

http://iupress.indiana.edu

Telephone orders 800-842-6796
Fax orders 812-855-7931
Orders by e-mail iuporder@indiana.edu

The paper used in this publication meets the minimum
requirements of American National Standard for Information
Sciences—Permanence of Paper for Printed Library Materials,
ANSI Z39.48-1984.

MANUFACTURED IN THE UNITED STATES OF AMERICA

Library of Congress Cataloging-in-Publication Data

McDonald, Marianne.
The living art of Greek tragedy / Marianne McDonald.
p. cm.
Includes bibliographical references and index.
ISBN 0-253-34231-7 (cloth : alk. paper) — ISBN 0-253-21597-8 (pbk. : alk. paper)
1. Greek drama (Tragedy)—History and criticism. 2. Greek drama (Tragedy)—
Presentation, Modern. I. Title.
PA3131 .M38 2003
882'.0109—dc21
2002152285

1 2 3 4 5   08 07 06 05 04 03

To my father,
Eugene Francis McDonald Jr.,
who taught me the value of
learning something new every day.

CONTENTS

P R E F A C E

Ancient Athens in the fifth century B.C. produced the first written dramas in the Western world. Apart from their intrinsic merit as some of the greatest plays ever written, their ideas still shape Western thought until this day. Primal questions are raised about life and death and about what constitutes a life of excellence. These plays are as relevant today as they were in antiquity, when they were considered a necessary part of a good citizen's education. Sadly, they are sometimes presented as museum pieces and can be deadly dull. This introduction will make suggestions about performing Greek tragedy in a way that makes these plays vivid and exciting for contemporary audiences.

In teaching ancient drama to both graduates and undergraduates in a department of theater in California, I have not found any brief introduction that presents a balanced overview, adequately covering both performance and textual analysis. Some writers put too much emphasis on the text itself and neglect performance or consider performance paramount with little regard for the text. Others try to combine both, but often without knowing the original Greek or, at the other extreme, without practical knowledge of theater. Many write about the physical characteristics of the Greek theater without having visited the sites. Others write about the subject without an in-depth experience of theater-going. And there is the pseudo-conflict about fidelity to restaging the original as opposed to creating something new. Some stress the religious aspects and neglect the drama.

There are questions to be addressed about language, translation, acting, movement, and set design. How long should the play be, and how should the choruses be handled? Should there be an intermission? (Personally, I am against them for Greek tragedy.) All these questions and more arise when one wants to bring an ancient Greek tragedy to life with all the danger and immediacy that good theater requires.

What I shall do is offer a short, practical guide that gives suggestions and general information, but not prescriptions. I shall begin with some background for the thirty-two Greek tragedies and the one satyr play which survive. I shall touch on the plot, some of the ideas, and make some suggestions about performance. The translations are my own. I shall also include some information about some of the most significant modern versions and performances in addition to a short bibliography. There is no study yet in English that covers the major versions available.

This small book should serve as a stepping-stone for directors, playwrights, actors, designers, and others in the theater who would like a brief introduction to the world of Greek tragedy and some of the works it has inspired. I give brief plot summaries, which should facilitate choosing a text. In the sections on the original plays, I shall refer to some recent productions and list even more in the sections called "Performance Tradition." I shall select a few for more detailed descriptions. In the sections following Seneca, the versions of the individual plays will be arranged chronologically, following the chronology of the modern versions, and then arranged according to plays. For instance, if Seneca wrote a *Medea* (which he did), I include this as the earliest surviving version after Euripides. The later versions of *Medea* follow. Since Seneca wrote no version of *Alcestis,* in this section *Alcestis* comes after *Medea,* although Euripides wrote *Medea* earlier. Then some more versions of *Alcestis* are arranged together. The arrangement is both chronological and thematic where possible. The translations are my own, unless indicated.

Greek tragedy has something to say to everyone. Greek tragedy raises questions and suggests answers but never insists. What these magnificent plays do is to let us look at our deepest fears and continue to live in spite of them. These fears can come from circumstances that are external to us: the threat of war; the threat of a crippling or fatal disease; and the pain of living with poverty or under an oppressive government. Then there are the internal reasons for fear: that clock ticking inside of us all that tells us that we shall not live forever. The fear of death can be crippling or, if we believe the existentialists, liberating.

Nietzsche used the image of Perseus, the Greek hero who slew the Gorgon Medusa, fierce with her head of snakes. If a person looked at her directly, he would be turned to stone. Perseus was able to slay this monster by looking at her reflection in a shield that the goddess Athena gave him. He saw Medusa's image in the shield and cut off her head. Nietzsche said that Greek tragedy allows us to look at Medusa and not be turned to stone.

We can look at our deepest fears through the reflective filter of Greek tragedy. We identify with the people whom we see suffering. We live their lives as we sit in a theater and watch the action unfold. When the play is over, we feel slightly drained: this is the experience that Aristotle called catharsis. We experience the suffering of others and pity the victims. We know that we could be those victims. When we leave the theater a strange thing happens. Instead of feeling depressed, we feel refreshed and renewed. Our lives have changed, and they have changed for the better.

This is a known effect of great drama, and Greek tragedy is great drama. Its survival for over two thousand years proves this. The language is glorious. Of course, it is best in Greek: learn Greek and you will then have access to the most beautiful poetry ever written. You may ask, what about Shakespeare? What about Dylan Thomas? Seamus Heaney? You are right to ask. Later poetry may equal the poetry of the ancient Greeks, but it is not better. Nor has any drama ever surpassed Greek tragedy.

Modern productions can vary, and there are many approaches by different directors. Some try to return to a primitivism and to include rituals as practiced in various places in the world. Peter Hall's use of mask is said to invoke this primitive tradition. Others use a Freudian approach and emphasize the psychological nuances of the characters. Yet another approach updates the play to make the contemporary allusions obvious (e.g., putting Creon in a Nazi uniform when Anouilh's *Antigone* is staged or setting my translation of Euripides' *Trojan Women* in Vietnam). The original language can be eliminated or reshaped (Stravinsky's opera *Oedipus Rex* is in Latin so that people will not understand it, but will instead concentrate on the ritual and the music).

The comments that I make about setting, staging, or acting are not meant to be prescriptive. Obviously there are many decisions which are up to the individual director. There are many factors that enter the mix and can make the modern staging either exciting or dull. I like a certain naturalism which allows one to understand the text and concentrate on what the ancient author was saying. Stravinsky aimed for the opposite and was very effective in his *Oedipus Rex*. With no attempt at naturalism, Ninagawa's majestic *Medea* is the best staging I have seen so far. What I say about staging and performance should only serve as a platform for further thought.

The Greeks began their theater to educate their citizens. As is well known, the ancient Greeks were the first to question theological explanations of the universe. They enjoyed their myths, but they wanted more than myths to explain the riddles of the world they saw. They wanted to know the reasons for the observable universe.

When the ancient Greeks said, "I know" (*oida*), they used a word which means "I have seen" (based on the Indo-European word *wid*—from which we get *video*). The ancient Greeks looked at the world and at the same time as they told the stories of the gods creating it, the philosophers gave scientific reasons. Democritus developed the first atomic theory. Ptolemy gave us a treatise on astronomy, and Euclid, geometry. Anaximander (sixth century B.C.) drew the first map of the world. Aristarchus of Samos (third century B.C.) claimed that the earth was spheroid and orbited around the sun. This lesson was forgotten until Galileo proved it, risking his life because he challenged the geocentric explanation which most of the theologians accepted. Because this was the time of the Inquisition, challenging theologians could be dangerous to one's health.

I owe special thanks to my painstaking readers, James Diggle, Francis Lovett, Thomas MacCary, and Michael Walton, and for the helpful suggestions from my editor, Michael Lundell, and from Tony Brewer and readers chosen by Indiana University Press. I also want to thank Jimmée Greco for her brilliant and generous editorial work. For the illustrations, special thanks to Tania Kamal-Eldin, Richard Higgins, and Barbara Rubin. Finally, my heartfelt thanks to Athol Fugard for a general education in theatre.

The Living Art of Greek Tragedy

Introduction

Background

We can say that dramatic storytelling in Greece began with Homer who told stories to nobles while they ate and drank. In the *Odyssey,* Demodocus also sings before the public at the games (8.266 ff.). Aristotle says that the particular form that Greek tragedy took was derived from the singing and dancing of the dithyrambic chorus in honor of Dionysus, the god of theater and wine. It developed when the chorus leader separated himself from the rest and created the possibility of a dialogue. The first performance of a tragedy is attributed to Thespis, circa 534 B.C. in Athens.

At first there was no such thing as theater professionals. Every citizen could enter the competition to have plays accepted, and every citizen could be an actor. The playwrights competed and the citizens voted on the winner. The audience also did not hold back its response, so one did not have to wait for the critics to write up their reviews. The prizes were awarded at the festivals. This drama was democracy in action.

There are three major tragic playwrights whose works still exist: Aeschylus (ca. 525–456 B.C.), seven of whose plays survive out of approximately eighty; Sophocles (ca. 496–406 B.C.), with seven plays out of approximately one hundred twenty-three; and Euripides (ca. 480–406 B.C.), with nineteen out of approximately ninety. Elaborating on the theatrical evolution, Aristotle tells us that Aeschylus added a second actor and that Sophocles added a third, creating more possibilities for interchange and conflict.

The Athenians took their theater seriously, and proof of this can be found in the location of their theater. They built it on one side of the highest hill of Athens. On the very top, the acropolis, they built their temples dedicated to the gods, and the greatest one of all was the Parthenon, dedicated to their patron, Athena, for whom the city was named. Below the temples, the Greeks built their theaters. The first was dedicated to Dionysus, the god of theater, inspiration, and wine. At the bottom of the hill, the people carried on their business and politics. The people themselves lived around this pulsing heart of the city. Theatre came just below the gods, and the plays educated a citizen in what it means to be a good citizen. There was always an ethical component, even when belief in the gods had begun to wane.

The Athenians invented theater as we know it, but they gave us more than that: the rudiments of science and philosophy, in addition to the political system called democracy. They overthrew their tyrants and by the fifth century had a workable democracy, although women were deprived of the vote (we should remember that they only got the vote in the United States in 1920 and in France in 1945). Slaves, acquired through wars and purchase, serviced the homes and the general economy. There was a population of about three hundred thousand in Attica (Athens and the area immediately surrounding it). The population was comprised of male citizens, women, children, slaves, and foreign residents. It is likely that only males attended dramatic performances. The theater of Dionysus seated about fifteen thousand to eighteen thousand people and featured a circular playing area called the *orchestra*. It may have had an altar in the center. This theater was outdoors, and one had a sense of a performance as part of the world to a greater degree than if the audience sat in an indoor theater.

The main Athenian dramatic festival was called the Greater Dionysia, in honor of the god of theater, Dionysus. The Greater Dionysia was held in early spring, on the ninth through the thirteenth days of the month *Elaphebolion* (March–April), when the seas were calm and Athenian allies could safely make the sea journey and attend. On the first day there was an elaborate show of tribute from the allies, war orphans were paraded, and prominent citizens were given awards. Going to the theater was a social, civic, and religious event. One purpose of the festival was to impress foreigners.

Three or four days of the Greater Dionysia were devoted to plays. The performances began at dawn and lasted all day. There are several plays whose action begins at dawn or even in the dark.

A secondary festival was the Lenaea. It took place on the twelfth day of the month *Gamelion* (January–February), when there were many storms. It was likely that foreign visitors were not able to attend. Aristophanes comments on this: here one can speak to the locals without showing off for foreigners. More comedies were performed than tragedies. It is said that contests took place from around 440 B.C.

Three playwrights were selected to put on three tragedies and one satyr play, which comically dealt with tragic themes. Aeschylus gave us satyr plays which seem to be related to the preceding trilogy. A comedy by a different playwright followed or was shown on a different day. Aeschylus preferred the connected trilogy (sometimes tetralogy), which allowed the development of a concept, such as the workings of divine justice over several generations. The only connected trilogy that has survived is Aeschylus's *Oresteia*. Sophocles abandoned the practice of writing connected trilogies and instead preferred to highlight one or two major characters in each of his three single plays. Euripides probably did not write connected trilogies either, but instead of emphasizing one heroic character, as Sophocles did, he usually divided his emphasis and created a more socially directed drama.

A prize was given for the best tragic poet and for the best comic poet. The audience was part of the performance and openly expressed its feelings and reactions, which very likely influenced the judging. The *chorēgos* (a person who paid for the costuming and training of the chorus) was also given a prize if his playwright won. The jury was selected from the citizens.

All the actors were male and masked, playing both male and female roles. Masks, with their stylized features, allowed the characters to be better recognized by the audience in the large outdoor playing spaces in which the tragedies were originally performed. The three actors were later called protagonist, deuteragonist, and tritagonist (first, second, and third actor), and the roles were divided between them, the major roles being taken by the protagonist. There were also supernumeraries (extras), or nonspeaking parts, such as attendants and children. At first all the actors were nonprofessional, and the playwright acted too. It is said that Sophocles' weak voice prevented him from acting in his own plays. He probably remained as director. Eventually acting became professional, and prizes were then awarded to actors too.

The chorus probably numbered twelve at first (as in most plays by Aeschy-

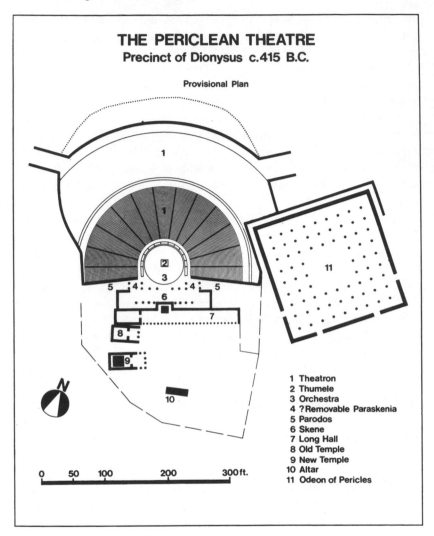

THE PERICLEAN THEATRE
Precinct of Dionysus c.415 B.C.

Provisional Plan

1 Theatron
2 Thumele
3 Orchestra
4 ?Removable Paraskenia
5 Parodos
6 Skene
7 Long Hall
8 Old Temple
9 New Temple
10 Altar
11 Odeon of Pericles

0   50   100   200   300 ft.

The Periclean Theatre. Design by Lee Elliott. Used by permission of Michael Walton, from his *Greek Theatre Practice.*

lus) and later increased to fifteen (Sophocles). They members generally remained present throughout the performance after their first entrance and danced in the *orchestra* as they sang. The music was provided by the *aulos,* a reed instrument (like the oboe), and sometimes drums. Spoken portions of the drama, mainly in iambic trimeter (the rhythm closest to that of ordinary speech), alternated with the choruses, which were always in lyric meters and were usually arranged in strophes and antistrophes ("turns" and "turnings back," possibly referring to their danced accompaniment). Anapests (⌣⌣–;) create a strong marching rhythm in the texts that accompanies the initial entrance and final exit of the chorus.

The spoken part of a play could consist of a monologue, a dialogue between two or three characters, or some exchange with a chorus. Sometimes the dialogue took the form of one-line interchanges. At other times an actor burst out into an impassioned lyric aria. Sometimes there was a formal lament, usually sung by an actor with the chorus.

According to Aristotle, Sophocles introduced scene painting to suggest a visual background. Dead bodies could be displayed on a device called the *ekkyklēma,* which was rolled out from the center doors of the building depicted on the *skēnē* (backdrop, literally tent). This device showed stationary tableaux inside the *skēnē.* A *mēchanē* (machine, or mechanical crane) allowed aerial entrances and exits, usually of the gods. It is doubtful that Aeschylus used any of these devices before the *Oresteia* in 458 B.C.; Sophocles used them sparingly, and Euripides the most freely. They were very popular from the fourth century on. The use of side entrances and exits, *parodoi,* could indicate whether a character was local or from a foreign region, or going to or coming from a particular place.

Brief Textual History

How we come to have less than 10 percent of the plays written by the three great ancient Greek tragedians is a complicated story. The plays were selected for a single performance, but there were possibilities that some were also performed in the demes and abroad. The more popular plays were often revived in the fourth century. During these revivals they were vulnerable to adaptations and additions by actors and producers. Around 330 B.C., the Athenian politician Lycurgus prescribed that copies of the texts of the plays should be deposited in official archives, and that future performances should conform to these texts. These copies were lent to the Egyptian king, Ptolemy Euergetes I, and passed into the library at Alexandria to form the basis of the critical edition made by the librarian, Aristophanes of Byzantium (ca. 257–180 B.C.). He also affixed prefaces, or *hypotheses,* telling about the subject of the play and production details. Many details came from Aristotle's *Didascaliae* and Callimachus's *Pinakes.* For some of the plays of Euripides we have plot summaries which precede the plays in the manuscripts. They were perhaps part of a complete collection of "Tales from Euripides," composed in the Roman period. Byzantine *hypotheses* were much longer, probably for use in schools. The composition of commentaries (*scholia*) on the plays was begun in the Hellenistic period by scholars such as Aristarchus of Samothrace (?217–145 B.C.) and Didymus (?80–10 B.C.). Further *scholia* were added in the Byzantine period.

Although the performance tradition is not well documented for this period, it obviously continued. The plays continued to be widely read, and scholars in Alexandria wrote commentaries on them, parts of which still survive. But by the second to third century A.D., the number of plays that were being read had diminished. The seven plays of Aeschylus and the seven of Sophocles which survive were the only ones which were still commonly read at this time. Of Euripides there were ten such plays, but a further nine of his survive through a lucky accident, preserved in a manuscript which presents them in a quasi-alphabetical order (they evidently formed one part of a collection representing *The Complete Euripides*).

After the Athenian Academy was closed in A.D. 529, classical texts disappeared from sight for several centuries and did not reemerge until the revival of learning in the early Byzantine period. Very few manuscripts of the plays survived into this period. Those that did are now lost again, but before they were lost, they were copied and recopied, often by scribes who did not understand what they were copying. The result is that the manuscripts which we possess (dating from the tenth century onward) are usually very corrupt, and one is often unable to recover the playwright's original words. The plays that were most popular in Byzantine times were Aeschylus's *Persians, Prometheus,* and *Seven against Thebes,* Sophocles' *Ajax, Electra,* and *Oedipus Tyrannus,* and Euripides' *Hecuba, Orestes,* and *Phoenician Women.*

Printed texts of all three playwrights were available from the early sixteenth century on in Europe.

▌ Aeschylus

Aeschylus (ca. 525–456 B.C.) is the father of Greek tragedy. Large issues and the splendor of his choruses characterize his drama. His trilogies show divine justice acting over generations. He utilizes spectacle to advantage, coupling it with equally spectacular poetic words.

Aeschylus lived during the glorious period of the Persian Wars (490–89 B.C. and 480–79 B.C.), when the invading Persians were defeated. He fought at Marathon, as evidenced by his epitaph, which commemorates him as a soldier and not as a playwright. He never had to face the less-glorious Peloponnesian War (431–404 B.C.), which came about as a reaction by Sparta and other former allies against the expansion of the Athenian Empire. It is likely that he came from a distinguished family. He was invited by the ruler Hieron to visit Syracuse in Sicily, and he wrote his *Women of Etna* on the occasion of Hieron's founding of the city of Etna.

His plays had inspirational and educational value. In Aristophanes' *Frogs* (405 B.C.) the god Dionysus brings Aeschylus back from the dead so that the Athenians can enjoy good drama once more, and Aeschylus claims that his *Seven against Thebes* is "full of Ares" and that whomever sees it is anxious to be a warrior (*Frogs*, 1021–22).

Aeschylus is said to have written about eighty-two plays. The seven plays that survive are:

Persians, 472 B.C.
Seven against Thebes, 467 B.C.
Suppliant Women, not earlier than 466 B.C.
Oresteia: Agamemnon, Libation Bearers, Eumenides, 458 B.C.
Prometheus Bound (authorship of this play has been disputed, and there is no agreed date for it).

We are told that Aeschylus won thirteen victories, compared to the approximately twenty-four of Sophocles and four of Euripides during his lifetime and one posthumous. Fragments exist of many of the missing plays. The most substantial fragments come from satyr plays: *Diktuoulkoi* (*Netfishers*) and *Theoroi,* also known as *Isthmiastai* (*Spectators at the Isthmian Games*). There are few extensive fragments from the tragedies. The most we have are from *Myrmidons, Niobe,* and *Prometheus Luomenos* (*Prometheus Released*).

Aeschylus's plays have many exchanges between one actor and the chorus. As much as half of a play can be choral, and his choruses are visually striking. The chorus of Persians appeared in lavish Oriental costumes. The *Erinyes,* or Furies, in *Eumenides,* were so hideous in appearance an ancient biographer claimed that women miscarried upon seeing them and little boys fainted from fright. By the time that the biographer wrote his account (in the fourth century or later), women were attending the theater.

Of the three great tragedians whose work we have, Aeschylus gets the prize for poetry. He combines abstract usage and invented and rare words, coupled with bold metaphors. He is certainly difficult, if not impossible, to translate. He often takes an image and carries it throughout the play or trilogy, as, for instance, in *Oresteia* with the related images of net, hunt, blood, fertility, sacrifice, and war: public pursuits which lead to private disaster. This use of a repeated image in a play or a connected trilogy is not unlike the Wagnerian leitmotiv in opera.

Persians

Most tragic plots and characters come from mythology. In the *Deipnosophistae* (*Sophists at Dinner*) by Athenaeus, Aeschylus is quoted as saying "My tragedies are large slices from the great Homeric feasts" (8.347.e). The first tragedy that we know of that had a plot and characters entirely of the author's own making was *Antheus* by Agathon, toward the end of the fifth century.

Tragedies rarely dealt with historical subjects. Alone of the three great tragedians, Aeschylus deals with a historical subject in *Persians*. *Persians* was written and performed in 472 B.C., eight years after the defeat of the Persians, who had invaded Greece on two occasions (490 B.C. and 480 B.C.), intending to make it part of their empire.

Phrynichus had earlier written *The Capture of Miletus*, and it was said that he was fined because he reminded the Athenians of their recent sufferings. It was produced in 493–92 B.C. and told of an Ionian city seized and destroyed by the Persians in 494. An ancient writer claims that Aeschylus based his *Persians* on Phrynichus's *Phoenician Women*, which showed the defeat of the Persians in the opening scene. It is unlikely to have been as dramatically effective as Aeschylus's play, which built up suspense by revealing the disaster only later.

In his *Persians*, Aeschylus extolled the merits of Athenian democracy by comparing it with the Persian monarchy. When Atossa, the Persian queen, asks who rules the Greeks and who is their master, she is told the Greeks are slaves to no one.

This is a play about overweening pride (*hybris*), which Aristotle describes as "doing and saying things which bring shame to the sufferer" (*Rhetoric* 1378b23–24). This is a common theme in Greek tragedy and generally led to crimes, which Aeschylus, as many other Greeks, felt that the gods punished. In the Greek mind, an abusive tyrant was the embodiment of this type of pride, and Xerxes, the Persian king who attacked Greece, fits this model. He tried to bridge the Hellespont, the crossing from Asia to Greece, by boats chained together. Storms destroyed the bridge, and Xerxes had the sea whipped to punish it. He and his army pillaged shrines, and for these and other acts punishment from the gods followed. This play combines history with an important moral lesson. It nevertheless arouses sympathy for the Persians, because we not only see their suffering from their eyes, but we also see the suffering of Atossa, a mother, for her son, Xerxes.

Aeschylus is delivering useful political and philosophical commentary. One might take this as a warning to the Athenians not to overextend themselves, and not to be eager to acquire an empire, which could be a liability later. It is just after the Persian Wars that the Athenians were beginning this expansion.

Persians also advises against going too far: "Nothing in Excess" was one of the sayings of the sages affixed on a temple at Delphi. Victors can easily become victims, and this play advocates sympathy for the defeated. It is to the credit of the Athenians that they gave a first prize to this play that showed sympathy for a long-standing enemy.

There are effective dramatic moments, such as the first entry of the Persian chorus in their colorful and exotic costumes. We should remember also that they sing and dance. The queen mother enters in a chariot. The ghost of Darius, Xerxes' father, is invoked and rises from the dead in hopes that he can save the city. Xerxes himself finally appears in rags, the embodiment of defeat. The incorporation of ghosts and gods in modern stagings can contribute to the overall drama not only visually, but also through tapping into an age-old desire for additional explanations and recourse behind phenomena. Religion and religious awe, even in the most secular age, still seems based in the human psyche.

The staging would have shown a tomb, possibly in the middle of the orchestra. The location was Sousa, the capital of Persia. One of the left and right entries might indicate the palace and home, and the other, the direction of Greece or the "foreign" land.

Seven against Thebes

This play, like *Persians*, contains long choral passages of lamentation; in both plays the chorus has half the lines. It seems fitting that our very first tragedies to survive from antiquity transformed human suffering into beautiful poetic song. In *Persians* it was an Asiatic foreigner, the "other," who did the weeping, and in this play it is women, also regarded as "other" by the Greek males.

As in *Persians*, there is strong sense of the divine in the play and of the pitilessness of fate. *Seven against Thebes*, following *Laius* and *Oedipus* (which no longer survive), is the third play in a connected trilogy about the family of Oedipus. The satyr play that followed, *Sphinx*, was also connected in theme.

Seven against Thebes illustrates the tragedy that resulted from Oedipus's curse on his sons, Polyneices and Eteocles. According to most mythical accounts, these two sons were to alternate yearly as rulers of Thebes. Eteocles became the ruler of Thebes and refused to give up his rule when his year ended. Polyneices raised an army in Argos and attacked Thebes.

The play opens with Eteocles explaining that the city is about to be attacked. He probably addresses the audience directly. The women of Thebes weep and call on the gods because of the threatening danger. They speak about the terrible things that happen to women who are made prisoners and slaves.

Eteocles forbids the women on pain of death to continue such disheartening lamentation. Instead of a random battle, Eteocles declares that seven defenders should confront seven of the enemy at each of the city's seven gates. There is elaborate poetry describing these heroes, including even the iconography on the shields. The boastful claims on the attackers' shields were sure to attract the anger of the gods. In addition, Polyneices was attacking his own city, something no one should do. As usual in Greek tragedy, things are not simple. Polyneices has a claim on the throne, and Eteocles should have given up the throne to him when it was his turn to rule.

The women warn Eteocles not to fight when he finds out he must face his own brother at the seventh gate. He remembers his father's curse but stubbornly insists on fighting and fulfilling his mission as a defender of his city. He concludes by philosophically claiming that no man can escape what the gods have in store for him. Then a messenger comes to tell us of the disaster. Eteocles and Polyneices killed each other and many others perished, but Thebes is safe. The women now lament the dead. They say of the two "sharp-hearted" brothers that they "divided their property, and each received equal shares" (lines 906–907). The original play probably ended with this dramatic lament, but the manuscripts include further scenes. First Antigone and Ismene lament their brothers' deaths. Then a herald enters to tell them that Creon has forbidden burial of Polyneices. Antigone says she will bury him anyway. The chorus divides and half sides with Antigone and goes to help her bury the body, while the other half obeys the law and goes to bury Eteocles. It is most likely that a later writer added this passage, after seeing or reading Sophocles' *Antigone.*

This is a warning against any civil war, which often is the bloodiest type of all wars, if the American Civil War (1861–65) and the Greek Civil War following World War II offer any indication. Some say both those wars are still going on. The "troubles" in Ireland have gone far beyond the simple colonial model where the occupied fight against the occupier. When brother fights brother no one can ever win. Wars that oppose one family or family members against each other are as bloody as religious wars.

Seven against Thebes takes place right before and around the city. It is possible that there are statues of the gods at the back of the orchestra. We can assume that one entry, possibly audience left, indicates the area of the conflict, from which the messenger would arrive, and the other entry indicates the city center, either the shrines or the palace. When Eteocles addresses the "citizens of Thebes," extras could play these citizens. A polarity is established between male and female, between the men who run the city, make the laws, and declare war, and the women (the chorus) who are subject to those decisions and who suffer from them. The chorus of women enters after just having visited the shrines, probably audience right. These suffering, lamenting women are a key to the drama, which can be taken as a warning to Athens to avoid war and internal strife. One would need particularly good performers (skilled singers and dancers) for the female chorus. Modern productions, unlike the original production, often cast women in these roles. Aeschylus's complex and striking poetry calls for particularly clear delivery.

Suppliant Women

In this play, again, the chorus has a substantial role, singing over half the lines. The daughters of Danaus (said to be fifty) come with their father from Egypt to Argos, trying to escape marriage with their cousins, the fifty sons of Aegyptus. Since the original chorus of Greek tragedy may have consisted of fifty (which I doubt), this used to be regarded as the oldest surviving play by Aeschylus. We now know that it is not. The fifty must have been represented by a lesser number, perhaps the usual number of twelve, which became fifteen in later plays. The dithyrambic chorus usually consisted of fifty, and on one day of the Greater Dionysia they performed.

Pelasgus, the king of Argos, is confronted with a dilemma: either he accepts these suppliants and faces the risk of war with the sons of Aegyptus, or he turns them over to the Egyptians and offends Zeus, the guardian of suppliants. The suppliants claim that they are related to the ancient Argives; they also threaten to commit suicide and thereby pollute the land of Argos. Pelasgus takes the dilemma to his people (an unexpected decision since he is king, and this probably alludes to the democratic climate in which Aeschylus wrote). They vote unanimously in favor of sheltering the suppliants. Backed by an armed force, a herald comes to seize the women and return them to their Egyptian pursuers, but Pelasgus promises to defend them with his army.

The father gives some general precepts to his girls on how to conduct themselves in a foreign land. An Argive chorus, most likely of men (a supplementary escort), urges them to accept marriage, but they violently refuse. They pray to Zeus to preserve their virginity and their freedom. This exchange raises one of the debates between men and women. These young women are adamant that they want to retain their freedom and not be subjected to the further restraints that marriage puts on a young woman. Euripides' Medea later will articulate this loss of freedom in her address to the women of Corinth.

We imagine that the other plays of the trilogy continued the mythological story. The women are forced to marry the Egyptians. All but one follow their father's order to kill their husbands on their wedding night. For this they will be punished in Hades and must carry water in leaky sieves for eternity.

The women's adamant stand against marriage and threats of violence are harbingers of the violent ending of this myth. This play shows a male-female polarity. The women are both attacked and protected by men. This play is also a lesson in a citizen's duty to protect a suppliant. It raises the dilemma which can confront a city: whether to wage a war to defend itself or to be cowardly for the sake of peace. It is obvious that Aeschylus, who himself fought at Marathon and at Salamis, is on the side of an honorable war. He shows this by opposing Pelasgus's democratic defense of freedom and justice against the herald's claim to tyrannical "might makes right."

Pelasgus claims that he has uttered plain words. (Free speech was something that characterized democracy.) He also makes a couple of rather silly claims, not only of the superiority of the gods of Greece over the gods of Egypt, but also of the superiority of men who drink fermented grapes over those who drink fermented grain, namely wine instead of beer, a sophisticated snobbery.

The language is as usual richly poetic and metaphoric. Dust is called the "silent messenger of an army." The women compare the soldiers who manhandle them to nightmarish spiders and serpents.

One can take dramatic advantage of the women threatening to kill themselves with nooses in hand, made out of the belts that held their clothes together. Then again there is more excitement when the herald (backed by the suitors) arrives to drag the women away, literally kicking and screaming. His defeat at the hands of the king who arrives with his men just in time to save the women illustrates how right can occasionally overcome might.

An altar is prominent, and probably once again there are statues of the gods. There would be entrances from the city and from the direction of the Argive coast on which the sons of Aegyptus have landed. The contrast of dark-skinned Egyptians in their exotic costumes with pale Argives in plain Greek clothes adds to the visual excitement in a typically Aeschylean way. Once again Aeschylus shows himself sympathetic to the foreigner, a useful lesson for the Athenians and for any conscientious citizen.

Oresteia: Agamemnon

Oresteia is the only trilogy that survives from antiquity. It is unfortunate that we have lost the satyr play, *Proteus*, which completed the tetralogy. Proteus was the "old man of the sea," a minor sea god and prophet. He was captured by Menelaus on his return from the Trojan War and was forced to answer his questions.

The trilogy form allows the development of a theme, and in *Oresteia* the main one is that the person who commits crime will be punished. Aeschylus charts the transition from personal blood feud and murderous vengeance to a public law court which will impose penalties.

Aeschylus's *Oresteia* shows us about vengeance and its consequences. Clytemnestra murders Agamemnon because he sacrificed their daughter so that he could be successful in the war Greece waged against Troy. He won the war but lost his life on his return. Orestes murders his mother to avenge his father, and he is tried by the first law court. This is a civilized response to murder:

reparations are made instead of killing following killing in an endless cycle. The cycle of vengeance creates a hydra, that ancient monster which grew another head when one was cut off. If a dictator is killed, there will always be someone to replace him. One needs to understand the reasons behind events, not simply assassinate leaders.

This trilogy is named after Orestes, the son of Agamemnon and Clytemnestra, the king and queen of Mycenae, or Argos. *Agamemnon* gives the background for Orestes' murder of his mother, which takes place in the second play of the trilogy. The first play is by far the longest that we have of Aeschylus's surviving plays. As usual, the chorus has about half the lines.

Agamemnon is set in front of the palace in Argos and opens with a watchman, posted by Queen Clytemnestra to look for a beacon which will signal that the Trojan War is over. He sees it and tells her. A chorus of old men relates how the war began and how Agamemnon sacrificed Iphigenia, his daughter, to secure fair winds for his voyage to Troy.

Clytemnestra tells the chorus that the war at Troy has ended, but it doubts her information. A messenger comes on foot confirming this, and then King Agamemnon himself enters on a chariot, bringing Cassandra, his war trophy and captive. What Clytemnestra says is influenced by Cassandra's silent presence. Clytemnestra welcomes him and entices him into walking on a crimson carpet. After he enters the house, she murders him in the bath and boasts about the murder to the chorus as she displays his corpse and Cassandra's next to him. Clytemnestra says she killed him because he murdered their daughter and brought a mistress home, and because she is fulfilling an old curse. Aegisthus, Clytemnestra's paramour in Agamemnon's absence, appears and explains how Agamemnon's father had killed his father's other children and served them up to him at an ungodly banquet. Thyestes (Aegisthus's father) had seduced the wife of Atreus (Agamemnon's father), and this was his vengeance. The old men of the chorus blame both Clytemnestra and Aegisthus, but the latter, with guards at his side, bullies them into silence.

The play and the trilogy show the working out of a curse in generation after generation. Modern parallels might be found in genetically inherited diseases such as hemophilia or alcoholism, which haunt families for generations. The chorus of old men propped on staves, who refer to themselves as "shadows walking in daylight," convey a sense of futility and helplessness in the face of powerful forces: fate, the hatred of Clytemnestra, and the fulfillment of a curse.

In Greek tragedy, man was subject to fate but at the same time was responsible for his actions. A criminal suffers the consequences of his crime. Suffering teaches man to be wise and is called a violent grace, accorded by the gods to man (*Agamemnon*, 176–83):

It was Zeus that ordained that man
must learn through suffering; he drips memory-laden
pain in the heart of a person as he tries to sleep; so
finally even the unwilling learn to be wise. This is the
violent grace of the gods seated far above man on their holy thrones.

Aeschylus urges that man learn from his mistakes. In ancient Greek the word *hamartia* is translated as a mistake; in the New Testament it translates as sin. The ancient Greeks do not have this concept. They felt man could always learn and that there was no such thing as irrevocable as sin, particularly original sin. There can be pollution from crime, but that can be washed away with the proper rituals.

The lesson one learns from one's mistakes and the suffering that follows is an important one. Greek tragedy shows the pain of human beings and lets an audience learn from the suffering that it has seen.

The crimson carpet is a visual dramatic symbol, alluding, among other things, to all the bloodshed at Troy, beginning with the blood that flowed from Agamemnon's own child. This carpet is made up of precious tapestries, which, as Agamemnon admits, are suitable only for the gods. His walking on it is an obvious challenge to the gods, and he will lose.

He is seduced onto the carpet by Clytemnestra, who plays on his vanity. By walking on the carpet, Agamemnon shows his lack of restraint and his contempt for public opinion. Like an animal victim in ancient sacrifices that nods its head when water is sprinkled on it, just before its throat is cut, Agamemnon, when he walks on the carpet, symbolically consents to his own slaughter. This carpet has offered directors an opportunity for showing this important symbolism.

Cassandra's mad scene before she enters the palace is a *coup de théâtre*. It is only topped by Clytemnestra's mad exultation after killing her husband and his concubine. The sexual imagery of her speech builds up to the climax of her saying that she was refreshed by his blood pouring over her as the crops in spring are refreshed by the rain. The denouement when Aegisthus appears and Clytemnestra calms him is seen to be merely the lull before the next storm. Agamemnon may have committed the first crime, but Clytemnestra has committed the next. It calls for vengeance.

Libation Bearers

In this second play in the Oresteian trilogy Orestes has a genuine dilemma, and no solution is good: kill his mother and satisfy the command of Apollo but violate the laws of man and be hounded by his mother's Furies, or not kill her and suffer from not avenging his father as commanded by Apollo. Orestes opts for following Apollo.

This play is the tautest dramatically of the three and is an exciting adventure story: we are in suspense for fear Agamemnon's children will be apprehended, and at the same time we are eager to see how they will achieve their vengeance. The chorus (of young Trojan female servants) again has the most lines, and it takes an active role in the drama. It is unlike the chorus of old men in the first play who do nothing to help Agamemnon when he cries for help.

The play opens with Orestes praying to Hermes, the guide to the underworld, to help him avenge his father. The chorus enters with a grieving Electra. Clytemnestra has had a nightmare about a snake biting her breast and blood flowing from the wound. She sends the chorus to offer libations (hence the title) to propitiate the dead. Orestes interrupts their prayers and reveals himself to Electra. His tokens of proof are a lock of hair similar to her own, a matching footprint, and a piece of cloth that she wove for him when they were young. They continue their prayers and are urged on by the chorus. Orestes and Pylades, his friend, go to the palace, pretending they are strangers from Daulis, and tell Clytemnestra that Orestes is dead. Clytemnestra is dismayed to hear of her son's death but graciously provides lodging for the strangers. Orestes' nurse, Cilissa, mourns his death. The down-to-earth realism of her descriptions of how she had to wash his wet diapers is comic. She is to summon Aegisthus, and the chorus convinces her to tell him to come alone, without his guards. Aegisthus is slain by Orestes, who then confronts his mother. Clytemnestra asks vainly for a "man-killing" ax, and then appeals to Orestes by baring a breast, a reminder that she bore and nursed him: he owes her his life. He has to be urged by Pylades to kill his mother and fulfill the commandment of Apollo to avenge his father. Orestes stabs his mother and the chorus and Electra rejoice, but he sees the avenging Furies of his mother approaching. He is the only one to see them. The chorus prays for an end to the suffering.

The set is the same as in the first play. We are in front of the palace. The tomb of Agamemnon will be in the orchestra. Many images from the first play are repeated, particularly the "net" (a type of bathrobe?) in which Agamemnon is killed. Orestes displays this "net" at the end to justify his brutal act. The choral entry of foreign women carrying offerings provides a vivid spectacle to the audience. They turn a lament into a prayer for vengeance.

The two travelers are welcomed by Clytemnestra, who speaks of warm baths inside, and one remembers that Agamemnon was killed in a bath. The dramatic irony is comparable to Clytemnestra's first welcoming speech to Agamemnon, but now her son is in charge and conceals his intended purpose.

The audience has been won over to him in a way that builds sympathy for him. Clytemnestra's impassioned appeal to Orestes as she bares her breast, followed by Orestes's taking her off to be killed, are moments of high dramatic tension. Clytemnestra dies silently, in contrast to Agamemnon crying out. There is acute psychological commentary and there are parallels between the first play and this one. The staging should make it clear that Orestes is angered by Clytemnestra's concern for Aegisthus's body and her mourning over it. Orestes is jealous and angry when he sees his mother's concern for another man, particularly the man who killed his father. The analogies to Hamlet are obvious.

The deadly cycle is made visible, particularly by parallel scenes, like the revelation of two bodies in both the first and second play. Orestes' mad scene at the end of the play is comparable to Cassandra's in *Agamemnon* as a harbinger of doom.

Eumenides

The final play of this trilogy ties up loose ends. Somehow the chorus of Furies must be appeased and an end brought to this cycle of vengeance. These women are strikingly horrible in their appearance, monsters with snakes for hair. They have the most lines and are the only divine chorus in Greek tragedy, except for the daughters of Oceanus in *Prometheus Bound* (in that play all but Io are divine). The transformation of the Furies into Eumenides, or "kindly ones," constitutes one main action of this play. Naming the third play *Eumenides* expresses the wish that this transformation will take place when the Furies accept the honors offered them at the end.

The first scene takes place in Delphi. A priestess enters the temple of Apollo (the central door of the *skēnē*) only to run out again in terror because she has seen the sleeping Furies and Orestes clasping Apollo's *omphalos* (sacred navel stone) to hold them at bay. The Furies are asleep, but the audience hears them loudly snoring, sometimes yelping like hunting dogs hot on a chase. Apollo leads Orestes out of the temple and tells him to go to Athens and appeal to Athena. The ghost of Clytemnestra enters and wakes the Furies up, telling them to pursue their victim. The Furies enter the stage from the temple. Apollo tells them to leave his sacred space. The scene shifts to Athens, first to Athena's temple on the Acropolis and then to the court on the Areopagus hill. Such a striking change of location within a play is unparalleled in surviving tragedies.

The Furies surround Orestes, dancing and singing a "binding song," a song of black enchantment and curse. Athena enters and she volunteers to be the judge of a trial. She leaves to bring back jurors, citizens of Athens.

The case is argued. Orestes pleads that Apollo ordered him to kill his mother. Apollo acts as the defense attorney and argues that a wife cannot be allowed to kill her husband, and that a mother is actually not the parent of a child, because she is simply the soil in which the father's seed is planted. So only patricide is a true blood killing, and matricide is not. The jury votes, and the votes are equal. Athena takes Apollo's side, claiming she is "for the male" since she was born with no mother out of Zeus's head. She admits her bias in the decision, saying that she is on the side of Orestes' father, the murdered husband. The Furies are naturally enraged, and it takes Athena a long time to win them over with an offer of a shrine, gifts, and worship. They reluctantly accept and take the title of Eumenides. Women and girls from the city join them, and all leave in a torchlit procession. The cycle of blood feuding has ended and justice is now sought in a court of law.

This is a wonderful parable for a democratic city. It closely echoes events which had only recently taken place in Athens. This trilogy was performed three years after democratic reforms took powers away from the conservative institution called the Areopagus and transformed it into simply a court of law dealing with homicides.

The solution, as presented in *Eumenides*, however, is not as neat as it seems. Although quite a few modern critics are satisfied with the "happy ending," I think reflective people and Aeschylus himself had more doubts. Some of the best modern productions reflect this doubt.

Orestes' flight from the shrine of Apollo in Delphi and arrival at the temple of Athena in Athens, in addition to the frightful chorus, are powerful theatrical images. The change of scene may occur in the imagination or by some sort of scene painting that might show the different locations. We have a chase scene and a trial. The trial may seem rigged, since the judge is biased, but it still holds our interest. Once again, as is typical of Aeschylus, the dramatic devices are exciting and the poetry is powerful.

This play teaches us not only that learning comes from suffering, but also that civilized alternatives to violence exist. Getting man to put these alternatives into practice is an ongoing problem for the human race. Athena's vote for civilization rings true and clear, but man is always ready to introduce his own cacophony.

Prometheus Bound

Although it appears with his other plays in the manuscripts, scholars have questioned whether *Prometheus Bound* is by Aeschylus. It is possibly by his son. This is the only Aeschylean play that has more lines for the main character (over half) than the chorus. This play may very possibly be the first in which the *mēchanē*, or "flying crane," appears. The authorship may be in question but not, I think, the brilliance of the play. It has been the favorite of many: Johann Wolfgang von Goethe, Karl Marx, Lord Byron, Percy Bysshe Shelley, and that Romantic of all Romantics, Victor Hugo.

Aeschylus shows us god confronting god in his *Prometheus Bound*. Prometheus the titan brought fire to man: this fire represents creativity and imagination. Prometheus taught man to build houses and ships and the arts of religion, healing, and letters. We are told that all arts that we associate with civilization come from Prometheus. For this gift, and for tricking Zeus, who would have readily destroyed man, Prometheus is punished. He is the first freedom fighter, and he is accused of loving man too much. We see Zeus as the first tyrant.

This is a play that indicts the tyrant, the king of the gods who abuses Prometheus, the humanitarian. Prometheus not only saved mankind from destruction by his gift of fire, but he also brought it all the arts and sciences, from medicine to navigation to soothsaying, even poetry and letters. Zeus punishes him for his defiant act and, even worse, for boasting about it. An eagle constantly feeds on his liver, and at the end of the play he will be thrown into an abyss. He refuses to act subserviently to Zeus or to reveal the details of a prophecy about the fall of Zeus. He is the rebel par excellence. No wonder he has been a model for revolutionaries!

The play opens with a scene of violent torture. Prometheus is nailed to a rock. The daughters of Oceanus, who are his cousins, come to visit him. They sympathize but keep their distance and advise him to make peace with Zeus. He is the physician who taught medicine to man, but he cannot heal himself. Oceanus enters and pompously tells Prometheus to do what Zeus wants and to secure his freedom through compromise. Io, another victim of Zeus, enters and is told her fate by Prometheus, who can see the future. She was raped by Zeus and is forced to wander the world in the form of a cow and to be stung by a gadfly sent by Zeus's wife, Hera. The gadfly is like the eagle that will torture Prometheus. The difference is that Io has no choice, except perhaps to kill herself. Prometheus gives her hope by telling her that her suffering will end when she finally reaches Egypt. There she will be welcomed; she will resume her original shape and bear Zeus's son Epaphus (great-grandfather of Danaus). Besides this, another descendant of hers (Heracles) will eventually free Prometheus from his torment. The hope that Prometheus gives Io is what he earlier gave men out of sympathy for them.

Hermes, Zeus's messenger, comes on the scene to threaten Prometheus with more torture if he will not reveal to Zeus what he wants to know. This wins the chorus members over to Prometheus's side, and they choose to share his fate at the end. They also opt to be heroic in their loyalty to their friend. Prometheus will not compromise, but as he is hurled to the depths, he calls on his mother and the sky to see what undeserved suffering he has to bear.

The parallels with Christ are obvious, from the suffering of the innocent to the pains of having hands and feet nailed. Even Prometheus's final words have a curious resemblance to Christ's complaint to his father when he is nailed to the cross. Both gave their lives for mankind. Prometheus advocates love, whereas Zeus prefers power. Prometheus is filled with love for man and is willing to suffer for it. He ends up being crucified for his defiance of those in authority.

Prometheus and Io are comparable to victims who suffer from slow, progressive, painful diseases. A director might choose to show the relationship to AIDS or other diseases in his or her particular production. Many remarks show psychological acuity: there is reference to a "talking cure," which characterizes talking as relief of pain.

The location is somewhere in the Caucasus Mountains, or Scythia. Prometheus is usually represented as a large figure who is nailed to a cliff and remains there. The fact that the actor is silent for so long is also dramatic and is typical of Aeschylus. In Aristophanes' *Frogs,* Aeschylus is lampooned for his use of an actor who is silent for long periods. Prometheus's silence at the beginning while he is obviously in excruciating pain builds up sympathy for him and antipathy toward the tyrant who ordered this. Significantly, Zeus never appears in the play but just sends lackeys to carry his messages. It is a pity we do not have the whole trilogy. It is possible that Zeus learned through his own suffering and that some compromise was affected, so that the final play may have resembled *Eumenides* in the *Oresteia.*

Other characters come and go: the daughters who make up the chorus and their father, Oceanus, on something called a "hippocamp." He may be flown in by means of the mechanical crane. Io is said to be in the form of a cow. The staging varies from production to production, sometimes simply by horns on the actress's (or actor's) head. Io is all motion, in contrast to Prometheus's stillness. Everyone except Io may have had flying entrances, since they are divine. Such an entrance for a chorus of fifteen might look ridiculous, if it were even possible, although it has been suggested.

A static Prometheus is a strong symbol for the rebel who will not give up his cause. The cataclysmic end could be done many ways, either imagined in the mind, danced by the chorus in some symbolic way, or actually staged as in many productions of Mozart's *Don Giovanni,* where Giovanni is literally plunged into flames at the end. The Greeks probably relied on the imagination. Words are sometimes the most powerful mise-en-scène. The two stage entrances probably signify messengers from Zeus on one side and sympathetic visitors on the other.

Performance Tradition

This is a very selective list to give some idea of the way Greek tragedy has influenced drama over the centuries. The separate translations, adaptations, and performances will be listed chronologically up to the twentieth century. Then the individual plays will be grouped and listed chronologically in that subcategory.

When Aeschylus died a state decree was issued allowing his plays to be revived at the tragic festivals in competition with living playwrights. Aristophanes' *Frogs* shows us that Aeschylus was still held in high repute after his death, since he is shown as victorious over Euripides. Throughout the centuries, Euripides gradually became more popular.

Oresteia

In Rome during the first century A.D., Seneca's plays based on Aeschylus (*Thyestes* and *Agamemnon*) were bloodier versions than the originals. Senecan drama heavily influenced Renaissance tragedy, including Shakespeare, and has proved influential since then, up to and including the visions of Antonin Artaud. It is not clear that Seneca's plays were actually performed in antiquity. Their lengthy descriptions and philosophical ramblings do not show the tautness of drama that we find in the ancient Greek tragedians. The violence shown onstage also was contrary to the ancient dramatic conventions and might have been difficult to enact. T. S. Eliot, in "Seneca in Elizabethan Translation," claimed that Seneca's plays were written "for declamation before an imperial highbrow audience of crude sensibility but considerable sophistication in the ingenuities of language." Eliot considered Seneca the ideal playwright for radio drama.

Thyestes was probably written during the time of Nero. Seneca, born in Spain in 4 B.C., was Nero's tutor but lost favor when less-demanding advisors were available.

Thyestes begins with Tantalus, the Ur-criminal-ancestor of the house of

Atreus, urged on by a Fury to inspire his descendants to surpass his own crimes. This play is an expansion of the story about the adultery of Atreus's wife with his brother Thyestes, and how Atreus took a brutal vengeance on his brother (all this is alluded to by Cassandra, the chorus, Clytemnestra, and Aegisthus in Aeschylus's *Agamemnon*). This may have seemed relevant in contemporary Rome: Nero very possibly murdered his own stepbrother, Britannicus, and even his own mother.

Seneca's plays show his Stoic leanings. In them, life is fundamentally chaotic and unpredictable, and even the gods cannot surpass man's inhumanity to man. Seneca has his choruses say again and again that they would rather have a life of obscurity, in hopes that fate will overlook them so that they can live in peace. They speak of the perfect ruler being free from fear. They themselves would like to share the inner peace that only man can create for himself. Atreus on the other hand prefers power: he compares himself to a god when his vengeance is complete: "No god remains, but only myself" (*The Tragedies* 1.76). What the king wants and what his chorus wants is very different. This was parallel to the difference between what Nero wanted and what Seneca wanted and has been repeated throughout history. Plato suffered a similar disappointment in Sicily when he wanted to train a "philosopher-king" who adamantly wanted to remain a king, not a philosopher.

In this play, Atreus serves Thyestes his own sons in a human stew at a banquet and then, with rhetorical flourishes, reveals to Thyestes that his sons were "within"—not within the house, but within his own stomach. Many plays, including Shakespeare's *Titus Andronicus*, show the influence of this play. The descriptive details of the murder of the children—their being sliced up for cooking and then consumed by their father—remind one of the worst moments in any film about Hannibal Lector.

Seneca's *Agamemnon* differs from Aeschylus's in its many descriptions of violence and threats of torture. The prologue is delivered by the ghost of Thyestes. Scenes from other plays are intermingled with Aeschylus's *Agamemnon* to pack in as much dramatic clout as possible. A nurse wanders in from *Hippolytus* or *Medea* to admonish Clytemnestra on her proper duties as a wife. Hecuba visits from *Trojan Women*. Electra helps her brother Orestes escape. Strophius, Pylades' father, has his own lines.

The choruses now are made up of women, in contrast to the old men who comprised the chorus in Aeschylus's *Agamemnon*. There are two choruses, local women and prisoners from Troy. The first advocates Stoic acceptance of what fate brings. The latter describes in detail the taking of Troy and the massacre that followed. This expands on Euripides' similar description in *Trojan Women*. The messenger also describes the horrendous storm and wreckage of ships that followed the taking of Troy when the Greeks tried to sail home. The accounts of human misery reach Senecan heights. This is a universe which naturally would look to a Stoic solution. One can see how these plays were used by Seneca as parables for Stoic lessons.

Aegisthus has a larger role and must convince Clytemnestra, who is having second thoughts, that her only way to stay alive is by killing Agamemnon. He claims someone is bound to tell Agamemnon about their affair. Then he delivers the first blows when Agamemnon is entangled in the net-like robe offered him by Clytemnestra.

Tantalus is described as horrified at the crimes that have surpassed his own. Clytemnestra knows about Cassandra and Agamemnon's excesses before he returns. The spy system is as advanced in ancient Greece as in Nero's Rome.

Electra smuggles Orestes out after the murder but is threatened with being thrown into a dungeon unless she reveals where he is. This is a good precedent for the brutal treatment of Electra in Strauss and Hofmannsthal's opera. Seneca's play also abounds with maxims which suited the rhetorical taste of the time. When Agamemnon says, "This is not Troy," Cassandra quips, "Wherever there is a Helen, there is a Troy" (1.199). Strophius, who protects Orestes, says: "good fortune invites friendship, while ill luck demands it" (1.204). When Electra asks, "What can be worse than death?" Aegisthus answers, "Life, when you wish to die" (1.207).

Aeschylus's plays can be used for political commentary. In 1993, the American director Peter Sellars performed Aeschylus's *Persians*, in a translation by Robert Auletta, in Salzburg as a protest against America's bombing of Iraq. The production featured the impressive music of Hamza El Din, with its Middle Eastern instruments and dancing. Sellars said that he used microphones as types of masks, "offering both a hiding place and instant public exposure" (p. 6). Each of the seats was wired so that each person had access to what sounded like an intimate, yet artificial, voice.

Sellars tried to end on a note of celebration and quoted in his introduction to the play Darius's words, "Try in the midst of devastation to give joy to your souls, for wealth, and pride, and anger, are useless to the dead" (p. 7).

Oresteia had special appeal in the twentieth century. Max Reinhardt directed a monumental performance in 1911 in Germany. It was revived at the Grosses Schauspielhaus in 1919 in which he replicated, in part, the ancient Greek theater. It certainly was large and in a semi-circular shape; however, his roofed theater could not duplicate the acoustics of the theater at Epidauros. Nevertheless, *Oresteia* was a good choice: a monumental play for a monumental theater. Reinhardt wanted to revive interest in the Greeks and their values just after the World War I. This first production was Hofmannsthal's *Electra* in 1903, but he was more success with his *Lysistrata* (1908) and his *König Ödipus* (1910), his two earlier ventures into Greek drama, in addition to his even earlier *Ödipus und die Sphinx* (1906). His *Oresteia* suffered from a lot of cutting. Nevertheless it made good use of repeated key words and was couched in a language accessible to moderns.

In 1926 Terence Gray directed an *Oresteia* at Cambridge influenced by Gordon Craig, with minimal and suggestive sets. He used a single large wheel placed against the back wall to signify Agamemnon's chariot.

Eugene O'Neill's *Mourning Becomes Electra* (1931) linked Aeschylus with Freud and presented a new emphasis on guilty sexual relationships. The three sections, *Homecoming, The Hunted,* and *The Haunted,* replicate Aeschylus's *Agamemnon, Libation Bearers,* and *Eumenides.*

Ezra Mannon (Agamemnon) returns from the civil war. His wife, Christine (Clytemnestra), has never loved him. There is no reason given for Christine's hostility against her husband, neither a murdered child (Iphigenia) nor an imported mistress (Cassandra).

She takes a young lover, Adam Brant (Aegisthus), the child of a slave woman who had been the mistress of both Ezra's father and his brother. The father cheated his brother out of his inheritance, and the brother began to drink and finally committed suicide. When Adam's mother was sick and impoverished and needed help she appealed to Ezra. He refused it and she died. Adam never forgave Ezra for this, and he swore vengeance.

Lavinia (Vinnie), the Electra stand-in, wears black and rejects her suitors, even before Christine kills her father. The reason seems to be a pathological attachment to her father and jealousy of her mother. She follows her mother to New York to prove that she is having an affair with Adam. She confronts her mother. Christine's revelation of the affair to Ezra precipitates his final heart attack, after which she administers poison pills that Brant was able to get for her.

Lavinia finds the pills she correctly assumes her mother used to kill her father. She convinces Orin, the son who also has just returned from the war, to spy on their mother, and they find her meeting Adam on his ship in Boston. Orin shoots Adam, making it look like a robbery. His words over Adam's body reveal he is as attached to his mother as Electra to her father:

> If I had been he I would have done what he did! I
> Would have loved her as he loved her—and killed
> Father too—for her sake! (p. 366)

When Christine learns of Adam's death, she shoots herself.

The audience sees that Lavinia wants to replace her mother. She dresses like her mother and, like her father, gives orders to Orin. Even though they go on a South Sea cruise, nothing cheers up Orin. He is haunted by ghosts and guilt and is quite reminiscent of O'Neill, who blamed himself for his mother's death-in-life affliction of morphine abuse.

Orin writes an account of the Mannon crimes but turns it over to Vinnie after he exacts a promise from her never to marry. She had been intending to marry Peter, her childhood suitor. One can see Orin's attachment to his sister: "He [Orin] touches her hair caressingly. She pulls violently away" (p. 411). Lavinia rejects his advances and also his suggestion that they confess to the murder of Brant. She rages at him, "I hate you! I wish you were dead! . . . You'd kill yourself if you weren't a coward" (p. 412). He then follows his mother in suicide, shooting himself with his father's pistol.

Lavinia decides to live alone in the mansion haunted by the ghosts of people whose lives that she has either directly or indirectly destroyed. This is her expiation of the family curse. One feels their heavy fate is a result of genetics rather than a divine source: as Orin says, "I find artificial light more appropriate for my work—man's light not God's—man's feeble striving to understand himself, to exist for himself in the darkness! It's a symbol of his life—a lamp burning out in a room of waiting shadows" (p. 397). This is a combination of Nietzsche and Freud. Jealousy and envy are at the root of the action in this play, in addition to a self-reliance devoid of God. This differs from Aeschylus's grim tale of crime and divine retribution, followed by a resolution that allows for hope. This is *Crime and Punishment,* with most of the guilt internalized and drawn out to eternity. One can imagine the restless ghosts. O'Neill's poetic language and haunted insights into a dysfunctional family create another type of masterpiece and are a rehearsal for his even more poignantly autobiographical *Long Day's Journey into Night. Mourning Becomes Electra* was performed as an opera composed by Marvin David Levy in 1967.

The 1936 production in Germany by Lothal Müthal of *Oresteia* was notoriously pro-Nazi, with its emphasis on centralized authority. In its favoring of Agamemnon, the play propagandized Hitler as a good leader for the people. The way that this was done was through making Agamemnon's (Hitler's) arguments seem reasonable and his appearance heroic. Clytemnestra on the other hand was overly made-up and showed the signs of a decadent life at home. Cacoyannis also did the same thing to Clytemnestra in his *Electra.* Costuming and makeup can enlist audience sympathy or hostility.

In the same year there was possibly the first translation of the *Agamemnon* by an Irish writer, Louis MacNeice. His *Agamemnon* was performed in England at the Westminster Theatre in 1936 with music by Benjamin Britten. Aeschylus and MacNeice have in common a lack of sympathy for Helen and Clytemnestra, unfaithful and murderous women, but this antipathy leads to felicitous poetry: the poetry of hatred can sometimes be more splendid than the poetry of love. Clytemnestra lies to the returning Agamemnon, "I know no pleasure with another man, no scandal, / more than I know how to dye metal red" (pp. 83–84). This is one of the best translations I have found, for both its accessibility and poetic sweep. We all know how Clytemnestra will dye a sword red.

MacNeice's primary reason for translating *Agamemnon* was respect for the brilliant poetry: he could read the original Greek. In this play, MacNeice speaks often of god as if he was the Christian God, and speaks of "The grace of God" (p. 32) or "asperging" something (p. 50), or of Helen as a lion cub "sent by God as a priest of ruin" (p. 38), or "To give the glory to God" (p. 251).

MacNeice wrote of his own concerns about class as he grew up. We find allusions to Cassandra as "a fortune-teller, a poor starved beggar-woman" (p. 56), and to Orestes as an "exile, and tramp and outlaw" (p. 56).

The language is poetic and engaging, although now somewhat dated. MacNeice speaks of the "money-changer War" that sends dust and ashes back for men (p. 27). The later poet captures the allusiveness of Aeschylus as the chorus expresses its awe toward the justice of God: "There is something cowled in the night / That I anxiously await to hear" (p. 28).

T. S. Eliot's *The Family Reunion* (1939) translates *Eumenides* into Christian terms. It is a story of Harry (Orestes) returning home to fulfill his mother Amy's dreams of his taking over the house, Wishwood. Harry made a marriage that took him away from home, and he may have pushed his wife off of a cruise ship, but the death was listed as an accident. His mother wished the death of this wife. She is rather like Apollo as we discover in her confrontation with Agatha (Athena) at the end of the play. Harry sees Furies, but gradually they become inspirational and are turned into Eumenides. Harry leaves in search of a type of spiritual expiation. This decision is followed by his mother's death. The final ritual is conducted with prayers and incantations as the women (Mary and Agatha, like the Eumenides) chant and walk clockwise around a table:

> This way the pilgrimage
> Of expiation
> Round and round the circle
> Completing the charm
> So the knot be unknotted
> The cross be uncrossed
> The crooked be made straight
> And the curse be ended
> By intercession
> By pilgrimage

By those who depart
In several directions
For their own redemption
And that of the departed –
    May they rest in peace. (p. 293)

This Orestes symbolically kills his mother and isolates himself from female contact. It is as if killing one's mother is the original sin for the human
race that may be expiated by certain human beings dedicated to a spiritual
quest. Harry must escape all maternal influence and seek his own spiritual destiny through a life of sacrifice and searching. This is a philosophical and religious rewriting of *Oresteia* as a myth for any son who tries to escape the
influence of an overwhelming mother. This liberation is as essential as the
Oedipal one signified by the symbolic murder of the father. Harry's liberation
is also beyond the dross of human life, or as he says on p. 281, "I must follow
the bright angels" (transformed Furies?). This is a modern Freudian and Christian myth, mingled with an ancient tragedy. A production was well staged by
Peter Brook in 1956 at the Phoenix Theatre in London. Both Eliot and Seneca
suffer from an intellectual approach to drama. The staging needs a creative
director to give life to this text that poetically rambles at times. Some judicious
cuts do not hurt the production. Eliot's mastery of language, however, justifies
the effort of staging this play. It is more contemplative than dramatic, as one
might expect from this poet.

Jean-Paul Sartre's *Les Mouches* (*The Flies,* 1943) has Orestes defy God
while discovering existential truths. *Les Mouches* was written during the Nazi
occupation of France, but like in Anouilh's *Antigone,* the occupiers did not
realize that they were the subject of a dramatic critique. Zeus controls the city
of Argos through fear, and the flies are his Furies. Aegisthus has ruled for
fifteen years. The city has been plagued by flies, and the people, by their own
sense of remorse because of Aegisthus's crime of slaying Agamemnon with
Clytemnestra's help. Zeus encourages fear, because that is the source of his
power. Orestes returns to Argos and Zeus tries to dissuade Orestes from stay-
ing, but after he has seen his sister living in drudgery, he decides to fulfill the
vengeance his sister prays for. He is immune to Zeus's threats because he has
discovered that he is free. After he kills Aegisthus and Clytemnestra, he assumes responsibility for his actions and refuses to repent; in existential terms
he exhibits no bad conscience. His is the existential nightmare and glory of
the soul that realizes it is free and human. Orestes leaves the city and takes with
him the flies that have plagued it. (He is comparable to Seneca's Oedipus who
leaves with the city's plagues and miseries in tow.) This Orestes compares
himself to the Pied Piper. It is now up to the inhabitants to assume freedom

and its consequences for themselves. This is an existentialism that could have been dangerous for the Nazis if the Parisian citizens had acted on its precepts.

In 1955 Jean-Louis Barrault staged an *Oresteia* which used voodoo rites that he had seen in Rio. It returned the drama to the religious and ritualistic; drums and music enhanced this effect. It also signified a return to "primitive rawness" which was associated with Greek tragedy in addition to an early attempt at the multicultural vision that Mnouchkine and Suzuki will realize even more fully.

In 1966 Tyrone Guthrie's *Oresteia: The House of Atreus* tapped into the tradition of the monumental through its use of elaborate masks. He established a festival to revive ancient Greek tragedy at least every ten years at his theater in Minneapolis, Minnesota, and occasionally at Stratford, Ontario. His *Oresteia* was revived in the nineties.

Jean Anouilh's *Tu étais si gentil quand tu étais petit* (*You Were So Nice When You Were Little*, 1972) is the story of Orestes, modeled on Aeschylus's *Choephoroi*, with a resentful Electra who, because she suffered as a child, wants to make others suffer.[1] Orestes tells Electra at the end:

What had to be done now is done. You must leave me now, and leave off your hate also. You stuffed me with hate, that old man and you, so now I am repulsed by it, and it makes me vomit. I am free now, and everything's fine. . . . I have some good advice for that old patriot, who, stinking of fries, and red wine, courts the mob's acclaim in the street in the midst of his tricolors, . . . he better keep clear of me. Actually he disgusts me more than Aegisthus. I am faster than he is and I can teach him what I've learned from him with a knife. I haven't forgotten his hitting me. Goodbye little hate-filled [*haineuse*] sister, grow up if you can. Our childhood is over. (pp. 143–44)

Each night Aegisthus and Clytemnestra are sentenced to replay their drama. At the end, the two old actors start to leave, and Clytemnestra removes her crown. Aegisthus sees Electra and they stop. Aegisthus asks, "What is she doing there? It's over." She answers, "No, it's not over. Everything will begin all over again. I am waiting for Orestes" (pp. 156–57). For Anouilh, life is a drama and drama is life. He said, "Theater is life as it really is" (in Lewis Falb, *Jean Anouilh*, p. 130).

In *Tu étais si gentil quand tu étais petit*, a band, comparable to the one Anouilh's mother played in when he was young, functions as a chorus that gives commentary. Anouilh claimed, "La vie, c'est un bastringue! Et la tragédie

---

1. Many of his works have classical references, and here we might include his adaptation *Les Dégourdis de la onzième*, a comic film that features a soldier played by Fernandel. The colonel of a camp puts on a play that his sister wrote called *Roman Orgy*, and an inspector shows up to find his soldiers dressed up like Roman virgins.

grecque, pareille!" ("Life is a dance band, and so is Greek tragedy"; *Pièces Secrètes*, p. 42). The pianist talks the other musicians out of punishing Orestes. These Furies are Eumenides.

The confrontation between Aegisthus and Orestes is like that between Creon and Antigone. Aegisthus understands how Orestes is vindictive because of what he has heard and does not blame him. In this play everyone has understandable reasons for what they do. (There is another *Hamlet* scene where the young Orestes finds his mother in Aegisthus's arms. One remembers how Aeschylus's Orestes was furious when he saw his mother upset at seeing Aegisthus's corpse, rather than focusing on the wrongs he himself, her son, had suffered.) The pianist argues for tolerance, and so does Anouilh.

Steven Berkoff's *Agamemnon* (1976) is "freely adapted" from the original. Berkoff's text of *Agamemnon* in the Amber Lane Press edition appears along with *The Fall of the House of Usher,* which he was working on at the same time. This is a poetic treatment, often with rhymes and half-rhymes, such as "house" with "murderess." There is an emphasis on violence and sex, with an explicit description of grotesque and shocking moments. The play begins with a long inner monologue on the way Thyestes felt when he had eaten his own children. He knew what he was eating, but he concealed his feelings so that he would not give satisfaction to his host, his brother, Atreus. There is a curse on the house of Atreus, just as there was one on the house of Usher. Both texts are manuals for dysfunctional families. Berkoff also brings in modern psychological observations, as in this chorus:

> Sea is the colour of paradise
> Sea is the colour of Helen's eyes
> The sea's depths are the deep unconscious
> That drag over our stone and wear us down to sand. (p. 15)

He reduces choruses or rewrites them, and includes scenes from mythology, such as moments from the *Iliad* with graphic battle descriptions or an erotic tableau of Helen and Paris with explicit commentary from the chorus, as he conflates lovemaking with war:

> The Trojan boy who
> kidnapped her will be paid with thrust for thrust/
> Exchange cold steel for rape hard flesh/ steel
> does not wilt/ insatiate weapon/. . . . (p. 14)

The language is modern. Clytemnestra describes Agamemnon's final moment:

> Then for luck I shoved the third and final thrust
> deep in his guts/ then he retched forth his life/ in
> one swift jet/ its fountain soaked me in its

drizzle like spring rain from heaven/ I do not blush
to tell/ he then went down stiff and down he
    FELL! (pp. 31–32)

If this version is well acted, with the miming, musical, and alienation techniques that characterize Berkoff's work, this can be an exciting anti-war meditation. That is probably different from what Aeschylus intended, but modern playwrights often use ancient Greek tragedy as an alphabet or grammar for their new sentences. That is the case here and it is benefits from being performed along with Poe to express hatred within a family. Both plays have a dreamlike quality. Personal and public hatred are shown to be living nightmares which haunt generation after generation. And no hatred is stronger than that between people who have once loved each other.

In 1977 Andrei Serban staged *Agamemnon,* with music and libretto by Elizabeth Swados. It was in oratorio form and featured a masked chorus and three main characters. The Vivian Beaumont theater in New York was made into a theater-in-the round. Agamemnon came out from a wire cage which used to be the pit. Papp performed this version in the park during the summer.

Peter Stein staged a notable *Oresteia* in Berlin in 1980, revised in 1994 with a Russian cast. He followed in the footsteps of Reinhardt but brought new insights. Like Reinhardt, he made the language easily understood. In *Agamemnon,* he directed the old men in the chorus to speak in a conversational way; he did not use the formal choral declamation which is the ruin of so many productions. He used the theater space of the Schaubühne Am Halleschen Ufer in interesting ways, so that it hardly resembled a conventional theater. Actors could enter from the back of the hall from behind the audience, as did Agamemnon, and the chorus often addressed the audience in the middle aisle, which became a stage area. The chorus was part of the people, separate from the isolated palace at the end. The palace that was approached by stairs was often closed. Through this visual imagery, the people (the chorus and audience) are separated from the elite who are in the palace.

His 1980 production was also spectacular in its lighting effects, which seemed to come from German Expressionism, particularly in film: Friedrich Wilhelm Murnau's *Nosferatu* or Robert Wiene's *The Cabinet of Dr. Caligari.* Darkness prevailed, which increased the gloom and terror. The music and strange human noises produced by the cast meaningfully punctuated the drama.

At the end, the chorus members voted halfheartedly for acquittal and then wrapped themselves in the same purple cloths that had covered the corpses earlier in the play, and also which constituted the purple rug that Agamemnon walked on to his destruction inside the palace. This symbolically showed the price of peace and reconciliation.

In Stein's Russian version, at the end of *Eumenides,* the chorus members were wrapped in cloths that made them resemble mummies and were stored on shelves in what seemed to be a museum. After the actors leave the stage at the end, the mummies begin to stir. We see a hand, then a foot, then a head. We know from this production that the Eumenides had indeed become once again the Furies. Germany certainly had a vivid experience of blood and vengeance. I find Stein's a much more intelligent reading of this ancient text than optimistic ones.

Tony Harrison's translation of *Oresteia* in Peter Hall's masked production was performed in London in 1981 and in Epidauros in 1982. Hall wanted to stress the primitive, ritualizing quality of the ancient drama. Harrison respects the original dramatic poetry of Aeschylus. His own translation seems at times to sink into a Beowulfian heaviness and explicitness. Nevertheless his language is musical, filled with alliteration and the repetition of sound and meters which echo the heartbeat. His translation contains words which drop heavy loads on the lines, compound words including lots of dooms, grudges, and blood: "doom-drum"; "doom-ague"; "doomgroom" (for Paris); "mangrudge"; "grudge-demon"; "bloodgrudge"; "bloodkin"; "blood-guzzling grudge-hound"; "bloodclan"; "bloodslicks"; "bloodflow"; "blood-bride" (Helen); and many others.

Aeschylus also made up words and invented his own compounds, for example, "plotting like a man" to describe Clytemnestra's heart. Harrison repeats phrases such as "Batter, batter the doom drum, but believe there'll be better!" capturing Aeschylus's alliteration (p. 183). Harrison translates Aeschylus's image of the sea blossoming with corpses into a sea "mushroomed with corpses and shipwreck" (p. 206). There are multiculturally derived words and slang:

> Such prostrations, such purples suit pashas from Persia.
> Don't come the Khan's courtiers, kowtow or cosset.
> Don't grovel, suck up, salaam, and stop gawping!
> Such gaudy displays goad gods into godgrudge. (p. 212)

His constant rhymes and hypnotic language can distract from the dramatic action. He also omits lines, such as those in the first chorus which talk of Zeus teaching man through suffering, the violent grace of the gods.

Harrison is more sexually explicit than Aeschylus. His Clytemnestra describes Agamemnon:

> Look at him, Shaggermemnon, shameless, shaft-happy,
> ogler and grinder of Troy's golden girlhood.
> Look at her, spearprize, prophetess, princess,
> whore of his wartent, his bash back on shipboard. (p. 225)

Peter Hall, the director, strangled the last life out of this vital text in his production. He gave masks to actors who were not sufficiently trained to use them, and the performance seemed to indicate insufficient rehearsal time. Hall insisted on the text being delivered according to the beats of the music. That may have been his idea of the "primitive." It was pure luck if anyone in the audience was able to decipher any meaning from the choruses. It was interesting, however, to see a cast which is entirely male, as in the original ancient Greek production. In the first performance Tony Harrison wanted to segregate the audience, with men on one side and women on the other, but the Royal National Theatre would not allow it.

Tadashi Suzuki took his *Clytemnestra* to Delphi, Greece, after it was performed in Toga, Japan, in 1983. *Clytemnestra* combined Aeschylus's *Oresteia*, Sophocles' *Electra*, and Euripides' *Electra* and *Orestes*. Suzuki's *Electra* was performed in Delphi in 1995. These plays show the potentially deadly power of the mother, in addition to the general breakdown of the family in modern Japan and the conflict of matriarchy with patriarchy. He reduces and rearranges texts drastically.

Clytemnestra deals more with the war of the sexes. It shows us a woman in a patriarchal society who fights back. Clytemnestra, after her son has killed her, returns as a ghost and kills him as he is locked in an incestuous embrace with his sister Electra. The latter incest is not an invention by Suzuki, because the implications may be seen in Euripides' *Orestes* (lines 1041–51). Clytemnestra is like a ghost from Noh: she is demonic in her jealous desire to have her honor reinstated. She will kill the living to achieve that.

This is also a meditation on sexuality and violence. Dressed in underwear with her legs spread apart, Electra castrates the "corpse" of Aigisthus. Orestes uses the same knife to kill his mother, embracing her and finally straddling her as he strikes her repeatedly. Electra tries to kill herself with the same knife, which Orestes snatches from her and then clasps her in his arms as he spits out his words in an orgasmic scream while embracing her.

This Clytemnestra is also symbolic of the Japanese mother who wields great power over the child but who as a wife is almost powerless. As in ancient Greece, she is confined to the home for much of her life, so her main freedom is in raising her child. It is through her child that she gains her freedom and her vengeance.

In the trial scene (from *Eumenides*), the gods Apollo and Athena (two men, with obvious facial hair) are dressed in traditional ancient Japanese feudal costumes. The Furies (also men) are dressed in black; Orestes and Electra are in informal modern dress.

Tyndareus, husband of Leda and Clytemnestra's mortal father, is dressed in nineteenth-century Meiji costume. He hits Orestes with an umbrella. Orestes

Clytemnestra. Adapted by
Tadashi Suzuki. Clytemnestra
(Shiraishi Kayoto) returns as a
ghost to kill her murderers
Orestes (Tom Hewitt) and
Electra (Takahashi Hiroko) as
they embrace. Photo: Miyauchi
Katsu. Used by permission.

throws the knife with which he kills his mother into a Marlboro wastebasket.
Modern Japanese music is combined with music from Noh. The past mingles
with the present, East with West.

In France in 1990–92 Ariane Mnouchkine mounted a multicultural production of *Les Atrides* (*Iphigénie à Aulis* by Euripides, translated by Jean Bollack and Mayotte Bollack, and *L' Orestie* by Aeschylus: *Agamemnon, Les Choé-
phores,* both translated by Ariane Mnouchkine, *Les Euménides,* translated by
Hélène Cixous). This production came to BAM (Brooklyn Academy of Music)
in 1992. She incorporated elements from Kathakali, Brazilian, Kabuki, and
Noh traditions. Mnouchkine's Théâtre du Soleil is no stranger to cultural di-
versity. She takes Greek tragedy and translates it into French, using actors and
actresses from various cultures—the European countries, the Middle East,
South America, and India. The varying accents add to the cultural blur. The
music, by Jean-Jacques Lemêtre, is itself a composite of Asiatic and European
traditions. It is played on two hundred and forty instruments from forty-one

different countries, with fifty-seven created by Lemêtre himself. The makeup derives from the Indian tradition, primarily Kathakali. Dances come from the various cultures: for example, the actress Nityanandan performs a dance from India and Da Cunha dances in the Spanish tradition.

Mnouchkine increases her mélange by prefacing the trilogy by Aeschylus, *L'Orestie,* with a play by Euripides, *Iphigénie à Aulis.* In this way, Mnouchkine couples her critique of violence with a feminist slant: she wins more sympathy for Clytemnestra by including Euripides, as the latter is more sympathetic to abused females. Seeing the sacrifice of Iphigenia, the audience understands why Clytemnestra would want to kill Agamemnon. Mnouchkine also cast the same actress in the roles of Iphigenia and Cassandra, both victims of Agamemnon. Her Clytemnestra strokes Cassandra's hair in a way that communicates to the audience that she is remembering her daughter Iphigenia.

Mnouchkine makes the Erinyes—the Furies—into barking baboons. Each of the plays ends with barking, and the end of *Eumenides* shows us the pack roaming at large, barely constrained by its leaders. After the three chorus leaders have sold out to Athena and have agreed to become the Eumenides, the pack that is left advances on the audience. This is as ominous an ending to *Oresteia* as the one presented by Stein with his mummies coming back to life, a visible rendition of the return of the repressed. This can also be translated into colonial terms and can signify the revolution of the oppressed.

The audience is involved in many ways. It is as if it is the jury in the trial of the final play. Everyone is implicated. As Hélène Cixous says in the program:

> Ta douleur me fait mal; tu me fais mal,
> comme je te fais mal—nous sommes des atomes
> d'un seul corps—ce qui arrive en Argos
> nous arrive à Paris.

> Your pain is mine; you hurt me
> as I hurt you—we are atoms
> of one body—what happens in Argos
> happens to us in Paris.

Both Mnouchkine and Suzuki are examples of directors who make Greek tragedy come alive in a way that speaks to moderns. They not only address modern political issues, but they also set the dramas in multicultural contexts.

Greek tragedy is best translated by a poet and best directed by someone who still respects words in this visually oriented age. Ted Hughes, the English poet laureate, turned to Greek tragedy in the last years of his life and translated *Oresteia.* This translation was successfully performed at the Cottesloe, Royal

National Theatre in London, to celebrate the millennium from 1999–2000. It was directed by Katie Mitchell, with a small company of actors.

Clytemnestra faulted Agamemnon's decision to sacrifice his daughter to obtain winds for sailing to Troy; this was one of her excuses for murdering him. Mitchell seems to be on Clytemnestra's side by keeping Iphigenia onstage throughout the first play as a gagged ghost. This ghost follows the other players on the stage, so the past is always present. At the end of the play, the ghost of Agamemnon appears as Iphigenia exits, a new ghost to haunt the living.

The actress who played Clytemnestra is feminine and charming but is also a beaming Maggie Thatcher. One feels the steel in her smile. Agamemnon is presented as a crude military type but as a plausible battle commander. The old men of the chorus are war veterans in wheelchairs.

Agamemnon returns in a "chariot," a cart that carried him and Cassandra, Troy's princess. The red carpet with which Clytemnestra welcomed Agamemnon home turned out to be made up of dresses for little girls. Agamemnon hesitates, not wanting to incur the jealousy of the gods, but finally concedes and walks on the dresses into the palace and to his own death, struck down by his wife in his bath. Clytemnestra appears before the chorus and exults in her crime: "Then the blood belched from him with a strange barking sound. / A foaming jet that showered the walls / And showered me, like a warm spring rain / That makes the new-sown corn swell with joy / And the buds split into blossom. / I felt my whole body exult" (p. 64).

At the end of the play, the chorus calls Aegisthus, Clytemnestra's paramour, a woman because he did not murder Agamemnon himself. He very sensibly answers that if he had tried to, he would have been recognized by Agamemnon. The chorus leader makes noises like a chicken as Aegisthus exits. Aegisthus turns around and shoots him with a revolver.

Through her use of the ghost of Iphigenia, Mitchell wins audience sympathy for a mother who has lost her child. This is more a Euripidean reading than Aeschylean; Mnouchkine as we saw also made use of Euripides for commentary on Aeschylus. Aeschylus wants us mainly to feel horror at the act of a wife murdering her husband. Euripides blames Agamemnon more than Aeschylus does, particularly for the death of Iphigenia.

There were many technological effects. Mitchell begins with guns shooting and bombs falling. This continues throughout the trilogy. Electra fiercely incites Orestes to kill his mother, and the ghost of Agamemnon is present, also egging him on. It is a parable of revenge, commemorating modern wars.

With only a small group of actors available, the Eumenides had to play other roles, including the jurors in an ingeniously staged scene. The threat the Furies posed was frightening enough, but there is a buzzing of flies at one point to recall Sartre's conceit in *Les Mouches* (The Flies). In my opinion, Mitchell strangely missed the opportunity to continue the theme of ghostly intervention by allowing Clytemnestra, Aeschylus's "real" ghost, to disappear from the action. As a result the conclusion offered simple reconciliation presided over by a black Athena, with none of the possible future threat that some critics and other directors have hinted at.

The production was presented in by far the smallest of the three theaters at the National. The staging was in traverse with the audience on two sides. At the end of the play, after the chorus had filed through, a huge door at the back of the stage area, which clanged open and shut throughout the performance, shut with a ringing finality. It was a play of ghosts and vengeance, followed by the optimistic ending often favored by the English.

The production was invested throughout with powerful images from past and present that allowed Hughes's striking if not always literal text to be given its full weight. All in all this was a far more impressive representation of Aeschylus's themes and apparent intention than the other production of *Oresteia* in 1981 by Peter Hall at the Olivier, Royal National Theatre.

Charles L. Mee Jr. has written a version of *Agamemnon* by Aeschylus (available on the Internet). It was produced by the Actors' Gang in Los Angeles in 1994 and was directed by Brian Kulick. He describes this play as follows:

Composed the way Max Ernst made his Fatagaga pieces at the end of World War I, some of the texts were inspired by or taken from the work of Hesiod, Herodotus, Thucydides, Homer, Aeschylus, Artemidorus, *The Book of Revelations*, Philip Vellacott, Slavenka Drakulic, Zlatko Dizdarevic, Zbigneiw Herbert, Pierre Klossowski, Georges Bataille, Sei Shonagon, and Hannah Arendt. (http://www.panix.com/~meejr/html/agamemnon.html; all of Mee's quotes are taken from this site)

It begins with a discussion between Herodotus, Thucydides, Homer, and Hesiod. They all have physical defects. Clytemnestra enters and reminisces on the war:

How can one person bring himself to kill another?
To take another human life.
Snuff it out.
This precious thing.
Destroy it.
Forever.
I don't understand it.

A messenger arrives from Troy and recognizes the old men as fellow veterans. Thucydides generalizes:

The Oresteia. Adapted by Ted Hughes. Directed by Katie Mitchell. A veiled Electra (Lilo Baur) rages for vengeance. She is as trapped in her past as her father was caught in the net/robe that enabled Clytemnestra to kill him. Royal National Theatre (1999). Photo: Neil Libbert. Used by permission.

The body is nothing
but a product of semen and of blood
which then becomes a meal for death
a dwelling place for suffering
a tavern for disease.
A man may know all this
and yet
from lack of judgment
drowning in a sea of ignorance,
he yearns for love, for women, and for power.

As is typical of a Mee play, the grotesque is emphasized with clinical precision:

The color of the dead:
faces changed from white to yellow-grey,
to red,

to purple,
to green,
to black,
to slick.

Or Agamemnon makes the following observations:

A human being can be thought of as a tree trunk on fire
You can lay them down screaming
on their stomachs or their backs—
or you can spare the fire
and lay them out on the beach
nothing more than breathless lacerations
shapeless silhouettes
half eaten
getting up or moaning on the ground
then you might say
the head—
the eyes, the ears, the brain
are the complications of the buccal orifice
the penis, the testicles
the female organs that correspond to these
are the complications of the anal orifice.
Thus one has the familiar violent thrusts
that come from the interior of the body
indifferently ejected
from one end of the body or the other
discharged,
wherever they meet the weakest resistance
as in war.

Agamemnon continues his commentary on humanity:

One group of soldiers
had caught a female ape
from the menagerie
tied up with ropes
struggling to break free
but trussed up like a chicken
legs folded back against her body
tied upside down to a stake
planted in the middle of a pit
howling and swallowing dirt
its anus screaming pink and pointing at the sky

like a flower
and all the men around the pit
stripped naked for the work and sweating with pleasure
and anticipation
armed with shovels
filling in the pit with dirt
burying the ape alive
its screams choked on the dirt
until all that remains
is the radiant flower of its anus
touched by gentle white fingers
its violent contractions
helpless as it strangles on the dirt
and all who stand around the pit and watch
are overcome by heat and stupor
their throats choked by sighs
and crying out
eyes moist with tears.

More brutalities and rapes follow, with much bodily mutilation. Agamemnon greets Clytemnestra, and a bruised Cassandra tells the chorus about more atrocities, the mutilation of infants.

She is killed with Agamemnon, and their corpses are displayed proudly by Clytemnestra. Aegisthus appears to share the gloating and revenge for his family wrongs. He graphically describes his lovemaking with Clytemnestra.

Hesiod concludes with a paean to human memory and human hearts:

This is the riddle of time:
the human capacity to achieve remembrance
is the capacity to transform time
into eternity.

Nothing human is forever;
everything perishes;
except the human heart
that has the capacity to remember
and the capacity to say:
never again
or
forever.

And so it is
that our own hearts
and nothing else

are the final arbiters
of what it is
to be human.

Mee shows us the horror of the human condition, without the grandeur that we found in Greek tragedy. Perhaps this is an apt reflection of modern times. It reflects the violence of American society with its daily shootings, to say nothing of the occasional war. This play is anti-war and yet luxuriates in the violent images of war.

This play resembles Sarah Kane's dramatizations of cruelty for its own sake. It is very like films that pander to an audience's taste for violence to increase their sales. Part of the glory of Greek tragedy was that it was very aware of the existence of evil in man and the violent side of human nature, but the violence itself was usually not depicted onstage, and the words themselves never delivered the grotesque monologues that savor violence. Something is destroyed here, something obscene is added, and these works offer entertainment comparable to the killings enacted to amuse the populace in Rome.

Charles Mee's latest play is *Big Love,* a version of Aeschylus's *Suppliant Women.* This was first performed in 2000 at the twenty-fourth annual Humana Festival of New American Plays and was revived in 2001 at BAM, directed by Les Waters. It is really the lost second play of the trilogy and describes the women marrying their cousins and killing them, except for one, Lydia. She is celebrated for following love. No one is punished: "for life to go on there will be no justice." Mendelssohn's "Wedding March" from *Midsummer Night's Dream* plays as Lydia and Nikos kiss. Lydia throws her bouquet to the audience and fireworks conclude the play. As Mee says, "Forty-nine of the brides murder their husbands and one falls in love, which is pretty good odds." I suppose this looks at modern attitudes toward love and marriage, but it owes very little to the Aeschylean predecessor. There is no idea of civic responsibility, the protection of suppliants, or a moral dilemma. It is also more comic than tragic.

Prometheus has inspired many adaptations, particularly in the eighteenth and nineteenth centuries, with movements arising to protest absolutism. Goethe was attracted by the theme of Prometheus as the Ur-hero, for which Goethe wrote a two-act dramatic fragment in verse in 1773. In this work, Zeus is called Prometheus's father, and yet Prometheus is not a god and boasts about his mortality, which he considers immortality since he has no memory of his beginning nor anticipation of his end. He is offered the rule of earth, but he would still answer to Zeus. He refuses. Another bribe offered was that the statues that he has created of men and women would be brought to life. Again, Prometheus refuses. Minerva becomes his ally. She rebels against her father and helps Prometheus find the source of life on his own. Men will also rebel. Zeus does not destroy them because he hopes they will be his worshippers.

The play ends with Prometheus teaching men the arts of building and healing, after they struggled over property. Pandora discovers love (for her companion Mira), which Prometheus calls death, but a temporary death, with a revival of desire. He describes it in terms similar to what Sappho describes in her poetic fragment (no. 31) in which the main character feels a flame running through the body, and then feels faint. Finally one clasps a world though heightened feeling. Both Goethe and Shelley see love as a major creative force, but Goethe links it with death and in this way prefigures existentialism. Goethe shows no punishment of Prometheus, only his rebellion and his glory in his imperfect creation, man. Both Goethe and Shelley opt for happy endings and their versions are not dramatic in a conventional way that endorses lively plot and dialogue; one might even say the same about Aeschylus's *Prometheus,* which is more of a poetic meditation than his other plays.

By 1820, Percy Bysshe Shelley had created a sequel to Aeschylus's play *Prometheus Bound;* he called it *Prometheus Unbound,* after the lost play by Aeschylus. It is very different from the received myth and shows Goethe's influence (both feature women finding love with their own sex). In this version Love is the triumphant force in the universe. Prometheus never tells Jupiter (Zeus) the prophecy: if he marries Thetis he will bear a son stronger than he is. Jupiter does marry her, and his son, Demogorgon, drags him off to the abyss. Prometheus is rejoined with his wife Asia (a stand-in for Aphrodite); man renounces evil and we have a new golden age of freedom:

> To love, and bear; to hope till Hope creates
> From its own wreck the thing it contemplates;
> Neither to change, nor falter, nor repent;
> This, like thy glory, Titan, is to be
> Good, great and joyous, beautiful and free;
> This is alone Life, Joy, Empire, and Victory. (p. 206)

.   Shelley considered this his favorite work; it contains his philosophical dreams. It luxuriates in vivid poetic language that describes the beautiful and the ugly, the unholy and the blessed, the vile and the good. Asia-Aphrodite's shell is described:

> See the pale azure fading into silver
> Lining it with a soft yet glowing light.
> Looks it not like lulled music sleeping there? (p. 192)

Equality among men is praised:

Sceptreless, free, uncircumscribed, but man
Equal, unclassed, tribeless, and nationless,
Exempt from awe, worship, degree, the king
Over himself. (p. 197)

Prometheus is the defiant Titan who wins freedom for man. One feels the drama of his struggle and admires his decision to wait out the years and to endure the worst of tortures so that finally he and man can be free and justice can triumph. This is a poetic adventure story well worth staging. Only the tragic end of *Prometheus Bound* is missing. But even that play had its sequel, and while the outcome might not have been identical, it was possibly a step forward in reconciling might, freedom, and justice. Who knows if the lost trilogy itself might have had a "happy" ending.

In 1927 Eva Palmer-Sikelianos revived performances of Greek tragedy at Delphi and began with *Prometheus Bound*. She trained the dancers in the chorus, and they executed Greek dances before the chained figure of Prometheus. She also designed the costumes and had them woven on looms. Her sister-in-law Isadora Duncan contributed to her approach to dance, although she differed with Duncan on the use of the chorus as an inspired ideal of group harmony as opposed to the isolated actor. The contribution of the body was considered as important as the ideas of the mind.

Palmer-Sikelianos had her chorus members show their profiles to the audience to replicate Greek vases and to show their involvement in ritual. People who saw this production (which used masks for the actors, not the chorus) commented on the compassion communicated by the emotive expressions of the chorus, which I can corroborate from the film I have seen of this production. The actors played on a raised stage above the chorus members, who danced in the circular space of the ancient theater. Eva's husband said this was a not a return to Greek tragedy but a resurrection. It was an attempt to convey the original emotions to moderns in a form of an art that used singing, dancing, dialogue, and spectacle. This put into practice much of what Nietzsche tried to articulate in *The Birth of Tragedy out of the Spirit of Music*. Aeschylus was Nietzsche's preferred playwright.

Prometheus's hands were spread to suggest a crucifixion, merging the ancient myth with Christian ritual. This merging is also done by Stravinsky in his *Oedipus Rex* (performed the next year, 1928) and in *Gospel at Colonus* (1982), which both use Oedipus instead of Prometheus as the Christ figure. It was a celebration of the human spirit through Greek art. Eva, an American heiress, and her Greek poet-husband, Anghelos Sikelianos, wanted to make Delphi a cultural center of the world, and it has continued in that tradition through revivals of Greek tragedy at international conferences held since 1981.

Festivals continue at Greek theaters in Athens, Epidauros, Syracuse, and Cyprus today following this vision.

In 1959 Rudolf Wagner-Régeny composed an oratorio with scenes called *Prometheus* in five scenes, which included not only an Aeschylus play in a libretto by the composer but also a recitation of Goethe's *Prometheus*. Carl Orff composed a *Prometheus* in 1967, which included ancient Greek. Orff tried to show not only the struggle between the gods, but also man against the gods and his fate in his trilogy that included *Antigonae* and *Oedipus der Tyrann*. These works are starkly rhythmical and use chanting and declamation. The music enhances the ritualistic quality, and its simplicity is meant to evoke antiquity.

Heinrich Miller had a performance of his French translation of Prométhée (written in 1977) in Paris in 1982. He simplified but remained close to the original. It is a faithful translation but lacks the poetry of the original Aeschylus.

Tom Paulin's *Seize the Fire* (1989) was also based on Aeschylus's *Prometheus Bound* and expressed the concerns by the Irish in the North about the British occupation. His play is a paean to liberty. Prometheus was purported to be the creator of man and stole fire for man after Zeus took it away to punish this audacious race. Prometheus is the freedom fighter who opposes tyranny; Zeus is the overweening tyrant. Paulin transforms Zeus into an imperialist, the capitalist who will use men as tools for his own self-aggrandizement. He is also the England that devours Ireland for its own pleasure. Prometheus stands for all who oppose such barbaric acts. "Seizing the fire" is a metaphor for regaining one's country, by the use of arms if necessary. It is a metaphor for gaining freedom not only from the tyranny of occupation, but also from the tyranny of dogma and of course—faithful to Marx—class. Prometheus calls himself one who loves man too much. Paulin communicates the difference between Zeus the tyrant and Prometheus the democrat: "Zeus said Exterminate! / I said Miscegenate!" (make love not war? p. 17). Power breeds hatred, or as Aeschylus has his Prometheus say, "There is a disease in tyranny that makes one distrust all one's friends" (lines 224–25). Paulin turns this into the biting line: "Power, it clamps like a frost on those that get it" (p. 19).

It is ironic that Prometheus is the healer who cannot heal himself, as Aeschylus's chorus points out. Paulin transforms this by having Prometheus say he cannot free himself, although he brought freedom to man. This shows us the new emphasis, with the disease of slavery as a legacy of imperialism.

Zeus tries to bribe Prometheus, sending Hermes with awards for Prometheus if he should reveal the secret only he knows: a threat to Zeus is about to be born. Other gods carry out his dirty work. Paulin's Hermes tries to bribe Prometheus with a medal, a post, and a title, "First Intellectual of the State."

The chorus chimes in, "The state's approval, / recognition— / that's what they'll give you!" Prometheus answers, "Just a contradiction! / They'd let me free / but freeze my mind" (pp. 55–57). Hermes offers more bribes: a chateau and a place for writing, with the leisure time to go along with it (most writers' dream). When bribes do not work, Hermes adds the threat of torture (but what can be worse than having one's liver consumed each day?). But hors d'oeuvres are not sufficient when a counterrevolutionary feast is possible. Hermes asks Prometheus to sign, like Michael Collins, "It's there you'll sign / two public texts— / a recantation / and a treaty" (pp. 54–55).

Paulin's *Prometheus* takes images from modern Ireland to make his points. Oceanus tells Prometheus, "I'll see you're freed." Prometheus answers, "More likely you'll get kneecapped" (p. 2). The tyrant Zeus excelled in a prison system, "a killing zone, / a meatgrinder" (p. 11). Paulin's Prometheus adds, "Had I not stole the fire / every last human body would be stacked up dead here" (p. 11).

Prometheus goes on to describe a revolution that will force Zeus to come to him: "Tanks on the lawn, new blackouts, / locked doors and panic— / those empty sinister blocked roads" (pp. 14–15), and immediately the North of Ireland comes to mind.

Io attacks Zeus in terms that evoke militant feminism:

> For I'm the cow girl, Io,
> who's watched,
> watched the while time
> by an audience of men's eyes.
> and this,
> (*Cupping hands*)
> this is the thing pokes out their flies
> —the flying prick
> that comes humming after me—
> oh, how it wants to sting sting sting me! (p. 35)

Her attack is so fierce that this can reduce audience sympathy for this victim. Nevertheless one is left admiring Prometheus's integrity and one hopes that Ireland remains as steadfast to its ideals.

There also have been several films made on plays by Aeschylus, such as *Prometheus in Chains* (Greece, 1927) by Costas Gaziadis and Demetrios Gaziadis; *Prometheus, Second Person Singular* (Greece, 1975) by Costas Ferris; *Prometheus* (England, 1998) by Tony Harrison; *Les Perses* (France, 1961) by Jean Prat; and *Notes for an African Oresteia* (Italy, 1970) by Pier Paolo Pasolini.

2 Sophocles

Sophocles was born at Colonus near Athens in about 496 B.C. and died in 406 B.C. He was spared the sight of Athens's final defeat at the hands of Sparta in 404 B.C.

Sophocles was a model citizen. He acted as *hellenotamias* (treasurer, 443–42 B.C.) in the league Athens organized after the Peace of Callias with Persia. After the battle of Salamis, he was said to have led a chorus, playing his lyre, and to have danced around the trophy. He also served as a general dealing with the Samian revolt in 441. Some say that *Antigone* earned him this position. Others suggest that Sophocles' disgust at the exposure of the enemies' corpses might have led him to write this play. These are speculations by ancient biographers, and sometimes modern scholars follow them. After the Sicilian defeat in 413 B.C. he was one of the *probouloi* (special Athenian officials) elected to deal with the political aftermath of the disaster.

Sophocles followed in Aeschylus's footsteps by serving his city when he could, in either a political or a cultural function. He lived to about ninety, and it is said that he was sued by a son, who claimed he was no longer capable of managing his own affairs. His defense was to read lines from the recently written *Oedipus at Colonus,* and he was acquitted. The story of a lawsuit is probably spurious, since there is other testimony that Sophocles got on well with both of his sons. Phrynichus (the comic poet) wrote that "Sophocles lived to a ripe old age, and he was happy and clever. After writing many excellent tragedies, he died well without suffering any serious misfortune" (quoted by Lloyd-Jones, *Sophoclis fabulae,* p. 15). Perhaps a fragment from one of Sophocles' plays may reveal his own outlook: "It is fairest to live justly, and most profitable to live healthily, but the sweetest is to have a bit of love each day" (quoted by Aristotle, *Nicomachean Ethics* 1, 9:1099a25).

The ancients regarded Sophocles as a man at ease with himself and contented with life. In Plato's *Republic* (329 B.C.), Sophocles is reported to have claimed that he was happy that he was finally free from that wild taskmaster, love. After his death he was said to have become a sacred hero like Oedipus and was worshipped as *Dexion,* roughly translatable as "he who receives," because of his association with the cult of Asclepius, which he had helped to introduce into Athens after the plague. He also was a priest of the healing spirit Halon.

Sophocles is the playwright of heroism. His Antigone is the first female character in drama to be a hero in the full sense of the word. She is the first conscientious objector. The play is often performed as veiled criticism of an abusive government to show that something is rotten in that particular state.

Even at his or her best, it is difficult to feel empathy toward a Sophoclean hero, who is both alienated and alienating, but one has to admire the single-minded pursuit of goals which so often entail self-destruction along with the destruction of others. As Bernard Knox says, "Sophocles creates a tragic universe in which man's heroic action, free and responsible, brings him sometimes through suffering to victory but more often to a fall which is both defeat and victory at once; the suffering and glory are fused in an indissoluble unity" (*The Heroic Tragedy,* p. 6).

Sophocles shows his characters struggling to right the wrongs they perceive in the world about them, and there is some objective justification for their struggles. What Sophoclean heroes do, they also do in isolation. Antigone goes to her death alone, as does Ajax. They die for ideals, which, although somewhat misguided in their one-sidedness, can still be respected. Sophocles celebrates the hero; Euripides (as we shall see later) laments the victim.

Sophocles is said never to have been placed third when he competed. He first competed in 468 B.C., when he defeated Aeschylus, and is said to have been awarded the prize twenty-four times (eighteen at the Greater Dionysia) in contrast to Aeschylus's thirteen and Euripides' four. Later writers claimed that he wrote about one hundred twenty-three plays.

Of the plays that survive, only *Philoctetes* and *Oedipus at Colonus* can be dated with certainty, and *Antigone* approximately, if we believe that it has some connection with the Samian War. The following chronology is very tentatively suggested:

Antigone 443 or 441 B.C.
Ajax ca. 442 B.C.
Women of Trachis ca. 432 B.C.
Oedipus Tyrannus ca. 427 B.C.
Electra ca. 413 B.C.
Philoctetes 409 B.C.
Oedipus at Colonus 401 B.C. (posthumous)

There are many fragments, including a large part of the satyr play *Ichneutai* (*The Trackers*).

I shall not be discussing these plays chronologically, as I do with Aeschylus and Euripides, but rather by topic so that I can discuss the Theban plays together.

Antigone

Antigone, Oedipus Tyrannus, and *Oedipus at Colonus* are often called the Theban plays. They were not originally performed together as a trilogy on a single day, but instead they span Sophocles' life. *Antigone* shows an idealistic youth battling what she sees as wrong. *Oedipus* shows us a search for identity and truth. *Oedipus at Colonus* shows us a man coming to terms with death and his god. These are the phases of every thinking man's life. It is interesting to see these characters in the varied contexts, and they do vary. One cannot ask that they be consistent except in the broadest way, as all three plays are written over such a long period. The disadvantage is in putting the expectations of a trilogy on all three plays. Each of these plays is a masterpiece and bears concentration on itself.

Another use made of Greek tragedy, in addition to teaching ethical lessons to a citizen about the good life, is to tell a government how to avoid excesses and how to avoid oppressing its people. All oppressive regimes should learn the lessons that *Antigone* teaches.

Georg Wilhelm Hegel said *Antigone* was "one of the most sublime and in every respect most consummate works of art human effort ever produced" (*Hegel on Tragedy*, p. 178). Although the play is from fifth-century Athens, the issues about human rights have everlasting relevance. The play is a human drama and a tragedy that shows the price of supporting these rights. Both Antigone and Creon are passionate people who have destroyed themselves and others. This is also a play about madness, hidden under the mask of ideals.

In her clash with King Creon, as Antigone defends the rights of the family, she invokes "the unwritten law of the gods" (my translation, lines 454–55) whereas Creon rests his case on defending the safety and security of the state against anarchy. Familial values and duty toward the gods of the underworld conflict with state interests and the interests of the Olympian gods, who back the authority of a king; personal issues confront public issues, and they radically influence each other.

The play opens after a war between Eteocles, the city's ruler, and Polyneices, his brother who has attacked the city. Both died in the encounter. Polyneices is condemned by his name: Polyneices means "the man of many quarrels," whereas Eteocles means "the man of true fame." The Greeks felt that names had power.

These are the two sons of Oedipus, and Antigone and Ismene are their sisters. Their uncle Creon, the new ruler, decrees that Eteocles should be buried, but not Polyneices. Against the warnings of Ismene, Antigone tries to bury Polyneices' body. For this act of defiance, Creon condemns Antigone to be walled up in a living tomb, in spite of the protests of his son Haemon, who is engaged to be married to her. The soothsayer Teiresias tells Creon he must bury the body of Polyneices. He reluctantly gives in. He finds Antigone has hanged herself. Haemon attacks Creon in the rocky tomb, and then falls on his own sword, embracing Antigone as he dies. Eurydice, Haemon's mother, hears of his death and stabs herself. Creon is a broken man at the end.

There are many conflicting interpretations of this play. For instance, many moderns see right only in Antigone and view Creon as a stereotypical dictator in the wrong. But things are not so simple. As Hegel suggests, two valid rights are opposed, albeit in an extreme fashion.

Creon opposes Antigone with the might of law on which he says personal happiness is based, namely via a well-controlled city. What Antigone does is the opposite of what Socrates did: in Plato's *Crito,* he declared that he would follow the city's laws even if they were unjust. With Sophocles' usual dramatic economy, Antigone is punished by the ruler and the *polis* she opposes, and Creon is punished by the loss of his own family, whose values he subordinated to those of the *polis.*

Justification can be found for Creon's refusing burial to an enemy, even though this view was unpopular in some circles. It was clearly acceptable law to refuse burial to traitors in the city. Just as heroes were celebrated, enemies and particularly traitors were punished. Polyneices chose to wage war against his native city, and even if his brother refused to share the rule of Thebes, as it had been arranged after the death of Oedipus, this was not sufficient justification to bring an army against one's own people.

Sophocles never presents us with black versus white, heroes versus villains. As Oscar Wilde said, "A thing is not necessarily true because a man dies for it" (*Complete Works*, p. 1161). One may even claim the play *Antigone* should be called *Creon*, because it is more his tragedy. In Sophocles' *Ajax*, the hero declares that a noble man ought either to live with honor or to die with honor. Creon did neither. He aimed at honor but missed through the excessiveness of the pursuit. He loses a son and his wife dies cursing him. He has lost honor along with his family. He is right to say that he is less than nothing, a walking corpse.

Creon is well named, because his name means ruler (or, the one who holds power) and he rules in an absolute way. He represents the law of the city, defends it, and finally yields to the pressures of the prophet Teiresias and the chorus. At first he is unbending, as Haemon points out, but he is constantly forced to modify his position, agreeing first not to include Ismene in her sister's harsh punishment, and then finally allowing Polyneices' burial and Antigone's release—but too late. His is the rigidity of the Sophoclean hero, the tree that will not bend to save itself when the river is in flood. The ruler who will not listen to his people, or even to his family, and claims he should be obeyed whether right or wrong may end up losing both, as does Creon. He gains in knowledge, accepts blame, and concludes that he is nothing, less than nobody. He does not have the grandeur of Oedipus, but he shares his suffering. Contrary to Oedipus he learns in spite of himself rather than because of himself.

Antigone is as unbending as her father and Creon. Both she and Creon pursued everything in excess. Her curse on Creon is fulfilled, and he is made to suffer what she did and worse. In this play Sophocles is suggesting that a humane city's laws should be based on recognition of the rights of the family and respect for the gods.

These opponents do not give up. Both Creon and Antigone suffer from their inability to compromise. Does that sound familiar? This play is a human drama and a tragedy that shows two passionate people who, in their determination to defend their positions, end up destroying themselves and others. The price of supporting their beliefs is paid in human blood.

Antigone shares her stubbornness with her father, who pursues the truth about his origin against the advice of those trying to save him, namely Teiresias and Jocasta. Creon, Oedipus, and Antigone are impatient and easily angered. They lash out at those closest to them. The chorus calls Antigone a law unto herself, and she resembles Creon and Oedipus in this also. One might even argue that what she did was totally ineffectual and, in fact, led to innocent deaths in addition to her own. It was only Teiresias and his dire prophecy that brought about Polyneices' burial.

Antigone kills herself rather than to wait and suffer more humiliation. Creon goes to release Antigone, but her suicide prevents his freeing her. Like

Romeo, Haemon arrives too late and decides to join his beloved in death. He dies in what seems to be a perverted marriage ritual, a "marriage to death." Antigone speaks of her marriage to Hades, and it may in fact be her veil with which she hangs herself (a veil figured in the marriage ritual). Haemon's name is derived from the Greek word for blood, and when he takes his life, his blood spurts out over Antigone's cheek in a type of marital consummation, a marriage through death.

Ismene, the sister who tries to dissuade Antigone from burying their brother, acts as a foil to Antigone. This allows us to appreciate the difference between a compliant citizen and a conscientious objector. Antigone is harsh and cruel toward Ismene, who is willing to die with her. For someone who claims that she is by nature one who prefers friendship to enmity, she is extreme in her rejection of Ismene.

In contrast to Antigone and Creon, Ismene represents what reasonable and sympathetic people do. She has neither the fanaticism of the heroes nor the mundane concerns of the guard and messenger. Ismene shows her loyalty to those she loves. Haemon also at the beginning shows himself to be reasonable and advocates compromise. At the beginning both are good and obedient citizens. Rather like Rosencrantz and Guildenstern, their fates are tied to the heroic monsters who direct the plot. The chorus also is made up of reasonable citizens who obey their ruler.

Center stage is the palace. One direction should indicate the battlefield, and another the city. The set should be something simple. The darkness of the first meeting should gradually merge into the day mentioned by the first chorus. This meeting takes place just outside the palace.

At the end, we have the dead Haemon carried in and Eurydice's body possibly displayed on the *ekkyklēma* (rolling machines for displaying bodies and interior scenes). Antigone's body is never seen, and this adds to her spiritual quality. I also think that Creon should not be demonized but rather made understandable, if not sympathetic.

Teiresias should inspire awe, and a director can do this in many ways. The other actors should regard him with respect tinged with fear. Some cast a woman in his role, and this can capture the sexual ambiguity. A boy should lead him in, but nonverbally it should be seen that he is leading the boy. Once he enters the stage area, his presence should dominate. This also applies to the next play.

Oedipus Tyrannus

Aristotle saw Sophocles as the greatest of the ancient playwrights and regarded his *Oedipus Tyrannus* as a model of dramatic construction. Clue after clue leads Oedipus closer and closer to the discovery of his identity. This is the

The Oedipus Plays. Translated by Ranjit Bolt. Directed
by Peter Hall. A blind Tiresias
(Greg Hicks) delivers his
spine-chilling prophecies to
Oedipus. Royal National
Theatre, Athens and London
(1996). Photo © Allan Titmuss.

greatest detective story every written. Each clue gives partial information
which can mislead the audience. Oracles give only part of the picture: Laius
is told to kill his child because his child will kill him. Oedipus tries to find
out who his parents are and is told that he will kill his father and marry his
mother, but is not told who his parents are. The puzzle pieces fall into place
only at the end: Oedipus insists on putting them together so that he can see
the final picture, even if it shows his own destruction.

This is a play about knowledge. Over the temple at Delphi was written
"Know Thyself" and "Nothing in Excess." If Creon fundamentally violated the
latter, Oedipus pursued the former to excess. Yet these violations were what
defined these heroes. Oedipus is supposedly the man of knowledge, the one
who solved the riddle of the Sphinx. He knew what went on four legs in the
morning, two at noon, and three in the evening: man.

A crowd of plague victims beseech Oedipus, their king, to save their city
once again. The oracle at Delphi tells the Thebans to find the murderer of
Laius. One clue comes after another, revealing the truth like pieces in a puzzle,
and Oedipus invariably misinterprets the clues. When Teiresias tells him he is
the murderer of his father, he thinks Teiresias is plotting against him. Oedipus
can solve riddles, as long as they are not about him. Jocasta recognizes the
truth, that she is his mother, and begs him to give up the search, but he stubbornly pursues it to the end. She hangs herself, and he puts out his eyes with
her two brooches. He asks to be exiled, but Creon sends off to Delphi to ask
what should be done. In this play Creon is pious, whereas one had questions
about his piety in *Antigone.*

This brilliant play shows us a man who will not give up, and who will live
even when it seems there is nothing more for him to lose. This play celebrates
human endurance and the will to discover the truth.

Sophocles is a master of imagery, and the connections between sight, insight, blindness, and ignorance in this play are important: in Greek, knowledge

The Oedipus Plays. Translated by Ranjit Bolt. Directed by Peter Hall. The polluter of Thebes, Oedipus (Alan Howard), addresses the chorus. Royal National Theatre, Athens and London (1996). Photo © Allan Titmuss.

and sight have close verbal connections. When Oedipus had sight he lacked insight; it was only when he blinded himself physically that he could finally truly see and understand. In *Oedipus at Colonus,* when he is blind, he becomes a guide to his last resting-place and finally a guardian for the land as a chthonic (earth-dwelling) seer and protective hero spirit.

Oedipus was the beast that he, the hunter, hunted. He was the child who slew his father and supplanted him in his mother's bed, Freudian fantasy as original nightmare. He was the disease that he, the doctor, had to cure. He was a marvel, endowed with skills, the riddle-solver who could not solve his own riddle. He helps his friends and harms his enemies, following the Homeric maxim. Finally as a protective deity he will save his friends, as he does the Athenians. In this way he paid back Theseus, the king of Athens who gave him shelter when he was an old man.

Oedipus chose to discover the cause of the plague in the city, in addition to finding out who he was, and ultimately that one equaled the other: he was the source of the city's tragedy. He tried to avoid what had been foretold, but he could not. His only real choice was to avoid the truth. This he chose not to do, and his dogged pursuit of the truth destroyed his public persona but defined him as a man. The relentless progression from revelation to revelation, moderated by false clues and orchestrated moments of release followed by scenes of gripping terror, are examples of Sophocles' mastery of plot. His use of language is subtle. When Teiresias accuses Oedipus, he uses the most striking metaphors to convey his point: "You are blind in your ears, your mind, and your eyes" (line 371). He spits out the words in anger: "*Tuphlos ta t'ota, ton te noun, ta t'ommat'ei.*" The succession of *T*s illustrates the anger by the sound of the speaker's tongue hitting his front teeth.

Oedipus tried to escape the oracle he had heard when he was young, namely that he would kill his father and marry his mother. But the more he ran the more he was trapped in the net, or the infernal machine, the trap that

Cocteau said was set in motion the moment he was born. Nevertheless, it is a mistake to see Oedipus as a simple victim of fate. The ancient view was a complex one, seeing man as responsible for his destiny in addition to being subject to controlling forces; Oedipus says himself, "Apollo brought these sufferings on me, but it was my hand that struck" (lines 1331–32). Oedipus may at this point only refer to his putting out his eyes, but it is even more interesting if he was also referring to killing his father. The claim of free will operating at the same time as fate may seem contradictory, but it is not so far removed from the modern view of man being genetically and environmentally determined yet also having a measure of free choice and of responsibility within that narrow framework. Man's having a choice distinguishes much of Western philosophy from Eastern, the Western drive to freedom from the Eastern fatalism and resignation to one's karma.

The play *Oedipus Tyrannus* not only shows the strength of a human being in enduring the suffering that comes from knowledge, but it also offers needed commentary on human happiness. It tells man not to rejoice overly in his happiness until his life is ended and he can see his whole life. Transient happiness is not enough. One has to see a life as a totality. Then one can weigh the good and the bad and see whether one has indeed merited the word happiness. This claim is a commonplace in Greek tragedy, beginning with the historian Herodotus. The Greek philosophers pointed out that wealth and power are not sufficient for happiness: goodness in the ethical sense is a necessary component.

Oedipus is a celebration of the human spirit. The play shows someone who will not give up searching for truth even when he suspects it may destroy him. He will also not give up life. Jocasta, when she learns what she has done, commits suicide. Not Oedipus. He will continue to live even after the gods have taken their best shots at him.

I tend to favor the actor playing Oedipus who emphasizes the little boy quality. After all, he is still living with "mommy." In the course of the drama he matures.

The set represents the palace. Exits stage right and stage left lead to the city and to the country. There are probably extras to constitute the crowd at the beginning who come to seek Oedipus's help. When Oedipus blinds himself at the end, perhaps he enters with a mask that shows his bloodied eyes.

Oedipus at Colonus

This play begins with the aged Oedipus arriving at Colonus, a city near Athens and the birthplace of Sophocles. It has been foretold that he would die here, in this place which is sacred to the Eumenides. Another oracle says that he will bring a blessing to the people who bury him. He will be their guardian hero and will bring disaster on their attackers. When he finds out where he is (Antigone is guiding him and discovers from the locals that they are at Colonus), he asks for Theseus to give him sanctuary in return for his blessing when he is dead. Theseus is summoned and readily accepts Oedipus's offer. Creon comes from Thebes to bring Oedipus home, or rather to settle him near but outside the border of the city so that Thebes could avoid pollution but benefit eventually from the dead hero. Oedipus refuses. Creon has his guards take as prisoners both Antigone and her sister, Ismene, who has arrived with news. Theseus saves the day and drives Creon out, returning the daughters to Oedipus.

The girls beg their father to listen to Polyneices, their brother, who has come to ask his father to help him regain the throne of Thebes. Oedipus curses him. Lightning and thunder fill the sky. Oedipus says it is time for him to leave this world, and Theseus should be summoned. He finds the grove unaided and takes only Theseus to the secret place, telling him further secrets which he must pass on to his successor. He is then transfigured in some supernatural way. Antigone would like to see his grave but that is forbidden. The sisters lament their loss, and Theseus offers to help them. The chorus says there should be an end to weeping.

Oedipus at Colonus shows us the aged Oedipus as more accepting on one level, but as an angry demigod-to-be on another. At the opening he says that three things have taught him to endure: suffering, time, and nobility. If this endurance is meant to imply patience, we find this refuted by Oedipus's rage against his son Polyneices, which clearly shows us that there is still some of the old Oedipus left. He curses his sons as he goes off to fulfill a blessing for Athens as the city's patron hero in return for refuge.

Besides hate, Oedipus shows love, which he says is the main gift he has given his daughters. He says they have been loved by him more than any man will ever love them, and this love compensates in part for their sufferings. Athens will give Oedipus hospitality and a welcome in *philia,* the love and duty one renders an honored guest. *Philia* has the meaning of both love, usually in a nonerotic sense, and affection. It can convey what one feels toward family members and friends, in addition to hinting at the notion of duty one feels toward them. Oedipus upholds the ancient creed of helping one's friends and harming one's enemies. At the end of his life, Oedipus rewards the faithful (his daughters, Theseus, and Athens) and curses the faithless (his sons and Creon). His final power is to bless and curse. Oedipus accepts his death, but he will not give up his right to choose. The rigidity he shows in not forgiving his sons is something shared by other Sophoclean tragic heroes.

The play is more contemplative than others. The hero's death and final relief from suffering can be seen to constitute a happy ending.

There is a development between the three Theban plays, which were written during a period of forty years, when Sophocles was aged between fifty and ninety. *Antigone,* which is written earliest of the three, shows a type of idealism which implies a belief in higher values to the point of sacrificing one's life to achieve them. *Oedipus Tyrannus* shows the folly and tragedy of rationality itself. It also seems to respect the hero's pursuit of truth, even when it entails his own self-destruction. Socrates claimed the unexamined life to be not worth living, but for Oedipus the examined life leads to a living death. Nevertheless, life and knowledge are reaffirmed, terrible though they may be.

Oedipus at Colonus shows a merging of god and man at the end of Oedipus's life, in addition to a certain sense of resignation. Religion is a salve for the pain of life. The earlier doubts are not resolved, but they are transfigured just as Oedipus is himself. God has become man, and man, god. The spirit of this irascible old man will protect Athens and inspire us. The sacred power to bless and curse inherent in someone who has committed crimes is something peculiarly Greek.

Sophocles has brilliant descriptions of nature, such as the ode to fair Colonus, a land of fine horses where the nightingale sings her melodious songs in the wine-dark ivy and sacred foliage. He uses nature symbolically, and one feels awe before the sacred grove of the Eumenides. Like the Eumenides, Oedipus becomes a protecting power.

The play was staged with the grove of the Eumenides center stage. One side indicates the direction of Thebes, and the other, Athens. Oedipus leaves the entrance of the grove to sit on a rock until the end of the play. The thunder and lightning described in the text can be rendered literally or imaginatively. This heaven-sent storm is like the heaven-sent earthquake described in Aeschylus's *Prometheus* and the one in Euripides' *Bacchae,* which results in the destruction of the palace. How literally this is done depends on the director.

Oedipus is blind throughout, but at the very end he no longer needs to be led. Creon here is not the pious good man from the *Oedipus Tyrannus* but is now like Odysseus in *Philoctetes,* believing that the end justifies the means. Some might say that Sophocles had second thoughts about Creon; nevertheless, he could be the same man as in *Oedipus Tyrannus,* now corrupted by power. Four actors are required in the final scene: Theseus, Oedipus, Antigone, and Ismene.

Ajax

Ajax also deals with a theme we find in *Antigone,* the burial of an enemy. Many of Creon's arguments are found in Menelaus's mouth as he praises law: "Laws can never flourish in a city where fear is not firmly established . . . and the ship of state will sink where men are free to transgress and do what they like" (my translation, lines 1073–74).

Odysseus has been awarded Achilles' armor and Ajax has set out to kill the Greek leaders, who in his eyes have rigged the decision. Odysseus is a versatile man who can both negotiate and fight. After the war, a new type of weapon will be called for: speech. Instead of confrontation and battle, negotiation and compromise will be the order of the day. The time for noble Achilles or Ajax will soon be over, and the day of Odysseus is dawning. Odysseus is both an effective strategist and a very powerful warrior, invaluable to the Greeks, for whom he will continue fighting mightily until the end of the war.

Ajax, in his fury over the loss of the arms of Achilles, decided to kill the Greek leaders. Athena drove him out of his mind and had him kill cattle instead. The play opens with Athena inviting Odysseus to gloat over Ajax in his madness. Ajax returns to sanity, and when he realizes what he has done cannot live with the shame. He kills himself. The second half of the play is the struggle over his burial, with Agamemnon and Menelaus refusing it. Teucer, Ajax's half-brother, is prepared to fight the leaders so that Ajax may be properly buried, but Odysseus finally convinces them to do the right thing. Ajax's funeral ends the play. Compromise carries the day in this ultimate ironic act: Ajax's bitterest enemy has negotiated his burial. But Ajax's death has gained him the glory of remaining uncompromised.

Can Ajax live in a world of peace and negotiation? He says to Tecmessa, "You are a fool if you think you can change my character now" (lines 594–95). This is the glory of a Sophoclean hero: the strength to create an identity in conflict with the way the world works. Man's adherence to his own desire becomes both his glory and tragedy. The Sophoclean hero is Achilles reborn in a world out of joint.

Ajax speaks of all changing with time: "Long and uncountable time brings all that is hidden to light and hides what is hidden, and there is nothing one cannot expect" (lines 646–48). But there is one thing that will not change with time: Ajax. As Thomas Rosenmeyer says, "The hero does not count, he lives, and when life becomes a sordid business of ticking off days, he sacrifices life" (*The Masks of Tragedy*, p. 168). Suicide keeps him faithful to himself. This shares much with the Samurai ethic. Some people call Ajax's speech to his men about time and change a *Trugrede* (a speech meant to trick the listener): delivered to enable Ajax to leave the stage. The ambiguity is such that Ajax could believe in most of it, except as it applies to himself. He will continue to live with honor or die with it.

At the beginning, Athena could speak from the top of the *skēnē* (stage building). The facade of the *skēnē* shows Ajax's tent (this could be done by scene painting). The tent can be opened to reveal him with the cattle he is torturing. There is a shift from the tent to the beach where he kills himself. This again could be left to the imagination, or could perhaps be done by scene painting which showed both locations, and we would imagine the distance greater than the size of the set. Change of scene is also demonstrated by the exit of the chorus, in this case right and left.

Ajax's costume is probably spattered with blood. There is the question of whether Ajax commits suicide before the eyes of the audience or behind a bush or something comparable. There is a convention in Greek tragedy that violence does not occur onstage. We see, nevertheless, various people being manhandled, such as Prometheus and the shepherd who is forced to reveal Oedipus's identity. I would prefer Ajax's death to take place behind a bush, which I believe was what was done in Sophocles' time, but this decision should be left to the director.

Ajax's body is said to be still bleeding at the end. The ancients did this in the imagination, but moderns seem to go for more physical realism. The limited number of actors in ancient Greek tragedy called for Ajax to take another role (probably Teucer), and so perhaps the "dead" Ajax would have been replaced by some dummy. Modern performances could simply add another actor. The director should think about how faithful he wants to be to the original performance.

Electra

Electra has fascinated generations, whether she is viewed as freedom fighter or as vengeful neurotic. It is probably the most controversial play that Sophocles wrote.

Electra resembles Antigone in prizing her relation to a dead brother (when she thinks he is dead) more than her relation to the living. Electra is under threat of imprisonment for her subversive remarks about the new rulers, her mother and Aegisthus, who had killed her father. Orestes returns home in disguise, claiming he is delivering news of Orestes' death. He finally reveals himself to his sister, and he kills his mother and then Aegisthus.

This play has generated many interpretations. Gilbert Murray describes the vengeance as a combination of "matricide and good spirits" (*The Plays of Euripides,* p. v). Others however see a darker side to the picture, claiming that Electra represents both justice and that evil side of human nature which delights in murder. Some, reading Sophocles in Euripidean terms, claim that both Electra and Orestes are no better than criminals, and that Sophocles's presentation is ironic.

Since we have not had *Agamemnon* to precede, showing Clytemnestra murdering Electra's and Orestes' father, modern audiences do not naturally have sympathy for these children killing their mother. But the ancient audience was well aware of the duty that Orestes owed his father, which in Aeschylus had been sanctioned by Apollo. Some fifth-century Athenians may have felt, as Euripides was to feel, that there is something uncomfortable in the portrayal of a god who sanctions matricide. Sophocles cleverly sidesteps this theological and ethical problem by having Orestes consult Apollo's oracle at Delphi not on *whether* he should kill his mother, but on *how* he should do so. This innovation has the further effect of enhancing the heroic stature of Orestes by showing that he acts of his own volition, without needing to be reminded to do his duty by a god. The audience is made to feel that at least the god of Delphi is on the side of the oppressed children. It is obvious an ethical problem remains, but Sophocles does the best he can to win audience sympathy for Orestes and Electra.

Sophocles also avoids some of the alienating effects of the crime of matricide by putting Aegisthus's death second. It is Aegisthus's death that remains in the audience's mind as the play ends, rather than the killing of the mother. Thus we have more sympathy for the children in Sophocles. Aeschylus and Euripides, in their versions of this story, put Clytemnestra's death last and thereby arouse horror in the audience with that final image of matricide.

Electra speaks to Chrysothemis, her sister, as Antigone did to Ismene, in an attempt to enlist her help when she thinks that Orestes is dead. She wants her to perform a bold deed (killing Aegisthus) to restore family honor, but she is rebuffed as Antigone was by Ismene, as a woman who does not know her place. Chrysothemis may agree with justice being on Electra's side, but she echoes conventional prejudice when she says, "Do you not see that you are a woman, not a man, and weaker than your enemies?" (my translation, lines 997–98). Sophocles gains sympathy from the audience because the target of their vengeance is Aegisthus, who is presented as a tyrant. The chorus condones the vengeance of the children by noting that justice is on their side.

Sophocles musters arguments in favor of Orestes and Electra for toppling tyrants; he underplays the matricide. At the end of the play, Orestes says, "Crime's punishment should be swift, and the penalty death: then there would not be so much crime" (lines 1505–1507). The chorus does not condemn him but rather congratulates him for attaining freedom, and this freedom may be the chorus members' own. There is a Homeric quality to the vengeance of the children. Honor is involved, as is a loyalty to blood relatives (we remember in Aeschylus's *Eumenides* that Apollo argued that the father is the real progenitor, whereas the mother just carries his seed).

The final scene is one of the most exciting and sadistic in Greek tragedy, but we accept the fact that justice is on the side of Agamemnon's children. Clytemnestra's body is wheeled out, covered with a sheet. When Aegisthus arrives he thinks this is Orestes' body. Orestes plays a cat-and-mouse game with him, having Aegisthus discover for himself that this is his wife's body. He then brutally postpones Aegisthus's death so that he can gloat.

This play may have a set similar to the one in *Libation Bearers,* but Agamemnon's tomb is nowhere in sight. A palace looms in the background and dominates the scene. Once again the two directions are from the city or to the city. The lamentation scene in which Orestes hands Electra an urn in which his ashes are supposedly contained gives a wonderful opportunity to an actress to express her sorrow. Just as the bow will be seen to be important in *Philoctetes,* likewise the urn is important here.

Of the three ancient versions of this story, this one is the most popular in modern times. It plays well on the stage because it is well constructed and full of surprises and suspense, it has a strong and effective heroine, and it satisfies a modern taste for blood.

Women of Trachis

Women of Trachis shows us Heracles, another hero who becomes a demigod, in his actions between god and man, but also in his actions between man and beast. He was a monster who slew other monsters, making a world safe for a civilization in which he could not share. He, like Ajax, Oedipus, and Philoctetes, is one who is needed and rejected; aside from their time of usefulness they are not considered fit for the conventional society of the Greek *polis.*

Heracles returns home after about a year's absence, and an oracle says that this time his wanderings are over: he will be either dead or at peace. His wife, Deianira, is elated until she finds that he has brought home a captive princess named Iole.

Hoping to regain Heracles' love, Deianira (whose name means "manslayer") sends her husband a cloak imbued with a drug (that she believes to be a love charm) given to her by the centaur Nessus (as he lay dying, slain by Heracles). A magic acid is released when this cloak is exposed to sunlight. Heracles writhes in agony when he puts it on. Deianira, realizing what she had done, commits suicide. Heracles dies slowly, prescribing his son's future, forcing him to marry Iole.

Heracles slew monsters but was defeated by erotic passion: "He defeated all by the strength of his hands, but he was finally defeated himself by Eros" (lines 488–89). He committed the fatal error of introducing a foreign princess into his house, as Deianira says, "to lie under the same blanket" with his lawful wife (lines 539–40). We, the audience, know what this can lead to, having had the example of Agamemnon, who brought Priam's daughter Cassandra home to be part of his household. So also in Euripides' *Andromache,* Neoptolemus imported Hector's wife as his concubine and mother of his only child. After this, he was not to rest easy in his home, and his wife, Hermione, Menelaus's daughter, arranged his death. All these men died because of their wives' intrigues. Not many wives are happy to meet a captive princess their husbands bring home.

Simulating the fire of love itself, with concomitant agony, sunlight activates the power of the drug in the cloak. It is fatal for Heracles and eats into him like an acid (or love). Heracles, in his single-mindedness, perpetuates his passion by insisting his son marry Iole. His desire shapes his son's destiny as he shackles the next generation. We can compare the cloak's fiery power to a disease with its concomitant fever. It can also symbolize Deianira's jealousy, as fatal for what she wanted as it was for Othello. In both cases the "disease" of love turns out to be deadly.

The final line of the play is "There is nothing here that is not Zeus" (line 1278) and, we can add, his incarnation in the Sophoclean hero. Greek tragedy shows us the paradox of god and man inextricably woven together, without man being released from responsibility. It is this which constitutes his human glory. Sophocles' heroes choose and suffer the consequences. The Sophoclean hero may learn through his suffering, but he will not change. Ajax will be Ajax and Heracles, Heracles. Even when he learns the truth, he still rails against Deianira, and like Ajax with Tecmessa, his final concern is his son, and for his son to help him achieve immortality, because he represents his future.

The staging is simple, with the house of Heracles in Trachis. We only see Heracles in his last tortured moments, and he and Deianira never meet. Heracles is played by the protagonist who played Deianira, which may add subtle commentary: possibly one can interpret the female who destroyed him as his own passion. The cloak, like Philoctetes's bow, is an important object and causes death. In Sophocles' *Philoctetes*, Heracles gave the bow to Philoctetes for his help in laying him on a pyre. Like *Ajax*, this is a double play, the first half being Deianira's and the second, Heracles'.

Philoctetes

Philoctetes is a late play, the only Greek tragedy with only male characters. It raises the issue of military victory and its price. Does the end justify the means? It shows a young warrior coming of age.

Philoctetes lives on an uninhabited part of Lemnos because of a wound that he received when he violated the precinct of a goddess. She sent a snake, and the wound it inflicted would not heal. It became so foul smelling that his comrades were forced to abandon him. Odysseus tells Neoptolemus that the bow of Heracles is necessary for victory at Troy, and at one point it seems sufficient that it be only the bow. But the oracle makes it clear that Philoctetes must go there himself (as Heracles verifies at the end).

Neoptolemus's presence is also required. Neoptolemus tells Philoctetes

Philoctetes. Adapted by Keith Johnson. Directed by William Gaskill. Odysseus and Neoptolemus try to take Philoctetes (Colin Blakely) to Troy against his will. The National Theatre at the Old Vic (1964). Photo: Zoë Dominic. Used by permission.

that his wound will be healed only when he goes to Troy. All this information is claimed to be oracular and is revealed by the characters at various points in the play. At these points there are variations, just as in the prophecies given to Oedipus. The story unfolds with lots of questions raised.

Odysseus persuades Neoptolemus to deceive Philoctetes to get his bow. At first Neoptolemus lies and betrays his own nature, but then he relents and returns the bow which Philoctetes has entrusted to him. Philoctetes then tries to shoot Odysseus, but Neoptolemus prevents him. Philoctetes and Neoptolemus are about to sail home when the deified Heracles appears to tell them that they must go to Troy.

Sophocles' genius is to show us Neoptolemus trying to compromise his nature. Only after experience and reflection does he see that the loss of self, or self-betrayal, is worse than the loss of Troy. His dilemma is like Antigone's; his loyalty to himself and the ideals that constitute his character is more important than his loyalty to those in power, particularly when his allegiance involves a loyalty to a higher truth.

The issue of truth versus falsehood is important here. In the *Iliad,* Achilles, the father of Neoptolemus, said, "As hateful to me as the gates of Hades is a man who says one thing and conceals another thing in his heart" (lines 312–13). Achilles lives a short life and gains honor; Odysseus lives a long life because of his lying. He also knows when it is in his own best interest to be a coward, and it is amusing to see the blustering Odysseus running away when Philoctetes regains his bow and tries to kill him. This is typical of Odysseus. He is true to himself, and he is a survivor. Such cowardice would have been unthinkable for Achilles.

In many of his plays, Sophocles replicates the hero in his strange majesty. Philoctetes and Neoptolemus are like two sides of Achilles: one, the irascible and wild nature of the devoted warrior, the other, his virtue and integrity.

When they are divided they lose; together, they defeat Odysseus. Heracles brings about this powerful fusion by forcing them back into the mythological track. This is one of the "happy ending" tragedies, but it is forcibly dragged to that ending by the strongman Heracles.

Both Odysseus and Philoctetes fight to gain the soul of Neoptolemus. Neoptolemus ultimately opts for the truthful Philoctetes, who most resembles his father. During the course of the drama he matures. Older heroes generally remain the same in Sophocles. This is a rite of passage for an adolescent. As the only Greek tragedy with an entirely male cast, it may have contained an important lesson for a young citizen (all voting citizens were male). Neoptolemus at last discovers his true nature. Neoptolemus is a reverse Oedipus in relation to the father: Oedipus kills his father, but Neoptolemus discovers his father Achilles in himself and adopts his values, which he sees are also his own.

Philoctetes, like Prometheus and Io, suffers intermittent agonies sent to him by a divine source. He is representative of all those victims who suffer from chronic illness. The bow itself is a prominent and magical symbol. It never fails. It is both a provider of life and a destroyer. Philoctetes says he cannot survive without it. The destruction that it will bring to Troy will also lead to peace.

The bare island of Lemnos wonderfully represents the craggy hero Philoctetes. His description of the island he is about to leave shows that he loved it as much as he hated it. Both Aeschylus (ca. 475 B.C.) and Euripides (431 B.C.) in their versions made it inhabited by Lemnians. Sophocles prefers the island deserted to point out his own isolated hero.

The set should accommodate the description of a cave with two entrances. This could have been done with scene painting. Heracles could appear elevated at the end, either on the *mēchanē* or speaking from the *theologeion* (a platform above the theatrical building, *skēnē*).

Performance Tradition

The Theban plays were popular in Rome: Accius (170–?86 B.C.) wrote a *Thebaid* and an *Antigone.* He also wrote a *Philoctetes.* Julius Caesar (100–44 B.C.) wrote an *Oedipus,* which is lost. Seneca wrote two plays based on Sophocles: *Hercules Oetaeus,* based on *Women of Trachis,* and an *Oedipus.*

Women of Trachis

Hercules Oetaeus shows us a Stoic hero. He also was a philanderer who rivaled his father Jove in his amours. The first half of the play shows Hercules return- ing home with Iole after having destroyed her home, Oechalia, because her father refused to hand her over. Deianeira rages against his affairs and vows revenge; her arguments resemble Medea's. Then she calms down and resorts to magic, which becomes her unwitting revenge. The centaur Nessus gave her some of his poisoned blood, which he claimed was a love charm. Here the mythological story returns to the known track. She sends the cloak to Hercules and he is burned in agony. She resolves to kill herself, but Hyllus, her son, does everything he can to dissuade her, to no avail. She dies by her own hand.

The second half of the play is all about Hercules and his death. Lichas, who delivered the cloak, dies from fear as he clutches an altar. This does not prevent Hercules from mutilating his body. Hercules learns from his son that Deianeira did not mean to kill him, but this hardly blunts his anger. Hercules is joined by Alcmena, his mother, who shows herself a Stoic by checking her tears. Philoctetes appears to set the fire and is given Heracles' bow and arrows. Hyllus is not asked in this play to marry Iole. Heracles bears the flames with Stoic resignation and dies while exhorting his followers. He asks Jove to give him a sign. Alcmena laments the loss of her son, focusing on how many of his victims will be trying to avenge themselves on her; *stabat mater* (the mother was standing), but this mother both weeps and complains. Suddenly Hercules' voice is heard: he has been translated to the heavens, proof of his divine origin. This apotheosis purges him of sin and guilt. He is not only a constellation, but he is also among the gods. This savior, the benefactor of mankind and the son of a god, is risen from the dead. His mother prays to him to save the world in its time of need.

This is more of a Stoic *exemplum* (parable) and philosophical tract than a play that excites an audience. The list of Hercules' labors gets a bit tedious. The play shows a Stoic hero overcoming passion and pain. Deianeira is the opposite and gives in to her passion, committing suicide as a gesture of despair. They show two alternatives to a human being's life. One wonders if Heracles' pain at the end really compensates for the pain he caused Deianeira and so many others. Moderns tend to feel sympathy for Deianeira.

Oedipus Tyrannus and *Oedipus at Colonus*

Horror and gloom oppress Seneca's *Oedipus*. The description of the plague is as gory as any description offered in literature. This description is coupled with a vision of Hades and bloody sacrifices. Seneca gives Teiresias a daughter, Manto, who is able to describe the sacrificial victims in bloody detail.

It is Creon rather than Teiresias who tells Oedipus he is the murderer of Laius, information that Creon gleans from the ghost of Laius, summoned from the underworld. It still takes shepherds to sort out that Oedipus is the son of Jocasta and Laius, and not the son, as he thought, of King Polybus and Queen Merope of Corinth. When he realizes the full extent of his crimes, Oedipus curses himself and puts out his eyes. This is again described in the most explicit detail: "His fingers clawed into his skull. His eyes wait, avid, ready for his hands, and rush to meet them, eager for the wound" (*The Tragedies*, p. 38).

Jocasta does not disappear to hang herself, as she did in Sophocles, but confronts Oedipus with the truth and when he refuses to kill her, she stabs herself fatally in the womb with his sword. This violence onstage is different from the ancient Greek predecessor.

Oedipus is sent into exile and willingly invites the fates, disease, the plague, and sorrow itself to be his guides as he leaves the city. He is the ideal scapegoat. The wordplay and irony is very different from the Sophoclean version, and the role of Jocasta is drastically reduced: the children never appear. There are no moments of cautious optimism. Magic, ghosts, cruelty, torture, and fear abound. This is a study in unmitigated darkness, not only of the sky, but also of the human soul.

In 1968 at the Old Vic in London, Peter Brook staged a production of Seneca's *Oedipus* in an adaptation by Ted Hughes. This ended with a demonstration of a six-foot phallus and featured a jazz band rendering of "Yes, We Have No Bananas." Steven Berkoff said that he shouted out "Rubbish!" during the performance. "It was an awful thing to do, but when they wheeled on this big gold cock I thought he was out of his tree. I have to admit I found the whole thing too eclectic for words" (*Free Association*, p. 110).

There was a famous performance of Sophocles' *Oedipus Tyrannus* in 1585 in Palladio's Teatro Olimpico at Vicenza: it was the first translation of Greek tragedy to be performed in the West. The music for the odes was by Andrea Gabrieli. Masks were not used in this production. An actress as young or younger than Oedipus played Jocasta, and this led to criticism. More criticism came from the fact that natural speech was used in the translation, and that the lavish set belied the poverty of a plague-ridden city. A chorus leader delivered the choral lines, and musical interludes punctuated the five acts. One can see how this was progressing toward opera, and how it was an aristocratic production for aristocrats. The criticisms of that production might be reasons to praise a modern one: intelligible choruses delivered by the chorus leader (as Ariane Mnouchkine did in her *Les Atrides*) and accessible language.

Oedipus Rex. Seneca's *Oedipus,* adapted by Ted Hughes. Translated by David Anthony Turner. Directed by Peter Brook. Jocasta (Irene Worth) and Oedipus (Sir John Gielgud) are caught in the trap that fate has set for them. The National Theatre at the Old Vic (1968). Photo: Zoë Dominic. Used by permission.

Versions of *Oedipus Tyrannus* were staged by Pierre Corneille in 1659 and Voltaire in 1718. Jean Baptiste Racine has a majestic *Thébaïde* (1664). After John Dryden and Nathaniel Lee's version in 1678 and its occasional revivals (such as in the highly altered version by Percy Bysshe Shelley in 1818 of *Swellfoot the Tyrant*), *Oedipus* was banned from the English professional stage until modern times because the theme of incest bothered the Lord Chamberlain.

Friedrich Schiller wrote *Die Braut von Messina, oder Die feindlichen Brüder* (*The Bride from Messina, or The Hostile Brothers*) in 1802–1803 as a Greek tragedy in five acts with choruses. Part of this is written in iambic trimeter, the usual language for dialogue in Greek tragedy. It drew on the Oedipus myth with the oracle, exposed child, and brothers who are rivals, in this case not for the throne but for their own unrecognized sister. Both brothers are killed, one at the other's hand, and the other through suicide as expiation.

Only in 1912 was Max Reinhardt given permission to stage *Oedipus* in London to a text by Gilbert Murray, following his successful staging of *Oedipus* using Hugo von Hofmannsthal's version (in 1910, in Munich). Reinhardt's performance was at Covent Garden, and it opened with a crowd that rushed through the audience to reach the stage at the beginning. This production also featured a chorus of dark-skinned slaves.

Sophocles' King Oedipus: A Version for the Modern Stage by W. B. Yeats was performed at the Abbey Theatre in Dublin in 1926, and his *Oedipus at Colonus* was performed in 1927. Yeats added accessible language to make the play more immediately dramatic for a modern audience. He also added recognizable Irish elements.

In *King Oedipus* sexual allusions are elaborated, as in the sowing metaphor from Sophocles:

> But, looking for a marriage-bed,
>   he found the bed of his birth,
> Tilled the field his father had tilled,
>   cast seed into the same abounding earth;
> Entered through the door that had sent him wailing forth. (pp. 510–11)

Yeats removed what he saw as difficulties in Sophocles, including much of the irony, many metaphoric or mythological allusions, and even long reflections, such as Oedipus's final despairing speech. For many years Yeats's "translations" served to introduce schoolchildren to Sophocles. Misleading as this might have been, it was compensated for by the quality of his language and his mixture of prose for the iambic sections and poetry for the choruses, which set a standard for many other translations.

In *Oedipus at Colonus,* the characters were transformed into the lasses and lads on an Irish countryside or in haunted woods: "The wine-dark of the wood's intricacies, / The nightingale that deafens daylight there, / If daylight ever visit" (p. 548). Yeats admits he is clearly describing Ireland rather than Colonus, "When Oedipus at Colonus went into the wood of the Furies he felt the same creeping in his flesh that an Irish countryman feels in certain haunted woods in Galway and in Sligo" (*Letters of W. B. Yeats*, p. 537). In the ode in celebration of Colonus, he also praises the intellectual and spiritual heritage of Athens, "The self-sown, self-begotten shape that gives / Athenian intellect its mastery" (p. 544).

Antigone's lamentation at the end was severely cut to concentrate on the mystery and spirituality of Oedipus's death and transfiguration. There seems to be a personal statement—as clear as Sophocles' own—in the way in which Yeats makes his Oedipus a proud hero who does not cling to life but, in the celebrated words of the chorus, utters "a gay goodnight and quickly turns away" (p. 561).

Jean Cocteau provided spoken interludes for Stravinsky's *Oedipus Rex* (1927), an operatic version in Latin. Stravinsky wanted modern audiences to concentrate on the music, so he used the Latin text as simply a percussive element that most people did not understand. The role of the diva also reinforces Jocasta, and she grows in presence and strength even as Oedipus is weakened. She is the heroic, tragic individual in this opera and must die. Her music as a coloratura mezzo-soprano enhances her as a queen. Her vocal line lends her a majesty and dignity that makes us understand that she is not only Oedipus's queen, but also his mother. The regal music which announces her also shows us who is actually in power. Oedipus's music is whining by comparison.

There are definite allusions to a mass. Oedipus's and Jocasta's music, which derives from Italian nineteenth-century opera, cedes finally to more ritualistic music. By conflating the mass with ancient tragedy, perhaps Stravinsky reveals his pessimism yet at the same time his hope for some type of redemption. As this opera shows his genius in the music, it also represents a quietism in its ritual optimism. The emphasis is on collective renewal and rebirth rather than on the death of the individual. The gentle farewell the chorus delivers mediates the horror and shock revealed by the chorus in Sophocles' play. Its final words, "Count no man happy until he die" (lines 1528–30), in that context imply that death will be the only possible release from this world's pain.

Julie Taymor directed an excellent performance of *Oedipus Rex* in Tokyo in 1992 with the Tokyo Opera Singers. This production combines Japanese theatrical traditions with modern Western ones. The monumental quality demanded by Stravinsky is aptly met by traditions from Noh, Kabuki, and Bunraku (the puppet theater).

This is a brilliant production starring Min Tanaka as the danced Oedipus, Philip Langridge as the tenor singing the role, and Jessye Norman as Jocasta. Norman fills the role with her rich, full tones. The set, staging, and movement create an unforgettable experience. George Tsypin is the stage designer, and his dark genius is perfect for this production. Japanese drama merges with Western opera and the result is riveting. The text is delivered by Shiraishi Kayoko, the talented actress who worked in Suzuki Tadashi's productions for many years. She begins with the introduction, which seethes with the unstated. She glides across the stage with the imperceptible movement that comes from the rigorous training of the Japanese Noh theater (a mastery of movement that the martial arts, like karate, try to imitate). She takes out a sword and handily rips open the curtain to begin the opera.

The major characters have pre-Cycladic masks above their made-up faces. The hands are also made of the same material and are larger than life. Teiresias has eyes painted in his hands. These characters appear monumental. The chorus members first appear covered with gray dust that suggests their skin is flaking off, as if they were victims of Hiroshima, but we are to understand that this is the plague that Oedipus will expiate. It is obvious that Butoh shaped the staging here, since white makeup gives the characters the appearances of corpses or ghosts. We remember that Butoh was the dance form developed after the Hiroshima disaster, and the actors featured shaven heads and bodies covered in white makeup to give them the appearance of corpses or ghosts, sometimes gods, who were to inspire the performances. Butoh aims to recreate the spiritually informed performances of Noh. It marries well with Stravinsky's recreation of a Greek classic.

Tanaka dances key portions, such as Oedipus solving the riddle and then killing his father and marrying his mother (all of which is performed in a tableau as Oedipus sings). Tanaka enacts the blinded Oedipus described by the messenger at the end. This doubling increases the aesthetic distance and the monumental aspect. Conventions are used from the Japanese theater, such as red ribbon flowing from Laius's wound and Oedipus's eyes to symbolize blood. There are other interesting touches using modern technology: when Shiraishi speaks of the unseen forces of fate governing Oedipus, we see a giant flying bird projected across the curtain.

The final scene in which the chorus bids Oedipus farewell is enacted in the rain, and we see Min Tanaka walk through a metal maze as he "leaves Thebes." The strange percussion of the rain is a fitting conclusion, a bleak purification, and the metal replicates the prison of fate, which is now provided by Oedipus's memories.

There was a production of this opera performed in the Carré Theatre in Amsterdam in 1984, with the conductor Bernard Haitink. It featured Felicity Palmer as Jocasta and Neil Rosenshein as Oedipus. This production replicated the spareness that Stravinsky indicated, with a simple set and the chorus in a row, but instead of wearing cowls and reading from scrolls, they were in formal suits with their faces in white paint, and they read from what seemed to be scores. The set, costumes, and masks (with the mouth area cut away) were all in black and white. The set showed a large rectangular door in a gigantic wall, and two triangles (the top white and the bottom black) intersected the door. This created an expressionistic angular space, not unlike the sets in the expressionist film by Robert Wiene, *Das Cabinet des Dr. Caligari.* (1920). The sets (produced and designed by Harry Wich) were probably the best part of this production, although Tsypin's in the Taymor production were still better. On the whole this was an undramatic performance and shows why this work was unpopular for so long. The brilliance of the Taymor production contrasts sharply with the dullness of this one.

Robert Edmond Jones staged this opera with huge marionettes and an invisible speaker (1931), and the music was provided by the Philadelphia Orchestra with Leopold Stowkowski conducting. This performance was criticized as being too understated and thus more impressionistic than classic: more Debussy than Stravinsky.

Cocteau's *La machine infernale* (1934) shows man caught by fate and Freud, truth and illusion, in addition to the absurd struggle of man who is only hastening to his death. Cocteau's introduction speaks of a wound-up machine waiting for its spring to unwind in a human lifetime. It is an ideal machine designed by the infernal gods to destroy man. Cocteau plays all the intellectual tricks for which the French are famous, but the essential Sophoclean drama with its tight plot and irony eludes him. He is more discursive in his four acts: they are both cinematic and epic, filled with sound bytes. All the events leading up to Sophocles' play are recounted in the first three acts, and only in the last one do we reach the beginning of Sophocles' original. In Cocteau's final act, Sophocles' entire play is performed in telegraphic fashion. The first act gives us Laius haunting the ramparts like the ghost of Hamlet's father, trying futilely to warn Jocasta that their son has killed him and is on his way to marry her. The mood is lighthearted for the most part; nevertheless, Jocasta's entanglement in her long scarf looks ominously forward to the means she will use to hang herself.

Jocasta is attracted to young soldiers. There is the implication that she has had an affair with Teiresias (called Zizi), who tries to keep her under his religious thumb. There are Marxist asides: the soldier says of the ghost being ignored by Jocasta, "now he's seen how hard it is to be heard by those in power" (my translation, p. 32).

The second act lets Oedipus confront the Sphinx, who is in the human form of a young woman. The Sphinx kills with the help of the Egyptian jackal-headed Anubis. She is tired of this slaughter, so she helps Oedipus, who is insensitive and ungrateful. She becomes Nemesis, a goddess of vengeance.

The third act shows Oedipus's wedding night, and he is horrified at Jocasta's story of a young girl who killed her baby because of the bad omens at its birth. The fourth act reveals that that baby is Oedipus. The prologue to this act mentions a plague. Jocasta kills herself after she learns that both Teiresias and Creon have tried to keep the truth from her and Oedipus. Oedipus blinds himself, and Teiresias tells Creon that Oedipus is now beyond Creon's authority. Now they belong to the people, the poets and the pure of heart. Antigone and the ghost of Jocasta lead Oedipus down the steps out of the city, the very steps that Jocasta found so difficult to negotiate at the beginning of the play.

This version is witty and filled with *bons mots*. It does not tackle all the major themes that Sophocles did regarding the search for truth and personal responsibility. Instead it shows that poetry, wit, and love are the main medicine man has to deal with the disease of fate. It has many more laughs than the original. A good director could polish the wit in performance.

André Gide's *Oedipe* (1930) is very amusing; like Cocteau's version, this is a play of ideas. Here is no driving, passionate Oedipus, eager for knowledge even if it will destroy him. He is inordinately self-confident, as Teiresias points out. Teiresias represents the gods and religion and, as Sartre also showed him, is limited. He admits that his authority is based on fear. He complains that

Oedipus is raising his children to be unbelievers, except for Antigone, who has decided to become anachronistically "a vestal." Polyneices and Eteocles are both shown to be incestuously interested in their sisters. Ismene is shown to be inordinately fashion conscious (at the end she says she will join Antigone, after she finds a suitable black dress). The boys are also ambitious to rule, and when their father is finally forced to leave the city, they are thrilled. This play is typically French in that we find asides on love and fashion.

Jocasta openly admits she was attracted to Oedipus, and that she was not at all upset about his killing Laius. Jocasta kills herself not out of guilt, but rather out of shame at the revelation. Oedipus claims he put out his eyes so that Teiresias could not boast anymore that his blindness was the source of his superior knowledge. To Teiresias's dismay, Antigone refuses to become a vestal as she said she would earlier; she will instead follow her own conscience and take care of her father. Oedipus is exiled until the people learn that the presence of his body can benefit them (one remembers this from *Oedipus at Colonus*). The people of the city are shown to be as self-serving as Oedipus's sons. Oedipus leaves with Antigone as his guide. Antigone emerges as a moral presence, and love binds her to her father.

Heiner Müller's *Ödipus Tyrann* (1966) is based on Friedrich Hölderlin's close translation of *Ödipus der Tyrann,* from 1804. Müller as usual creates a collage of fragments and takes a classical figure as a symbol for mankind. Rather than exalting the heroism of classical figures, he deconstructs heroes. He shows history winding back on itself and forming a net in which man is trapped. Oedipus tries to catch it, to "seize the hour," and realizes he himself is caught. In the myth of Oedipus, Müller stresses the futility of everyone's actions, from Laius vainly trying to kill his son to his son limping his way to a solution of his own riddle, which will be his destruction. Müller shows Oedipus as everyman, limping his way to death. Oedipus (man) is born from blood with the illusion he is free, but soon he is caught. He buries the world in his eye sockets and exchanges perception of the world for insight. He creates in his imagination, waving his hand in the air, grasping at emptiness. Müller excels in deconstructing hope, love, and happiness, all of which he considers "false consciousness," and gazing with exceptional rigor into the void. In vain do we search for Sophocles' vision of man's heroism and his search for truth; we have exchanged this for Müller's vision of his truth: a focused view on the abyss. He is a Nietzsche without hope, a Brecht without a blueprint for social reform. But one must admire his poetry of despair. He allows a director great leeway in interpreting his plays. The director can provide the social and political commentary that Müller said he shunned.

The Nigerian playwright Ola Rotimi's *The Gods Are Not to Blame* (1968) is based on *Oedipus Tyrannus* and incorporates ritual, folk sayings, and descriptions of tribal warfare. Rotimi claims that drama is a useful artistic medium for expression in Africa because it is not alien, like the novel. He also says, "I don't call [theater] a recreational pastime. I see theatre as a serious, almost religious, undertaking" (in Gilbert and Tompkins, *Post-colonial Drama*, p. 56). For his theater space he "prefers a small, round, outdoor theatre that incorporates the audience into a communal event rather than dividing it from the actors with an invisible fourth wall" (*Post-colonial Drama*, p. 157). The South African playwright Athol Fugard also prefers spaces like this, and he has written plays on Greek themes, showing their parallels with African stories. The Greeks, like these Africans, preferred outdoor, circular, and communal spaces.

After studying in Boston, Rotimi returned to Nigeria to establish a national theater, and his drama features Nigerian names and local atmosphere. He incorporates the Yoruba pantheon. This is an overtly political play, not dealing so much with racism or the experience of being occupied as with the bloodshed caused by one tribe fighting another. He takes the Oedipal tragedy of son killing father and applies it to the African situation. The killing here happens not because one man is trying to pass another on the road, but because a man from one tribe (Adetusa-Laius) is trying to take over the land occupied by a man from another tribe (Odewale-Oedipus).

A prologue sets out the background in mime. African choral singing with drums figures prominently. Ogun and the other gods of the Yoruba pantheon are invoked. We are told of tribes attacking tribes, and how Odewale overcame the Sphinx, in this case by freeing the country Kutuje from its invaders. We meet a very human Odewale, who, when the country is stricken with plague, produces his own children to show that they also are infected. He tells his people to use medicinal herbal cures instead of simply praying to the gods. As he says later, "Do not blame the gods" (p. 71). Although Odewale is clearly a victim of fate, he also speaks of man helping himself and is aware of human responsibility.

African chants form the choruses and in the printed text are given both in native Yoruban and English. Many are akin to incantations. Besides native magic, folk sayings are used and often accompany formal speeches, with homely proverbs such as "Until the rotten tooth is pulled out, the mouth must chew with caution" (p. 21), advocating that Odewale go slowly in rooting out the murderer of Adetusa, and "The monkey and gorilla may claim oneness but the monkey is Monkey and the gorilla, Gorilla" (p. 51), illustrating how one tribe will not accept another. New sayings come into being, rather like Homeric similes: "When the elders we esteem so highly can sell their honour for devil's money, then let pigs eat shame and men eat dung" (p. 27). With these words, this Odewale shows his dismay at the prophecies of Baba Fakunle (Teiresias).

Instead of Creon, we find another son by Ojuola (Jocasta) and Adetusa, to replace their lost son whom they thought they slew in accordance with the dire prophecy that accompanied his birth (that he would kill his father). This leads to sharper confrontations between "tribes" and two men roughly the same age fighting for the love of Ojuola.

Physical cruelty is emphasized here even more than in Sophocles' tragedy. The curse that Odewale calls down on the "murderer of Adetusa" is brutal:

I swear by this sacred arm of Ogun, that I shall straightway bring him to the agony of slow death. First he shall be exposed to the eyes of the world and put to shame—the beginning of living death. Next, he shall be put into lasting darkness, his eyes tortured in their living sockets until their blood and rheum swell forth to fill the hollow of crushed eyeballs. And then the final agony: we shall cut him from his roots. Expelled from this land of his birth, he shall roam in darkness in the land of nowhere, and there die unmourned by men who know him and buried by vultures who know him not. [Solemnly.] May the gods of our fathers—Ọbatala, Ọrunmila, Sango, Sọpọnna, Esu-Ẹlẹgbara, Agẹmọ, Ogun —stand by me. (p. 24)

How different is the Sophoclean original, where exile is to be the entire punishment of the man who confesses that he is the murderer of Laius.

Women and children are treated as inferiors. When the king enters, "children either kneel or prostrate themselves, according to their sex" (p. 37). Contrary to Sophocles' deference to her classical equivalent, Jocasta, Ojuola is treated like a servant.

When Adetusa and Odewale fight, it is a clash of strong magic on either side. Odawale "pulls out his tortoiseshell talisman pendant, holds it towards his assailants, and mesmerizes them" (p. 47). The old man curses Odewale and pulls out "his own charm of dried eagle's skull, vulture's claws, bright red parrot tail feathers" and prays (pp. 47–48). Odawale "staggers, his breathing becoming laboured" (p. 58), prays, and takes up a hoe after he invokes Ogun. With this he slays Adetusa.

Two tribesmen who saved Odewale as a child tell what happened. Odewale, in putting out his eyes, fulfills his own curse on the man who slew Adetusa. Aderopo, the second son of the original king and queen, will rule Kutuje, and he forgives his brother, Odewale, saying that all this is the fault of the gods. Odewale responds by saying, "Do not blame the gods . . . they knew my weakness: the weakness of a man easily moved to the defense of his tribe against others. I once slew a man on my farm in Ede. I could have spared him. But he spat on my tribe. He spat on the tribe I thought was my own tribe . . . I lost my reason" (p. 71).

Here is a parable for the intertribal fighting of Africa, with Xhosas against Zulus and Tutsis against Hutus, and naturally the war Rotimi knew best, the

Biafran War. Of course, this fighting is comparable to the wars of Ireland, Yugoslavia, and the Middle East. The play thus achieves a universal status, and yet it ends with Odewale leaving with all his children, saying,

When
The wood-insect
Gathers sticks,
On its own head it
Carries
Them. (p. 72)

In other words the gods are not to blame; man is, and when he recognizes this, he shoulders the responsibility himself. This is an effective reworking of the original to touch on both universal and local issues. In the original the dual motivation was more clearly delineated: "Apollo brought these sufferings upon me, but it was my hand that struck" (lines 1329–32). Some of the Sophoclean irony is lost, as is the taut, detective-story plot from the original, but this African play captures the fundamental lesson that comes from anagnorisis, or recognition of who one is and why one acts as one does. Performances can be cathartic and informative.

In 1978 Jean Anouilh wrote *Oedipus, or The Lame King, after Sophocles,* once again choosing a character who says "no" to his fate. His *Antigone, Eurydice,* and *Medea* all show rebellious females who, comparable to Oedipus, refuse to compromise. Anouilh presents his characters with psychological acuity. There are elements of modern religion and philosophy. As in most of the French versions, the characters speak explicitly about their sexual natures and experiences.

Anouilh is faithful to the original, with enough alterations to justify his claiming that it is "after Sophocles." At the beginning of the play Oedipus and Jocasta sit next to each other on a bench, and the chorus comments on them: "This man you see dreaming on this bench, seated next to his wife: he's Oedipus" (my translation, p. 9). The chorus (a single person) at first seems to be an all-seeing commentator rather than the elders that were part of the original play. He offers philosophical observations more than reactions of people, upset because of the plague. He also gives stage directions: "Finally, after silently looking at him for a long time—during the anxious silence of the crowd—the queen offers him her hand" (p. 11).

Oedipus and Jocasta discuss their first years together: how Oedipus slew the Sphinx, whom they call *La chienne chantante* (the singing bitch); how the queen never loved Laius, but this vigorous young man named Oedipus became her first real love. Over the years Jocasta felt Oedipus was becoming less ardent, and she sent him beautiful slaves to satisfy him. But he gave them up: "I took the path that I knew, towards that deep and hot chasm. . . . where I had no more fear . . . finally!" (p. 14). For a while they were happy. But the chorus tells us that the gods do not like human happiness, especially Oedipus's. The gods sent the plague on Thebes. A new group of peasants join the chorus, and they ask Oedipus for help.

Creon tells Oedipus that he must rid the land of Laius's murderer. He urges that Teiresias be sought. The chorus says that Oedipus now is both the hunter and the hunted beast: he is evidently omniscient.

Teiresias is piqued into revealing the truth to Oedipus that he is the criminal he seeks, and that before evening he will "see the light and lose it" (p. 35). The chorus continues to comment in a way that resembles Cocteau in his *Infernal Machine* and also the commentary that intersperses the episodes in Stravinsky's *Oedipus Rex*. It is obvious that Anouilh used Cocteau as a model, but he is ultimately more dramatically sound. Cocteau took too great a pleasure at times in verbal displays to create a moving drama.

Oedipus quarrels with Creon, who tries to teach Oedipus that he does not want the kingship, and that he does not suffer from the same disease that Oedipus does: a lust for power. He admits he trades political favors for those of a wife, a pretty slave, or some valuable that he craves; he believes that men have found no greater sweetener than pleasure for a life filled with meaningless hours.

The various oracles are revealed, and the peasant is sent for who witnesses Laius's killing. A messenger comes from Corinth, a rather amiable drunkard who wants to solve Oedipus's problems. Jocasta begs that the search be stopped. Earlier Jocasta comforted her son like a little boy. Now she begs him to imitate the beasts and accept happiness without questions. The stage instructions say that she appears to have aged, and her final words to Oedipus are, "My poor little one. I'll wait for you at home" (p. 77).

Oedipus discovers the truth about himself and finds that Jocasta has hung herself with her red scarf (the French pay attention to fashion details). Oedipus imitates his Senecan predecessor and blinds himself by repeated blows to his eyes: "'I do not want to see any more. I don't want to see anything any more.' He lifts his eyelids and strikes his eyeballs repeatedly: the blood spurts out and runs down his chin, not drop by drop but jetting like a black rain and a hail of bloody pebbles" (p. 88).

Creon returns, but not to gloat. Oedipus asks that Antigone lead him to Cithaeron and leave him there to die, just as his parents wanted. One should always obey one's parents. He also says he has forgotten his name: what should he call him who lived in the palace?

Oedipus entrusts his daughters to Creon: he says he never loved his sons, and since they are adults they should take care of themselves. He says their destiny is inscribed in their own hatred. Creon thinks he will have trouble with Antigone, just as he did with her father. He sees them as archetypes: "Oedipuses" and "Antigones," stubborn in their beliefs. He says that one should instead "try to avoid the attention of the gods: scratch out a little happiness each day without making any noise—dance while the music plays. . . . that's all" (p. 93). Oedipus says that is the path for the lowly, base cowards. Creon agrees with him but claims that is the only chance for man. As soon as man refuses to conform, as soon as he has an idea of his own, it becomes a massacre. Creon tells Oedipus, "bon voyage, old fool. I'll put things in order. One always needs someone to do that" (p. 94). He is rather like Creon in Anouilh's *Antigone*. Very sensible.

The chorus tells us that life has returned to normal. The plague will be just a memory the old people will tell their children. There are just as many deaths each day: "Unhappiness, like in the story of Oedipus that you have just heard, is not always so exceptional" (pp. 94–95).

This is a very moving play and touches the audience personally, at the same time that it deals in archetypes and universals. Anouilh does more than Cocteau ever did with his clever tricks. He has written a play about people with whom one identifies and about whom one is concerned. He also understands love. Only Berkoff has made an equally sympathetic and sexually attractive Jocasta.

In Steven Berkoff's *Greek* (1980), a modern version set in the East End of London, Oedipus ("Eddie") marries his mother, and he is perfectly happy to remain married to her. Berkoff has extended poetic passages, particularly when Oedipus reveals his love for his mother as a sexually exciting partner. Berkoff says of this that:

> *Greek* was my love poem to the spirit of Oedipus over the centuries. I ransacked the entire legend. So this is not simply an adaptation of Sophocles but a recreation of the various Oedipus myths which seemed to apply, particularly to a play about what I saw London had become. London equals Thebes and is full of riots, filth, decay, bombings, football mania, mobs at the palace gates, plague madness and post-pub depression. . . . *Greek* came to me via Sophocles, trickling its way down the millennia until it reached the unimaginative wastelands of Tufnell Park—a land more fantasized than real, an amalgam of the deadening war zones that some areas of London have become. It was also a love story. . . . In *Greek* every speech is an extreme feeling: of tenderness, of passion, of hate. (*The Theatre of Steven Berkoff*, p. 139)

The set was spare for this first performance of *Greeks* (London, 1988): a black wall in the back, and dirty white walls on each side. A table was in the center with chairs. The actors were in whiteface, a type of makeup mask which allows one to see the face. Actions were stylized, and at times the characters seemed to be puppets, somehow monumental. The Sphinx was a woman, also in whiteface, with enormous eyes which she kept crossed. Chorus members acted out the horrors they witnessed and duplicated deformities by pulling at their faces. There was a lot of humor. Mum: "More tea love?" (This is her solution to any crisis.) Dad: "What do you make of it son? You don't fancy your old mum do you son? You don't want to kill me do you boy?" (p. 30).

This is Oedipus with a happy ending: accept the violence, accept what fate has in store for you, and enjoy it! There is a biting edge to the satire, but there is genuine love poetry at the same time. The message seems to be that one can never have enough love, no matter where it comes from. An opera was based on *Greek,* composed by Mark-Anthony Turnage and first performed in 1988.

The first Chinese performance of Greek tragedy was an *Oedipus Rex* in 1986 at the Beijing Central Academy of Drama. It was translated by the pioneer scholar Luo Nian Sheng. Since then the entire canon has been translated into Chinese. It was performed at the Second Attic Drama Festival in Delphi and directed by Luo Jin Lin. The children were very moving at the end as they cried at the sight of their father and clung to him. The chorus members had shoes that made them the same height: there was both social and dramatic equality in this production from the People's Republic of China. Other productions followed of *Antigone, Medea,* and *Trojan Women.* In all of them they used the principal of "most expressed by least." They aimed at simple but faithful renderings of the original tragedies. In Oedipus they tried to show his heroic choice in defying his fate. The set had four Doric columns at the back of the playing area. The performances ended with a moment of silence to allow the audience members a moment to react to what they have witnessed. The plays also feature added prologues so that the Chinese could know some of the mythological background. Faithful to the Greeks, violence onstage was avoided. Oedipus puts out his eyes behind the chorus so he is not visible to the audience. He emerges with a black band covering his eyes. This also shows some of the stylization of traditional Chinese opera.

In the Chinese version of *Antigone* (1988, Delphi) the set was a simple war-scarred arch. Antigone buried her brothers in a type of stylized dance. At one point there were eight Antigones confronting Creon in dance. As Antigone goes to her cave, the chorus followed her waving silk ribbons (something again from traditional Chinese opera: the sleeve dance). At the end the ghosts of the dead return to haunt Creon for the rest of his life. This came from the opera *Madame Li Hui Niang.* It is rather like what Suzuki did in his *Clytemnestra*: the murdered mother returns to haunt Orestes and Electra, like a ghost from Noh drama. A recitative style of delivery in *Oedipus* and *Antigone* was used, also from traditional opera.

In 1985 Stephen Spender produced his *Oedipus Trilogy*, comprising the two Oedipus plays and *Antigone*. He began by writing a version in which all three plays could be produced in one evening at the Oxford Playhouse in Cambridge, 1983. From this he produced a longer version in a combination of prose and poetry. He cut and added where he felt there might be a chance of more emotional impact. Like Yeats, he focuses on poetic images: "Many are wonders and none more wondrous / Than man" (p. 168); "Know then, we should call no man happy / Till he has passed that frontier where all pain ceases" (p. 90); "Nightingales / Pour forth their throbbing song from hidden depths" (p. 93). Or Ismene's comment to Antigone: "You have a heart of fire for deeds of ice" (p. 160). Spender cuts the last chorus of Antigone and ends, "Come, blessed day, for me the day / That is my last, where I'll see no tomorrow. O, / Oedipus, / Blind, blind, blind" (p. 199). He brings the trilogy full circle back to Oedipus. This is a good example of a poet translating a poet: the later poet rewrites the earlier poet into his own modern idiom.

Timberlake Wertenbaker also translated the same trilogy (1992) with less poetry but more dramatic tautness. This trilogy was first called *The Thebans* and was performed at the Swan Theatre, Stratford-upon-Avon, in 1991. She abbreviates the choruses, sometimes using a telegraphic style: "Wonder / at many things / But wonder most / at this thing: / Man" (p. 102). Or "See what calamities have come upon him [Oedipus]. And seeing this, how can we say anyone is happy until he has crossed to the other side without suffering" (p. 45); "And in the deepest thicket, a world of nightingales— / propitious song" (p. 49). She ends the trilogy faithful to the original with the words of the chorus at the end of the *Antigone:* "Those who puffed themselves up with great words have been / dealt great blows. In old age, / they have learned judgement" (p. 137). It may have gained in fidelity, but it loses in poetry.

Rita Dove's *The Darker Face of the Earth* shows Oedipus as a slave in the American South and was performed in Oregon in 1996 and in 1999 at the Royal National in London. Secretly having had sexual intercourse with one of her slaves, the mistress of the house, Amalia, gives birth to a black child, and her husband and doctor take it from her. The husband wants to kill it but the doctor relents, and so the story of Oedipus begins again.

The child, Augustus, is educated by a kind ship's captain but is finally sold at the captain's death as a slave and makes his way back to the house where he was born. He is seduced by Amalia. Augustus kills a black man in a swamp (Hector), not knowing that Hector was his father, and finally, in a revolutionary coup, kills the master of the house who is married to Amalia. Augustus tells her what her husband began to tell him about his birth, and she finishes the story. Augustus realizes the truth: Amalia is his mother.

Amalia stabs herself, and the revolutionaries think Augustus has carried out his task of killing both the master and mistress of the house. He does not put out his eyes as the original Oedipus did, but a better future seems to lie before him, complete with a love interest in another slave. Here instead of a King Oedipus, ruling with Jocasta and concerned for his people, we find a slave who is a leader of others in their fight for freedom. Oedipus is conflated with American history, and Dove's poetry and passion deliver an impressive play.

In 1998 Dare Clubb's version of *Oedipus,* performed by the Blue Light Theatre Company, was called a "four-hour long orgy of self-indulgence," in spite of the excellent cast of Billy Crudup and Frances McDormand. A reviewer quotes an unintentionally funny line: when Oedipus is still in Corinth he propositions Merope, the mother who adopted him; she rejects him saying, "I can't marry you; I'm not your mother" (Hischak, *American Theatre,* p. 425).

Oedipus at Colonus has fewer versions or performances. In 1845 Friedrich Wilhelm IV of Potsdam performed *Oedipus at Colonus,* with music by Mendelssohn. T. S. Eliot's *The Elder Statesman* (1958) is based on *Oedipus at Colonus.* I believe it is the best of his versions of Greek tragedy, because it is the least pretentious. Nevertheless, it does not attain the majesty of the Sophoclean original, with its dread sinner going to his death in the grove of the Eumenides. This shows the story of a man who wears the mask of an elder statesman. As he is about to enter an old age home, two people from his past come to haunt him. One was a friend he had at Oxford, in whom he cultivated expensive tastes, and who subsequently became a forger to support those tastes. One night they were driving back to Oxford when our hero, now Lord Claverton, ran over a body and did not stop.

At the new home, Lord Claverton meets a woman who sued him for breach of promise and who took a settlement. Lord Claverton has gone to this home with his daughter Monica, who becomes engaged to a man named Charles. Michael, Monica's brother, wants to leave the country because of his debts. Lord Claverton gives him a moralistic speech but then sees the absurdity of it and gains the courage to tell his children about his misdemeanors (hardly the crimes of Oedipus: it turns out also, from a newspaper article, that the corpse was already dead when run over). The old friend, called Gomez (his new name), offers Michael a "safe" haven. This is Polyneices with a happy ending.

Lord Claverton leaves his daughter and goes for a walk alone; we have the feeling that he will not return from this walk alive. It is as gentle a way of leaving life as Oedipus's walk in the grove of the Eumenides at Colonus. Lord Claverton says as he leaves: "I've been freed from the self that pretends to be someone; / And in becoming no one, I begin to live. / It is worth while dying, to find out what life is" (p. 129).

Each discovers love in his or her own way. Lord Claverton reveals truths about himself and accepts the truths of others, including those of his children, something that every parent must discover. This is another case of Greek tragedy turned into domestic comedy, but one with serious lessons: the anagnorisis ("recognition") of the mask one assumes in society and who one actually is behind the mask. The play is also well written and amusing.

Lee Breuer gives us the highlights from Sophocles' *Oedipus Tyrannus* and *Antigone* as well as *Oedipus at Colonus* (circa 405 B.C.) in his *Gospel at Colonus* (1982). In the guise of a black revival service, Breuer draws on the rich Afro-American gospel tradition. Oedipus is blended with Christ: Oedipus is a "sinner" but achieves a type of salvation through suffering and offers hope to mankind in his death. The setting is a church with a cycloramic painting as background showing the Last Judgment: it is described as "more Africa than Europe . . . part Eden and part Colonus' Sacred grove" (p. 4). A preacher reads from "The Book of Oedipus." Some characters only sing, such as Ismene in accordance with her lyrical nature; others only speak, such as Theseus and Polyneices, following their less lyrical and more legalistic approaches to life. Oedipus and Antigone are each played by two people, one that sings and one that acts. Oedipus the singer is played by a blind man, the leader of a group called the Five Blind Boys of Alabama, which functions as his private chorus.

At the end, when Oedipus dies, he sinks down along with his quintet, all resting their heads on the piano, which is their bier. They disappear into an open grave. Then to the amazement of all, the bier reappears, ascending to a hallelujah chorus, and Oedipus and the quintet emerge clapping. Oedipus is truly immortal. We have seen him die and now he is resurrected. This is very different from Sophocles: in his play we do not see Oedipus return. There the mourning of Antigone will last.

No two performances of the *Gospel at Colonus* are identical, and the congregational choir interacts constantly with the other actors and singers. This is a communal creation and much is unpredictable, and spontaneous emotions add to every performance. This version also shows how Greek tragedy benefits from music in performance.

Antigone

An early version of *Antigone* in French was by Robert Grenier, *Antigone, ou La piété* (1580). *Antigone* was very popular in the eighteenth century and in the twentieth century. It has often been played when there is political unrest. In 1804 Friedrich Hölderlin's translation *Antigonae* coupled fidelity to the original with poetic flair.

In 1898 *Antigone* first was performed in Russia at the Moscow Art Theatre in a translation by Dimitri Merezhkovsky. There was an attempt to preserve the ancient ritual and ceremony. At the same time there was an attempt at realism and psychological fidelity to the characters, as had been developed in the theater of Chekov. There is an obvious clash in these two approaches, but this marked an experimental advance in Russian theater. No curtain separated the stage from the audience. There was an altar on the set with a flame burning on it throughout the performance. The young V. Meyerhold appeared as Teiresias. Meyerhold's theater later was based on the classical Greek theater.

Another French version of *Antigone* was produced by Jean Cocteau in 1922, with sets by Picasso, music by Arthur Honegger, and costumes by Chanel. Pound admired Antigone's accusation: "You have invented justice," or as she says literally, she does not think that "the caprice of a man can impose itself on divine law" (p. 26). In general Cocteau abbreviated Sophocles' splendid text and effectively eliminated the poetry. He simplified the text to make it more dramatically viable and to allow for various dumb shows (aptly named, with statue-like figures crossing the stage) in performance. For the 1927 revival he uses gigantic heads and masked figures: "The group suggest a sordid royal carnival, a family of insects" (my translation, p. 11). His choices eliminate Sophocles' suggestive ambiguity.

In the chorus, beginning, "There are many wonders in the world, but none more wonderful than man," Cocteau reduces this line to "Man is wonderful" (*inouï*, p. 23). This is typical of what was done throughout. When Creon answers Ismene's question regarding his killing of his son's fiancé, he says he will find other fields to plow, but Cocteau says, "He will find other wombs" (or "bellies," *ventres*). There is the usual Cocteau wit. When Haemon says, "That's the opinion in the streets," Creon answers, "So now the streets show me the way" (p. 37).

Cocteau's *Infernal Machine* and his prologue and interludes for Stravinsky's *Oedipus Rex* showed more wit and mastery for transforming the classics. His *Antigone* is naïve and reductive of the brilliant original.

Jean Anouilh staged his *Antigone* (1944) during the Nazi occupation of Paris; his even-handed presentation of both Creon's and Antigone's positions got it past the censors. Creon stands for life, with all its compromises. He speaks with the voice of rationality and conventionality. Antigone is a romantic young girl who says "no" to orders and convention. She no longer stands for the honor and right of the family and the gods of the underworld as she did in Sophocles. She is a stubborn little girl who insists on dying, although she is given many chances to escape. Creon even admits that the bodies of her brothers were indistinguishable, and his insistence on one not being buried is simply a political move to keep him in power. Antigone is shown attached to her pet, her nurse, and her fiancé, to whom she smuggles a final message.

We can only admire Antigone's act of not compromising, but we are never given the clear reason for this choice. Neither Anouilh nor Brecht gives to Antigone the heroic value that Sophocles did. Anouilh offers a play of intellectual tricks, and Brecht, ideological ones.

Bertolt Brecht's *Antigone* (1948) showed Creon overtly as Hitler, along with his aggressive son Megareus, who continues to fight and finally brings defeat on Thebes, an allusion to modern Germany. He succeeds in his *Verfremdungseffekt* (alienation effect), distancing us from all the characters, including Antigone. This alienation is a technique for distancing the audience members so that they can make an objective assessment of the action they are seeing and come up with a moral judgment. Brecht wants to enlist minds over emotions, but he does not always succeed. Brecht objected to what he saw as Antigone's pacifism. He thought she did a disservice to the memory of the German partisans who fought against the Nazis. Judith Malina's version from 1966 of Brecht's *Antigone* was performed in sixteen countries over twenty years, including Ireland, Franco's Spain, Poland, and Prague, all at politically crucial times.

In 1949, Carl Orff had his opera *Antigonae* performed, based on Hölderlin's translation. He returned to the Sophoclean original for its postwar messages. He had his work performed under the Nazis; like Anouilh's it contained veiled criticism. Although often simply remembered as an official composer for the Nazis, perhaps his *Antigonae* was a form of expiation, saying, "I have a sense of justice after all."

In 1967 the Caribbean writer Kamau Brathwaite set his *Odale's Choice* in Africa. Odale is Antigone, and she buries her brother against her uncle's decree (he is the ruler). Creon tries to exile Odale, but she insists on being buried next to her brother, Tawia. The play ends with Odale going to her death as she says, "Don't touch me! Of my own free will I will go" (p. 32). Earlier she said, "Either I had to obey your law, or the law of my gods" (p. 28).

Athol Fugard's *The Island* (1973) features black prisoners of South Africa's apartheid period playing out *Antigone* in protest. *The Island* was also staged in Ireland in 1986 after three Irish versions of *Antigone* (1984) and was revived in London at the Royal National Theatre in 2000 and BAM (Brooklyn Academy of Music) in 2003. Fugard's play opens with a scene that shows two inmates doing the horrible, futile work that was assigned to them on Robben Island. They are chained and forced to run in tandem; if they do not run fast enough they are beaten. In the cell they treat their wounds with their own urine to disinfect them.

Through drama the prisoners try to remain sane. They simulate news broadcasts and pretend to speak to their friends back home on an imaginary telephone. "John: 'News bulletin and weather forecast. Black Domination was chased by White Domination. Black Domination lost its shoes and collected a few bruises. Black Domination will run barefoot to the quarry tomorrow. Conditions locally remain unchanged—thunderstorms with the possibility of cold showers and rain. Elsewhere, fine and warm!'" (p. 196).

The prisoners are also allowed "concerts." In the concert that is the subject of this play, they intend to perform Sophocles' *Antigone*. One of the inmates, John (Creon), learns that he is going to be free in three months. The other, Winston (Antigone), is in for life. The agony of the latter gives fuel to the final performance of *Antigone*.

The inmates perform a scene from the drama that is highly rewritten. It is clear that Creon represents the oppressive power of apartheid and that Antigone represents human rights. Antigone says to Creon, "You are only a man, Creon. Even as there are laws made by men, so too there are others that come from God. He watches my soul for a transgression even as your spies hide in the bush at night to see who is transgressing your laws. Guilty against God I will not be for any man on this earth. . . . But if I had let my mother's son, a Son of the Land, lie there as food for the carrion fly, Hodoshe, my soul would never have known peace" (p. 226).

At the end of the prison concert, this character tears off his wig and says, "Gods of our Fathers! My Land! My Home! Time waits no longer. I go now to my living death, because I honoured those things to which honour belongs" (p. 227), a literal, albeit abbreviated, translation of Antigone's final words in Sophocles' play. We are left with an image of human triumph. Human oppression is overcome by the greatness of the human spirit.

Performing this play during the time of apartheid in South Africa was not only daring, but it also provided needed catharsis for the audience. It was first performed at the Space Theatre in Cape Town. If someone looked out the window at the back of the theater, he could see Robben Island.

In 1983 Miro Gavran had his (unpublished) *Creon's Antigone* performed at the Gavella Drama Theatre in Zagreb, Yugoslavia. He gives thanks to Sophocles, Anouilh, and Smole. It begins with Antigone reflecting on how she was arrested, without a trial and for no reason. Antigone pleads with Creon, saying she is harmless. Creon tells her to wait, with time she can become dangerous. The king comes to complain to her about his own troubles: the loneliness of ruling, the unending pace of his life and the demands put on him, the countless problems, and the people waiting for him to make a mistake.

Creon claims he prefers his subjects to hate him. It's more reliable. He says everyone wants to rule in his place, particularly his son and the queen, to say nothing of Oedipus's sons. They are all in prison now waiting for their deaths; he will only spare "harmless and foolish" Ismene. Creon tells Antigone that she is dangerous, because she has less of an odor of fear about her than others.

The Island. By Athol Fugard. Winston Ntshona (left) and John Kani, prisoners on Robben Island, "call home" in one of the fantasies which makes their imprisonment barely tolerable. The Market Theatre, Johannesburg, South Africa (1986). Photo: Ruphin Coudyzer. Used by permission.

The Island. By Athol Fugard. John Kani (left), playing Creon, and Winston Ntshona, playing Antigone, enact this age-old drama of human rights, for the defense of which they are both in prison. The Market Theatre, Johannesburg, South Africa (1986). Photo: Ruphin Coudyzer. Used by permission.

He says he will stage a scenario, which is basically Sophocles' *Antigone:* mercenaries will be hired to attack, and bodies will be placed in the appropriate places. Antigone says that no one will believe that she would risk her life to bury her brother. Then Creon explains her idealism to her. They both prefer Ismene's role. Creon threatens torture if Antigone refuses to play her part, so she agrees. He wants her to rehearse so she can play with conviction. He will torture her if she refuses. She has two weeks.

A week goes by. The second act shows us Antigone embracing her role. She no longer fears death. She says she thinks the play is a good piece of work, and that Creon should have been a playwright. She questions Creon about love and happiness. She knows that he lives with constant fear. She predicts an early end for him. He may kill five people now, but he cannot kill his whole kingdom, and one among them, one day . . . She takes out some poison and swallows it. She will be dead in a minute. She says that she has thwarted his play. But Creon says he predicted this also, and Ismene will play the part; no one will know (they resemble each other). Antigone calls him a monster, and he says to her, "Farewell, you who could not be king."

This play reflects the fear of people who live with a dictator and secret police. It villainizes Creon and also makes Antigone into a silly girl (rather as Anouilh did). Creon is triumphant at the end, but if Antigone had really believed what she said, she would not have been bothered by his saying that he had foreseen her taking poison. I find the ending rather weak and contrived. Both characters are undercut. Perhaps this way the play survived Yugoslav censorship (another lesson from Anouilh). This is no one's tragedy, except the country's. Creon as Milosovic does not achieve the stature of Sophocles' tragic figure, but this play is a good illustration of *Antigone* used to protest political abuse.

The Irish use *Antigone* to indict British occupation. In 1984, Tom Paulin's *The Riot Act* shows us an Antigone from Northern Ireland, and she is a freedom fighter, whereas Creon's words sound like Ian Paisley's. Aidan Carl Mathews's *Antigone* (1984, unpublished) has his heroine unjustly murdered, whereas official propaganda claims that she has been seen in another country. Also in 1984 Brendan Kennelly sees Irish relevance in his *Antigone*. He focuses on the power of words for both good and evil. Both Antigone and Creon speak to each other in a common language, but they do not understand each other. This is an ongoing tragedy in the peace negotiations between England and Ireland.

The memory of the dead is dangerous. Kennelly's Antigone says that she has more love for the mistreated noble dead than for the ambitious living. Antigone's acts lead to the downfall of a tyrant, and she is inspired by the dead of her past, as are so many of the Republican heroes who are conscious of the Fenian dead, besides the modern hunger strikers, such as Bobby Sands.

Creon here is Cromwell and is symbolic of England and its occupation. Antigone's moral superiority wins. We find the Catholic God in this *Antigone* as we do in many Irish reworkings of the classics.

The Polish director Andrzej Wajda produced a version in 1984 which set *Antigone* in a Gdansk shipyard and aligned her with the Solidarity movement. *Antigone* once again provided modern political protest.

In 1989 A. R. Gurney's *Another Antigone* was performed at the Old Globe Theatre in San Diego. It begins with a confrontation between a classics professor and a student who wants to write a play on the theme of Antigone, associating it with the nuclear arms race. The professor, Henry Harper, refuses on the grounds that it does not satisfy the requirements and is badly written. The student, Judy Miller, gets support from peace groups and is going to perform it the evening before graduation. Miller needs credit for this course or she will not be able to graduate with her class.

The dean tries to work out a compromise, but none seems to be possible between Harper and Miller. The dean raises the issue of Harper's dwindling enrollments in his classics courses and the fact that the student is Jewish: he might be prejudiced against her. The student, when interviewed by the dean, denies that the professor is anti-Semitic but then takes up the idea and makes Antigone Jewish in her play. Harper is asked to go on a leave of absence (a study leave in Greece), and Miller refuses a check that she is being awarded for her play. She is able to find a Jewish drama professor who would give her an A for the play and so she is able to graduate with her class.

Both Harper and Miller seem to lose, as indeed did the original Creon and Antigone, but the issues seem trivial. Harper at the end is willing to lower his standards so he can continue teaching; Miller seems to have learned nothing except how to politick and get her way. There is more sympathy for Harper, and in this sense the play is a precursor for David Mamet's *Oleanna*. Harper and Gurney himself also seem to misunderstand Greek tragedy when Harper says that tragedy arises when a person no longer has a choice; I think it is the opposite. The choices that people make and the knowledge that they are responsible for their choices are the sources of the greatest tragedy. Another political performance is *Antigone: A Cry for Peace* (1994). It was produced by Nikos Koundouros at the border of the former Yugoslavia with a military backdrop featuring tanks.

In 1999 Athol Fugard directed my translation of *Antigone* in Cork and Listowel, Ireland. Karen Carpenter directs it at the Globe Theatres in 2003. Antigone was played by Patricia Logue from Derry (Londonderry) in the 1999 version, and her accent clearly located the political thrust of the play. The chorus was played by Celina Hinchcliffe, an actress of Irish ancestry who was raised in England. Trina Dillon, who played Ismene, was of the same background. Creon was played by Damen Scranton, whose father was black and whose mother was white. Scranton teaches black students in New York and feels he can protect them most by urging them to obey the law. Steffen Collings, of English ancestry, played Haemon. The messenger and guard was Irish-American: Kelly Doyle. Our Teiresias was Ivan Talijancic, a Serbo-Croatian student. Two more Irish actors rounded the cast off: Norah McGettigan as Eurydice and Peter Sugrue from Listowel as Teiresias's guide. It was an international cast, and we were offering them a catharsis for many of their own fears. They brought their nationalities to play in their roles.

Fugard had the play begin with the lights shut off. Voices were heard saying names from the play: Acheron, Salmydessus, Dirce, Thebes, Dionysus. Four actors chose the names they liked and one began; the next followed at a lower decibel, and the next accordingly, in a fugal structure. Then Antigone said "Ismene" from one side of the stage, at first softly and then more urgently. Ismene waited a bit, and on the fourth "Ismene" answered "Antigone," likewise quietly one time, and then more urgently. As their volume increased, the four voices that began quieted down until one only heard the two girls who cried out to each other and ran into each other's arms.

As Ismene tried to speak, Antigone put her hand over her mouth and searched the area. The lights went up, but dimly. Only when the first chorus entered did the full lights fill the stage, to coincide with the sunrise described in the ode. When Creon first appeared he was greeted by a shout, "King Creon!" He was cheered at appropriate times in his first speech. All muttered agreement.

Just before the entrance of Teiresias, the ensemble made wind sounds. At the end the dead bodies were symbolically represented by an article of clothing. Haemon threw his coat at his father. Eurydice laid her cape down at Creon's feet. Finally, Antigone put her wreath next to the two "bodies." The four actors who began reciting the names at the beginning started again. These sounds faded away gradually. Ismene broke the final silence and called quietly, "Antigone?" three times. The lights went up. One would hope to convey by this question not only a sense of loss, but also of the need for Antigone and her sense of justice in the modern world.

Whereas *Antigone* and *Prometheus* have been used to express anti-authoritarian ideas, *Ajax* could be used to convey fascistic might, as it was by Pietro Aschieri in 1939. Peter Sellars set *Ajax* (1986, adapted by Robert Auletta) in front of the Pentagon and showed the corruption of generals who censor in-

Antigone. Adapted by Marianne McDonald. Directed by Athol Fugard. Belfast actress Patricia Logue plays Antigone, to whom her sister Ismene (Trina Dillon) urges a compromise she finds intolerable. Firkin Crane Center, Cork, Ireland (1999). Photo: Marianne McDonald.

Ajax. Adapted by Robert Auletta. Directed by Peter Sellars. Menelaus (Ralph Marrero) screams over the dead Ajax (Howie Seago) that as a traitor he will never be buried. A La Jolla Playhouse presentation of an American National Theater production (1986). Photo: Micha Langer. Used by permission.

formation and are power mad. Ajax was played by a deaf-mute, Howie Seago, who sloshed around knee-deep in blood in a large plastic booth. The chorus of soldiers delivered his lines.

Ajax

Heiner Müller created *Ajax for Instance: A Poem/Performance Text* in 1995. He was perhaps feeling his own irrelevance since he was not understood and was abandoned by the communists, whom he also felt had betrayed their own ideals. He was accused of working indirectly for the *Stasi,* the abhorred secret police. About this time, he had a rival for running the Berliner Ensemble in Peter Zadek (whom he quotes in this piece). It seemed to be that he was feeling his uselessness as a playwright, and thereby paralleled Ajax, who in times of peace was no longer a valued hero. As usual he deheroizes the hero, seeing him as a man tested by a goddess who played games with him. The piece claims that finally there is only the invention of silence; only the blood of Ajax is left. Müller is seen as an irrelevant man. One thinks of the ending of Hamlet: "The rest is silence." Müller is well versed in the classics—Shakespeare, Greek and Latin classics, and his own German ones—and his plays are patchworks of literary allusions.

Freud used Oedipus to represent what he saw as a universal complex in man. But the Sophoclean Oedipus is not the Freudian Oedipus of the Oedipus complex; Sophocles' Oedipus did everything to avoid having sexual intercourse with his mother. But we find the seeds of Freudianism in the comment by Sophocles' Jocasta, who says many men have had intercourse with their mothers in their dreams (lines 981–82).

Electra

The Electra complex may also be traced to Freud. Hugo von Hofmannsthal and Richard Strauss's opera *Elektra* emphasized the Freudian aspects to her character, including her obsession with her father. Jean Giraudoux wrote *Électre* in 1937 and gives it a modern setting with modern philosophical observations. At the end Électre pleads the cause of justice. She is the idealistic female heroine we find in other classical plays by Giraudoux, like Andromaque in *La guerre de Troie n'aura pas lieu* (1935), translated into English as *Tiger at the Gates* and about the Trojan War. Giraudoux's *Électre* ends with a hopeful sunrise. Andrei Serban's *An Ancient Trilogy,* which included *Electra,* was performed in Romania in 1989 as a critique of the Ceausescu family and regime.

Deborah Warner and Fiona Shaw presented a brilliant production of Sophocles' *Electra* in 1992 in Derry. At the end no one applauded, simply be-

Electra. Directed by Deborah Warner. Translated by Kenneth McLeish. Electra (Fiona Shaw with member of Chorus) rejoices in being reunited with Orestes, the brother she believed had been lost. Royal Shakespeare Company, Riverside Studios, London (1991). Photo © Allan Titmuss.

cause they were so moved. The audience stayed to discuss the play, because the issues raised were ones with which everyone was all too well acquainted. Mary Holland wrote of this performance: "At one level, last week was an awesome vindication of those who believe that this is what the arts should be about, and where they should be—close to the cutting edge of political argument. Fiona Shaw said: 'I do believe we must use the theatre to debate these danger-ous issues—justice, retribution, violence.'" Holland continues: "One woman spoke of the actress's performance as Electra: 'I thought of Mrs Kelly, whose son was killed on Bloody Sunday, and the way they would find her, even years afterwards, lying on his grave with her face smeared with earth.' Another talked of Electra's sister begging her to bow to the inevitable: 'I kept remem-bering the hunger strikers, when their families were trying to persuade them to give up the fast and accept the prison system'" (*Irish Times*, February 13, 1992).

Frank McGuinness's translation in 1997 toured England with Zoe Wana-maker as Electra, and it also had great success in New York. David Leveaux directed. Wanamaker had just lost her father, and she delivered an impassioned performance.

A throbbing, deep beat in the background greets the audience. The set shows us something like Bosnia, with devastated buildings, and a suggestion of ancient ruins with a column overturned. The dress is modern Sarajevo: suggestions of Moslem women in the chorus with their hair covered. Electra appears with her hair in tatters: hunks are cut out and she has bleeding sores. She wears an overcoat which may have been her father's. Fog and rain fill the stage; one drop ceaselessly falls and splashes throughout the entire performance. This is an apt set for this bleak drama of revenge about two children (Electra and Orestes) who kill their mother (Clytemnestra) because she killed their father (Agamemnon). The mother's excuse was that the father had killed their daughter, Iphigenia. When does the cycle of vengeance and violence end?

The best aspects of this performance are the silences, such as the unbearable silence when Electra and Orestes finally recognize each other. The urn scene, where Electra-Wanamaker thinks she is holding her brother's ashes, is also superb. Many in the audience wept. Wanamaker did this in a restrained, quiet way, contrary to much of the rest of her performance, which conveyed a neurotic and mad Electra. However, Sophocles' Electra is not mad. Euripides' is. Sophocles makes Electra and Orestes into heroes; Euripides shows them as deranged, egocentric monsters. In this production of Sophocles we recognize the words, but the acting works against the ancient text. Orestes resembles a British punk at a soccer game, shouting his taunts and commands to Aegisthus before killing him.

There are just too many cute devices; directors should trust the text more. The Bosnian set is innocuous enough, but by the end of the play, the endlessly dripping water becomes a Chinese torture for the audience. Electra comes out wearing a mask, removes it, and puts it on at the end of the play. Does this remind us that we are seeing a mythical character in an ancient play? We are also overwhelmed by the gore in the performance. Orestes and Pylades appear with their arms soaked in blood. Electra takes Orestes' dripping arm and licks up the blood. When Electra recognizes the *paidagogos* (tutor) to whom she gave Orestes as a baby, he lifts her up as she assumes a fetal position and passes out. Perhaps she mistook him for Agamemnon and she is returning to the embrace of her father. Perhaps she desires the protection of the womb. The audience is unsure. One thing the audience is sure about is the symbolism of the costumes: red for Clytemnestra, white for Aegisthus, and a slinky dress for Chrysothemis, against the war rags of the rest. Claire Bloom (Clytemnestra) contrasted her dress with a bland performance.

In spite of the criticism there were moments of genius in the occasional silences and in some poignant deliveries; for instance, Wanamaker screams in anguish as her mother screams in the agony of her death throes. For all their enmity, there is much in common between these two women, as indeed Electra points out in the play. But one would have needed a stronger Clytemnestra. Chrysothemis's moderation also made a lot of sense in this performance; however, as a result Electra appeared even more deranged. McGuinness wanted to show the madness of vengeance, particularly because he had firsthand experience of it in Ireland. He did that well with his adaptation and this director. Perhaps Sophocles was diminished a bit by the gimmicks and reinterpretation, but the greatness could still be seen.

Women of Trachis

Ezra Pound wrote a colloquial version of *Women of Trachis* in 1954. He considered this play to be symbolic of the cohesion of the universe, as contained in his revelatory phrase, "Splendour, it all coheres" (p. 50). Pound suggests that this play be staged with masks, and his Heracles represents "solar vitality" (p. 4) and Deianira is called "Daysair" (p. 5). He freely cuts and alters but is essentially faithful to the original. The loftiest language (mainly in the chorus) is linked with the most colloquial, which is also now the most dated. An example of the former is "Dian's beach / Neath her golden-shafted arrows" (p. 28), and the latter, "on the Q.T.," "screw-ball," or "me blubbering like a flapper" (pp. 17, 19, 45). Images are far-fetched, such as "put some cement in your face, reinforced concrete" (p. 54), along with some very felicitous ones, "Double yoke / Under one cloak" (p. 25), Daysair's phrase for sharing her bed with Heracles' Iole. There are also mistakes, such as "Alkmenes's son for Alkmenes's son" (p. 10). The occasional foreign phrase also does not add to the accessibility that seemed to be Pound's intent because he was writing in a dramatic medium. This differs from most of his other literary endeavors, which rarely catered to accessibility.

Philoctetes

Philoctetes has inspired many playwrights, who found it offered philosophical or political commentary on the present. André Gide's *Philoctetes, or The Treatise on Three Ethics* (1898) speaks of some philosophical problems. It shows the existentialist progression from love of one's country, to love of another, and finally to the most valid love: love of self. This is a play about love and identity. It is also a celebration of love between men and a rite of philosophical passage. Love and existentialism link this version with Cocteau.

More political and tough-minded is Heiner Müller's *Philoctetes* (1965, followed by another version, *Philoktet, der Horatier* 1968). This was his first play on a classical theme. He offers an impassioned ideological critique of a man in power who seeks more power with no ethical restraint. Odysseus is a soldier blindly following immoral orders. He resembles the Odysseus of *Ajax* more than the Odysseus of Sophocles' *Philoctetes*. He is more concerned about the communal good than about his own egotistic concerns. Philoctetes here is concerned with personal slights, and Neoptolemus is shown to be a liberal blunderer, first taking pity on Philoctetes and returning his bow, and then killing him so that he would not kill Odysseus. Müller removes the mask from power politics and seems to be saying that it is better to take a realistic look at the consequences of following a cause that demands the absolute obedience of its followers, particularly if that cause calls for sordid acts. The fact that the cause is a good one does not justify some of the means used to obtain its ends. Here Müller is faithful to Sophocles. He is not faithful in his total elimination of heroism. The communists were not pleased with this barefaced depiction of *machtpolitik*, with the obvious corollary that they also demanded absolute obedience and occasionally resorted to what most people would call crimes.

Also political but not so tough-minded is Seamus Heaney's *The Cure at Troy* (1990). It is based on *Philoctetes* and deals with the Irish situation and people's persistence in nursing old wounds. His play proceeds from and ends in optimism. It is a version that truly urges, believes, and hopes "for a great sea-change / On the far side of revenge / . . . that a further shore is reachable from here" (p. 77).

There is an exposition that not only locates the chorus in its mediating function, but also lays out the theme of the play: a focus on the wound rather than the cure. The play is about a man with a wound, and he will be cured at Troy. Heaney sees the Irish as obsessed with their wounds and believes that this obsession is hindering their reaching a lasting peace.

Heaney's optimism shines at the end in a speech delivered by the chorus leader. These words are not in Sophocles but in modern Ireland:

> Human beings suffer,
> They torture one another,
> They get hurt and get hard.
> No poem or play or song
> Can fully right a wrong
> Inflicted and endured.
>
> The innocent in gaols
> Beat on their bars together.
> A hunger-striker's father

Stands in the graveyard dumb.
The police widow in veils
Faints at the funeral home.

History says, *Don't hope*
On this side of the grave.
But then, once in a lifetime
The longed-for tidal wave
Of justice can rise up,
And hope and history rhyme. (p. 77)

The sufferings on both sides are mentioned. The hope is for a peaceful settlement and a healing of the wound of hate. The poetry is superb.

All three of these versions of *Philoctetes* by Gide, Müller, and Heaney
minimize Sophocles' emphasis on honor and a boy's loyalty to his own ideals.

Trackers of Oxyrhynchus (Reconstructed Satyr Play)

Tony Harrison shows the power of the lyre to celebrate creation or to warn of
destruction. The lyre can sing a joyful song or one that foretells disaster. He
has taken the Sophoclean satyr play and broken the classical mold, allowing
papyrological fragments to fuel a burst of tragi-comic fireworks in his *Trackers
of Oxyrhynchus*, based on Sophocles' satyr play *Ichneutai*. As the ancient play
is reconstructed in a modern frame, it becomes a commentary on elitist art
and society. Cultural imperialism is lifted from its ancient setting as modern
punks put a torch to the salvaged manuscript and the trackers obliterate themselves along with their masters—a bitter warning to those who would like to
reserve the benefits of art and society for themselves.

His play begins with Grenfell and Hunt and a team of fellahin searching
for papyri at Oxyrhynchus, Egypt. The fellahin chant syllables from the *Ichneutai,* including titles of Sophocles' lost plays, and their chant sounds rather
like an invocation. A rhythmic percussive background punctuates. Time is also
fragmented, and as pictures are taken the action is frozen (image and time
are pictured as fragmented papyri—pure rhythm without melody or flow).
Rhythm also seems the satyr's prerogative, whereas melody will be Apollo's;
the fellahin toss the papyri, showing their talent at sport, while Grenfell and
Hunt show theirs for scholarship (one throws group, the other reads).

Grenfell is possessed and Apollo gradually invades his mind. Hunt expresses concern for Grenfell's health. After a tedious going over of lists suddenly there's a discovery: Pindar's *Paean for the People of Delphi (Paean VI)*,
which the fellahin chant with passion. Apollo begins a frantic dialogue with
Grenfell and urges Grenfell to find the god's own play. Grenfell tries to shoot

Apollo in desperation, and a relay race ensues in which the chants of ancient spectators are heard.

Apollo-Grenfell emerges from the rubbish heap, and the *Ichneutai* begins with Apollo looking for his stolen cattle. He cries "Hunt," and Hunt answers from the tent, "Just a minute, just getting dressed" (p. 25). Then he emerges from the tent as Silenus, who promises, for a reward, to retrieve the stolen cattle with the help of his satyrs. The satyrs (former fellahin) are summoned with help from the audience, and they emerge from boxes which have been brought into the acting area and begin a vigorous clog dance on the flattened sides of the boxes, marked with the tracks of Apollo's stolen herd. The sound of the lyre is heard to the consternation of all. Silenus urges on his satyrs but leaves, saying he's too old for this, but he'll be back for the award. A stage is formed on the back of the satyrs, imitating the sculpture at the Theater of Dionysus in Athens, and Kyllene appears dressed as a caryatid from the Erechtheum in Athens. She tells of her predicament in caring for Zeus's child Hermes and finally reveals the secret of the lyre. She is tipped off her stage, and the satyrs become suspicious about the cattle being used to make the lyre. She falls, and as she retrieves her elaborate headgear, she finds herself suggestively astride a satyr: the group takes up an erotically rhythmic chant (not unlike the *Rite of Spring*). Kyllene exits while pursued by the satyric pack, protesting that she is not in the right play.

Apollo enters and confronts the baby Hermes (a full-grown man, although "Not yet six days," as Sophocles' fragments say). The baby finally admits the theft of the herd, but Apollo is so charmed by the sounds of the lyre that he is willing to take it in exchange. But he will not share his art with the satyrs. He gives them, via Kyllene, ghetto blasters instead. They look at them like primitives confronted with a product of civilization. Harrison says, "sometimes they are like Cheetah in the Tarzan films getting hold of a camera" (p. 57).

The satyrs exeunt dissatisfied and Silenus appears. He kicks in all the ghetto blasters. A powerful speech follows against the use of the satyrs to test things, because they do not have full use of those discoveries; Marsyas is the paradigm, the satyr that dared to play a divine instrument (the flute) as well as a god could. The satyrs here choose to destroy if they are ignored. The last of the papyri is used as a football. Apollo's first words are heard ending in omega, the final "O," a type of moan which is taken up by the eight thousand ghosts. Harrison writes of this, "There is the sound like a dying firework of *Ichneutes* off the Phaedriades [cliffs in Delphi, where *Trackers* was first performed]."

There have also been several film versions of Sophocles' plays. Tzavellas made a politically charged film on *Antigone* starring Irene Papas (1961), and Liliana Cavani's *I Cannibali* (1970) was also based on this play. We find Freud again in Pier Paolo Pasolini's powerful film *Edipo Re* (1967). There was also a filmed version of *Oedipus Rex* by Tyrone Guthrie (1956), with screenplay from W. B. Yeats, which emphasized the monumental in its use of masks, and another by Philip Saville (1967), which was more naturalistic in its approach. There have been several films based on *Electra:* by Ted Zarpas (1962); by Jean-Louis Ughetto (1972); and a revolutionary *Elektreia* by Miklós Jancsó (1975). Theodoros Angelopoulos's *The Travelling Players* (*Thiasos,* 1975) also wove its political theme around the Electra legend.

3 Euripides

Euripides was born in ca. 480 B.C. and died in ca. 406 B.C. He spent the last two years of his life a guest of Archelaus in Macedonia. He won his first victory in 441 B.C. and three others in his lifetime (including the trilogy which contained *Hippolytus* in 428 B.C.), and an additional one for the posthumous performances of *Iphigenia in Aulis* and *Bacchae* in 405 B.C. Although in his own lifetime he was not as successful as Aeschylus and Sophocles, he became the most popular of the three in later times.

In Euripides we see man opposing man, sometimes him- or herself. Belief in the gods has diminished, partially because of the teachings of Protagoras and philosophers like him, who claimed that "Man is the measure of all things." Some have called Euripides an atheist. Others have called him the first psychologist.

In the Euripidean universe, chaos and malevolent gods rule. Man's only recourse is to make an alliance with other men. This alliance goes by the name of *philia,* or love. Antigone claimed she was born to love, not to hate, and the word she used was a verbal form of *philia. Philia* is called a virtue by Aristotle, and it can also describe friendship and the duty one owes to one's relatives, one's friends, and one's rulers. In this it resembles the Japanese *On* and *Giri,* so important in ancient Noh and Kabuki plays.

Euripides made women, children, and slaves into heroes and tended to present the traditional male heroes in a very bad light. He showed us the heroism of the victims. He was also the greatest anti-war playwright of antiquity.

He was said to have written about ninety-two plays, from which nineteen survive. These include our only complete satyr play, *Cyclops.* It is possible that *Rhesus* is not by him but by a later poet. In addition, there are extended fragments of several other plays, in particular, *Antiope, Alexander, Archelaus, Bellerophon, Cresphontes, Cretans, Erechtheus, Hypsipyle, Captive Melanippe, Wise Melanippe, Phaethon,* and *Stheneboea.*

The dates of performance for eight of his surviving plays are known, and others are tentatively proposed on the basis of evidence provided by ancient writers or through his own developing metrical practice:

Alcestis 438 B.C.
Medea 431 B.C.
Children of Heracles ca. 430 B.C.
Hippolytus 428 B.C.
Andromache ca. 425 B.C.
Hecuba ca. 424 B.C.
Suppliant Women ?424–20 B.C.
Electra ?422–16 B.C.
Trojan Women 415 B.C.
Heracles ca. 415 B.C.
Iphigenia among the Taurians ca. 414 B.C.
Ion ca. 413 B.C.
Helen 412 B.C.
Phoenician Women ca. 409 B.C.
Orestes 408 B.C.
Iphigenia at Aulis 405 B.C. (posthumous)
Bacchae 405 B.C. (posthumous)
Cyclops (uncertain)
Rhesus (possibly post-Euripidean)

In Aeschylus god can confront god, and major questions are raised about conflicting rights. Sophocles shows man confronting god and a world which can never be entirely knowable. Euripides shows man confronting himself, and sometimes he is a source of his own defeat. In his universe, the gods could be actively hostile to man. Sophocles presents us with the hero, and Euripides shows us the anti-hero. According to Aristotle, Sophocles claimed he depicted men as they ought to be, but Euripides depicted men as they are (*Poetics* 1460b33–34). Euripides was not as politically active as Aeschylus or Sophocles and left Athens in old age. He had a bleaker view than his predecessors. The main recourse man has in the chaotic Euripidean world is friendship or human alliances. Heroism is dead, at least as it was known to Aeschylus or Sophocles, or even earlier, to Homer. Women are central to his universe.

Longinus praised Euripides' depiction of madness and love (*On the Sublime*, 15.3). Euripides questions traditional beliefs and attitudes, and his plays feature the kind of debates which were popular among the sophists of his time. In these debates both strong emotions and strong intellectual positions are expressed; examples are the confrontation of Hippolytus with Theseus (*Hippolytus*) and of Hecuba with Helen (*Trojan Women*). These intellectual contests bothered many critics in the nineteenth century, who would have preferred inspired emotionalism without philosophical debate. Nietzsche condemned Euripides for just this rationality, which he considered a debasement of the noble goals of tragedy.

Aristophanes' *Frogs*, which highlights a contest between Aeschylus and Euripides, shows the latter as an innovator and iconoclast. It is from Aristophanes that we get the dubious idea that Euripides was a misogynist. He was instead a scientist of the emotions and focused on unconventional, passionate women. It may have been his idea to have Medea kill her children, the ultimate revenge against the husband she hated. His psychological characterization is outstanding.

Euripides' language is accessible and at times colloquial. His structure varied from the most organized and conventional (*Bacchae, Iphigenia among the Taurians*) to loose and episodic (*Trojan Women, Iphigenia at Aulis*). He specialized in arias to enhance emotional states; he also excelled in debate as a revelation of character. His choruses can range from being highly connected to the play to somewhat irrelevant, at least to the action in the play. This may reflect a trend of the time in the development of the chorus, which became less and less relevant to the main drama.

Alcestis

This play is typical of Euripides in that it shows a woman acting more heroically than the men who are conventionally considered heroes. It was performed after three tragedies which have not survived (*Cretan Women, Alcmaeon in Psophis,* and *Telephus*) in place of the usual satyr play. It has comic elements and a happy ending, which it shares with these types of plays.

The story is set in Pherae, Thessaly. Apollo gives the background in the prologue: Zeus killed Asclepius, Apollo's son, because he was raising the dead.

Apollo retaliated by killing the Cyclopes who made Zeus's thunderbolts. As punishment, Zeus required him to serve as a herdsman to Admetus, the king of Pherae. Admetus was a kind master, and as his reward when he was fated to die, Apollo tricked the Fates into agreeing to accept a substitute. Admetus looked far and wide for someone to die in his place, even his aged father and mother, but finally only his wife, Alcestis, was willing to do this for him. The play opens on the day that she is to die. After the prologue, Death and Apollo debate, but Death remains adamant. The chorus enters and laments. Alcestis appears on a couch with her children and her husband beside her. Admetus promises he will not remarry. She dies and her son sings a song of mourning.

Heracles arrives, and Admetus greets him and insists on entertaining him, claiming the deceased is only a distant relative. The chorus initially blames Admetus for this deception, but it ends up singing his praises.

At the funeral, Admetus and Pheres, his father, argue over the body. Each unmasks the other, and they are seen to be selfish and self-serving. Admetus claims his father is old and soon to die anyway, and should not have let a young person die. The father argues that a parent is not obliged to die for a child. Pheres indicts Admetus's own selfishness in asking his wife to die in his place.

Heracles drinks too much and is chided by a servant. (A scene like this is typical of the satyr play.) On discovering that Alcestis is the person they are mourning, he leaves to wrestle with Death, and he wins. He returns with a veiled woman, saying he won her as his prize, and he begs Admetus to keep her for him. Admetus at first refuses but then gives in to his guest. Heracles unveils her, showing that it is Alcestis. She is silent but her silence will last only three days (the time needed for a dead person to regain speech). Husband and wife are reunited.

This is a play about a woman's sacrifice. Admetus must learn through suffering, that lesson reiterated throughout the *Oresteia*. He is certainly lucky to be able to recover his wife. His hospitality gets him into trouble but also leads to the happy ending. He is a warm host and a good human being in his treatment of Apollo and the rest of his servants. This may be set against his selfish acceptance of his wife's sacrifice.

Like *Helen, Alcestis* shows a genuine reciprocal love between husband and wife, and this is rare in Greek tragedy. It has a happy ending, with love figuring in the equation. This is the type of play that leads to the New Comedy written by Menander. However, we see the actual sordidness and consequences of asking another person to die in one's place.

Alcestis is shorter than the usual tragedy. There are several comic scenes, between Apollo and Death, Heracles and Admetus, and Heracles and the servant. Heracles is a comic figure: the conventional strongman, but boastful and drunken. He is very different here from the Heracles in Euripides' other surviving play about him (*Heracles*), in which he is driven mad and kills his children. Here he gets his revenge on Admetus for deceiving him by putting him to a test. Admetus fails the test: he does not keep his word to Alcestis in accepting another woman into the house.

Most of the men are shown as stupid (Heracles should have seen earlier that someone more important than "a distant relative" had died since the whole household was in mourning) and self-serving (particularly Pheres and Admetus). It is significant that immediately after Alcestis dies, it is her child who laments her in song rather than Admetus. The song of the child is sure to provoke tears and shows Euripides' ability to stir sympathetic emotions in an audience. Admetus laments only later when he finally feels the full pain of his loss, the intensity of which was quite unexpected. Admetus is described as shedding more tears than hero in Greek tragedy.

This is one of the few plays in which a death occurs onstage. Another is *Hippolytus* and possibly *Ajax*. Alcestis is carried off the stage before the arrival of Heracles and then is carried in on a bier for the funeral scene.

Admetus's house is in the center with one main entrance. Apollo can appear above the house and Death below, but it would be possible to have them arguing just before the front door. After all, Death has come to take Alcestis away and his home is the underworld, not the upper Olympian one of Apollo.

Medea

Medea tells the story of a woman who not only carries out her vengeance against her husband (who has left her for a younger woman), but who is able to escape afterward to a better life. She is the worst nightmare of every philandering husband. This is Euripides' passionate heroine Medea.

Medea struggles in a monologue with herself. Only she can stop herself. Her gentler impulses lose and she kills her own children. She also escapes with impunity. Medea is a foreign princess who gave up everything to support her husband. She is the wife who supports the future doctor or lawyer and now is turned in for a younger and more socially suitable model after the man is successful, through much of her efforts. This play with its dark ambiguities has haunted the human imagination for centuries. She kills the ruler of Corinth, his daughter (her husband Jason's new bride), and then her children and escapes to lead a new life. The whole idea of child killing taps into the primal horror of a mother slaying rather than nurturing, coming with a knife instead of milk.

Medea is a Sophoclean (or even Homeric) hero. Like heroes in Homer, she says that she acts as she does so that her enemies cannot laugh at her. "Help your friends and harm your enemies" was an ancient Greek maxim, and Medea does just that, although she is not Greek.

Jason's quest for the Golden Fleece is a theme for epic. He was successful,

Medea. The chorus try to dissuade Medea (Nuria Espert) from the vengeance which will entail killing her own children. Rosas de Otono, Athens Festival, Greece (2002). Courtesy of Hellenic Festival S. A.

with Medea's help, and married her. He brought her from her native Colchis (in the Caucasus region at the far end of the Black Sea) to Corinth after a series of adventures. While their two sons were still young, Jason decides to leave Medea and marry the royal princess of Corinth. This is where Euripides' play begins.

The play starts with Medea having heard the news that her husband is to abandon her. We can hear her weeping and screaming in the house. She comes out and addresses the women of Corinth. She swears them to silence. Creon pronounces a sentence of exile on her. She begs him for a day's delay, and he finally assents. Jason appears, and she outlines all that she did for him and asks him how he could break his sacred oaths to her and the gods. He claims that she has nothing to complain about because she is now better off than in barbaric Colchis.

Medea formulates her plans, and when Aegeus, the king of Athens, arrives on his way home after consulting the oracle at Delphi, she asks him to provide her with a refuge in Athens. He agrees and takes a solemn oath. Medea summons Jason again and is all sweetness and light. She gives him gifts for the princess: a diadem and a robe, given to her by her grandfather Helios, the sun. She wishes the help of the princess in persuading her father to allow the children to stay. The children deliver the gifts, and when the princess puts them on, they burst into flames which (as Euripides puts it) melt her flesh so that it drips off her body like sap from pine. Her father dies a comparable death as he embraces her burning body. Medea then kills the children. After taunting the helpless Jason, she escapes in a dragon-drawn chariot, his curses following her.

Medea has calculated the worst possible vengeance. A Greek man wanted fame, fortune, and offspring. She arranges it such that that Jason has no offspring, not only by killing their own children, but also by destroying the possibility of future offspring from the princess. Then she predicts that his death will be inglorious. He, the once glorious hero, will be killed by a rotting piece of timber falling from the ship *Argo*, in which he sailed on his quest for the Golden Fleece. She destroys his fame that he has worked so hard to earn, in addition to his children and his fortune.

Why does Medea decide to kill the children? Creon says he fears Medea because of the danger to his daughter. Jason says that his new marriage will benefit his children by giving them royal brothers. Aegeus tells Medea he consulted an oracle on how he might have children. From all this, Medea sees how important children are to Creon, Aegeus, and Jason, so they show her that this is the best way to avenge herself on her husband. The sons are in the image and likeness of their father. When Medea looks at them she sees Jason. One wonders if Medea would have killed daughters.

Initially all our sympathy is with Medea. She has been victimized by Jason, who owes her everything. She has no place to return to. But by the end, the sympathy of the audience has shifted because of Medea's final brutal act against her own children.

As he said, Jason may have simply wanted to secure their position in the new city. He speaks a different language from Medea. Jason's is the language of the *polis* (the city), money, and power; Medea's language is of the *oikos* (the home), honor, and the heart. One argues for the outside world, the other for the inside world.

What makes Medea particularly horrific is that she is sane. She debates her every action, and she plans rationally. She is a woman who loves and hates, but her main concern is her honor, and that she shares with many male heroes. It is very hard for many directors to accept Medea's actions as those of a sane woman. They prefer to see her as a romantic victim, driven mad by her suffering, rather than as a wronged princess who coolly plans her vengeance.

Nor is Euripides' Medea a witch, like Seneca's Medea. It is important that the actress playing Medea play her as human: it is a mistake to demonize her. It is equally important not to demonize Jason but to make him as plausible as possible, and finally sympathetic at the end of the play. His caustic comments to Medea should merely reflect the great pain he is suffering.

Medea says, "I know what I am about to do is wrong, / but my passion is stronger than my reason" (lines 1078–79). She also tells herself to forget her children for the short time needed to kill them but then to mourn them for eternity. When Jason asks how she could bring herself to kill her own children, she answers, "At least, now you cannot laugh at me" (line 1362).

Medea is heroic and deadly, sympathetic and appalling. She uses the devices which the Greek playwrights traditionally ascribe to women: lies, deceit, and plots. These devices are sufficient to destroy the rulers and the man who oppressed her. This is why this play is often performed to express the discontent of those who perceive themselves as abused. A victim can be victimized

Medea. Directed by Deborah Warner. Translated by Kenneth McLeish and Frederic Raphael. Medea (Fiona Shaw) appears in her blood-stained shirt after she has killed her children to avenge herself against Jason. Queen's Theatre, London (2001). Photo: Neil Libbert. Used by permission.

only so long before fighting back. That fight can be successful. It is obvious how the play can function as a political parable. There have been many productions where Medea is played by a black actress.

The staging shows Medea's house. One entrance comes from the city and palace, and the other from the exterior, such as Athens. Medea appears above Jason, either on the roof or possibly in the *mēchanē* at the end, just like a god. But it is important to remember that she is a woman and not to think that she is a divine monster because she departs at the end in a dragon-drawn chariot. I have seen this staged with an actual chariot, comparable to the machinery regularly used in baroque opera. Alternatively, Medea can simply speak from an elevated height, so that the imagination must fill in the details. The safety of the chariot (whether the chariot is shown or imagined) allows the final exchange with Jason to take place. If they were on the same level, she would be vulnerable to attack.

Euripides allows us to see Medea gloating. This completes her vengeance and makes her even more shocking. Like a Homeric hero, she does not show her grief in front of Jason but merely relishes her triumph over him. However, the audience knows Medea's triumph is her tragedy. A performance that does not convey this ambiguity is not a good performance. Medea is not a heroine without faults, nor will she be immune from the suffering that follows the loss of her children.

Euripides has created one of the most powerful roles in the history of drama, and among operas there are over fifty which feature Medea.

Children of Heracles

This play is about war, vengeance, and the heroism of a young girl—frequent themes in Euripides. The story begins in Marathon, where Heracles' sons and daughters are fleeing from Eurystheus, the king of Mycenae, who persecuted their father and continues to persecute them. Their leader is Iolaus, Heracles' right-hand man. A herald arrives from Eurystheus and asks Demophon, the king of Athens and son of Theseus, to turn over these suppliants. Demophon refuses and war is declared.

An oracle demands the sacrifice of a child; otherwise Demophon will be defeated by Eurystheus. Macaria (unnamed in the play: her name means "blest," a term which is often applied to the dead) is one of Heracles' children, and she offers herself as the victim. Iolaus insists on fighting, but his attendant has doubts about whether he can even reach the battlefield because of his age. This scene offers comic relief. During the battle, Iolaus's youth is restored so that he fights valiantly with the others, and they are victorious. Iolaus takes Eurystheus prisoner and turns him over to Alcmena, Heracles' mother. Alcmena would like to kill him, her archenemy, but the chorus says it would be unjust to kill a prisoner. Eurystheus reveals an oracle that when he is buried in Athenian soil he will be a protective spirit, fighting against the Argives if they ever attack Athens. Alcmena takes charge, gives him to her guards to kill, and asks that his body be thrown to the dogs.

Here we see how suffering can brutalize a person. We will see this in several of Euripides' plays, notably *Medea* and *Hecuba*, in which women exact a cruel vengeance from their oppressors. All three of these dramas turn the audience against the woman who goes too far.

This play is dated around 430 B.C., a year in which Thucydides tells us that some Spartan envoys were summarily executed by the Athenians (2.67.4). It illustrates the violence actions of which the Athenians often were guilty. Euripides does this again in *Trojan Women*, just after the Athenians massacred the men on Melos and enslaved the women and children. Euripides, like Socrates, indicted the Athenians and raised questions about the wrongs he witnessed. Like Socrates, he was not popular; Euripides, we remember, spent the end of his life in Macedonia, far from his native Athens.

Macaria is like Iphigenia (*Iphigenia at Aulis*) and Menoeceus (*Phoenician Women*), children who willingly sacrifice themselves for their people. They are young idealists and by contrast show up the self-serving and corrupt adults who surround them. Macaria's generous act contrasts with Alcmena's ungenerous one.

The comic scene of the elderly Iolaus struggling to the battlefield is comparable to Teiresias and Cadmus, two elderly men in the *Bacchae*, trying to play the role of bacchants and dancing in their worship of Dionysus. Making the elderly into comic figures is another way that Euripides introduces elements which will appear in the New Comedy of the next century. Such scenes also relieve the tragedy for a while, only to intensify its return. Iolaus being restored to youth is a touch of the supernatural which delights audiences. It is always exciting to see Clark Kent become Superman. Iolaus in the battle resembles Heracles himself.

This play is staged in front of the temple of Zeus in which Alcmena and the children take refuge. Alcmena's brutal revenge gains in enormity because it takes place in front of a temple, in a land where she has been given sanctuary. This play illustrates vengeance and at the same time is a lesson in heroism. An old man and a young girl are ready to give their lives for what they believe and they are rewarded for their acts.

Here we find some of the optimism still possible in the early years of the Peloponnesian War. The optimism will fade as war-weariness sets in, and by the time of *Trojan Women* the only heroism left is that of the victims in the face of slavery or death.

Hippolytus

This play is most likely a reworking by Euripides of one of his earlier plays. The first *Hippolytus* does not survive, but we can guess from various pieces of evidence that it was too shocking for its original audience. Euripides had represented Phaedra as a dangerous woman who attempted to seduce her stepson, Hippolytus. In the reworked version he showed Phaedra not as a scheming seductress but as a virtuous wife, a helpless victim of a passion which she cannot resist. In the later versions, she is a woman to be pitied, not condemned.

Aphrodite says in the prologue that she is angry with Hippolytus and that she intends to punish him, because he refuses to worship her and worships only the virginal goddess Artemis. She will punish him by making his stepmother, Phaedra, wife of King Theseus, fall in love with him. Aphrodite knows how disastrous the consequences will be. She says she knows that Phaedra is innocent, but her vengeance is more important to her. This is terrorism on the divine level.

In the earlier part of the play, Phaedra fights against her passion for Hippolytus and refuses to tell anyone that she is in love. But her nurse extorts her secret and tells it to Hippolytus, and he, thinking that she is acting on Phaedra's orders, denounces Phaedra. In order to preserve her own reputation, Phaedra commits suicide, but first she writes a letter to her husband in which she falsely claims Hippolytus tried to rape her. Theseus believes her accusation and curses his son. They debate in a way reminiscent of the sophistic debates popular in Athens at the time. Theseus accuses his son of aiming at the throne, which his son vehemently denies. Hippolytus's defense, claiming he prefers not ruling, is believable. His defense that he was not attracted to Phaedra omits the possibility of an overwhelming passion. Theseus conducts his examination of Hippolytus like a prosecutor in a law court. The arguments do not take adequate account of the irrationality of love.

As Hippolytus drives his chariot along the shore, a bull rises out of the sea, frightening Hippolytus's horses, who run out of control and smash their master against the rocks. Artemis convinces Theseus of Hippolytus's innocence, something that no mortal could have done. Hippolytus's battered body is brought to his father, whom he forgives just before he dies. He has only a few moments to bid farewell to his beloved Artemis. She hastily departs lest she be polluted by death.

It is easy to see in *Hippolytus* how the warring goddesses represent warring forces in human nature. The person who denies Aphrodite, both love and lust, will be torn apart, as indeed Hippolytus is. A sexual drive can no more be easily suppressed than Poseidon's bull from the sea can be tamed.

In this pre-Christian world it is *human* to forgive and *divine* to bear a murderous grudge. Aphrodite is relentless and unforgiving; Hippolytus, on the other hand, forgives his father with a gesture of great generosity. In a harsh universe ruled by cruel gods, humans best endure through mutual bonds. Euripides often delivers this message. The servant early on urges Hippolytus to worship both Aphrodite and Artemis. Hippolytus refuses, so when he exits from the stage, the servant prays that Aphrodite will forgive him, claiming that gods should be wiser and more tempered in their judgment than mortals. The action in the play shows that gods are as guilty of excess, passion, and violence as humans, a lesson taught again in *Bacchae*. In that play Cadmus says that gods should not equal men in their passions and anger.

This play warns against hasty judgments and irrevocable actions that follow those judgments. It is a story of false evidence and jealousy; one can see how Shakespeare's *Othello* has a similar plot, and Theseus knows the same agony as Othello. Aphrodite is like Iago in bringing about the destruction of innocents on a matter involving personal pride and honor and in the feeling of being slighted.

Phaedra did all that she could to overcome her love for her stepson. Nevertheless, her false accusation is hard to forgive. Hippolytus earns a punishment, but he hardly deserves the violent death that he finally suffers at the hands of his father's curse because of Phaedra's lie. A major theme of this play and many others by Euripides is the suffering of the innocent.

In antiquity Hippolytus was probably regarded as the hero. Phaedra was always under suspicion because her mother was Pasiphae, who fell in love with a bull and gave birth to the Minotaur, another victim of a god's wrath. She and her mother gave a bad name to Cretan women, who subsequently were regarded as lustful.

Phaedra is guilty of an innocent's death. Nevertheless she was still the victim of Aphrodite, who made her mad for Hippolytus in the first place. Many modern audiences are on Phaedra's side.

I think it is important to try to maintain a balance between the two main characters. Both Hippolytus and Phaedra should be played as people who are in over their heads, and both are innocent in their own ways. One might think Theseus is more to blame because of his absences and infidelities. Many modern reworkings take this tack, as did Racine's. But Euripides makes this Theseus's tragedy as much as anyone else's. He loses his son and his wife through his own rash judgments, but these judgments were natural given the circumstances.

Theseus's son forgives him, but it is hard to believe that Theseus will ever forgive himself. He blames Phaedra, in spite of Artemis exonerating her. Hippolytus's misogynist remarks were unremarkable in antiquity. Hippolytus can be looked upon as a boy who does not want to enter the adult stage, rather a Peter Pan of the hunt.

Euripides' Phaedra is an Ajax, but now love is the battlefield; both Phaedra and Ajax are fierce in their passions and jealous of their honor. Like Ajax's, Phaedra's suicide is heroic and her vengeance is Homeric. She also resembles Medea; her choices are made in the heroic mode.

In staging this play, the goddesses could appear on the roof of the stage building. We also see their statues because Hippolytus worships one and slights the other, against the good advice of his servant. The servant admonishes the goddess statue also and tells her to be forgiving, because gods should be wiser than men.

At the beginning, Phaedra is carried in prostrate on some sort of litter. At the end, Hippolytus is likewise carried prostrate to his father, so it is seen that the positions have reversed in this play. The scene in which Phaedra hears Hippolytus denouncing her is probably the most difficult to stage. Hippolytus and the nurse argue in front of the house; Hippolytus does not address Phaedra, and it is not clear that he sees her, but she is clearly present. She could join the chorus in the orchestra or be off to the side. Alternatively, Hippolytus could see her but choose to ignore her. Phaedra's letter, written on a tablet, is also an important prop. Phaedra is silent in death, but her written message is deadly and effective.

Some of the main thematic images have to do with the opposition or relationship of word to deed. Hippolytus claims his mouth swore but not his mind: his speech act is different from his thought. Aristophanes quotes this line out of context as an example of sophistic quibbling. Hippolytus never in fact broke his word. In this play words become deeds. As Phaedra's letter is fatal for Hippolytus, so Theseus's verbal curse is soon translated into action. The insults that the father hurls at the son are even worse than the physical trauma. Theseus's apology and Hippolytus's forgiveness heal the verbal wounds as best they can.

There is a second chorus, males who accompany Hippolytus on his hunt. The main chorus is made up of women who serve Phaedra and who are sympathetic to her.

Andromache

This is another of Euripides' plays which shows the superiority of the "barbarian" woman to a "civilized" Greek one, in this case the Trojan Andromache to the Spartan Hermione. In the prologue Andromache gives the background. She speaks of the taking of Troy by the Greeks ten years after Helen had been stolen from her Spartan husband, Menelaus, by Paris, son of Priam, the king of Troy. Andromache was married to Hector, the greatest warrior of the Trojans and another son of Priam. After the war, their son Astyanax was killed by the Greeks, hurled from Troy's walls lest he be a future threat. Andromache was awarded to Neoptolemus, the son of Achilles, the greatest warrior of Greece. She is now living in Phthia, Achilles' birthplace in Thessaly. Peleus, the father of Achilles, lives nearby.

Hermione, Neoptolemus's lawful wife, is jealous of Andromache because she has had a child with Neoptolemus, whereas Hermione, as yet, is barren. She accuses Andromache of casting spells on her. Andromache has taken refuge at the altar of Thetis, the goddess of the sea and the mother of Achilles by Peleus. She has hidden her child in a neighboring house. A bitter debate ensues between Hermione and Andromache, but Andromache holds her own and says that Hermione should be a docile wife and not imitate her mother, Helen, who was unfaithful to Menelaus, her father. Menelaus appears with the child and tries to get Andromache to leave the altar, saying otherwise he will kill him. She leaves her sanctuary, and Menelaus ties both of them up, awaiting the pleasure of his daughter. Menelaus and Hermione are about to execute them when Peleus arrives and accuses Menelaus of treachery. He frees Andromache and her child. Menelaus slinks off.

Hermione now appears with her nurse. She has tried to kill herself. Orestes arrives and takes her to safety. He has also set up a plot to kill Neoptolemus, who has gone to Delphi to make reparations to Apollo for earlier accusing him of being responsible for his father's death at Troy. Menelaus had promised Hermione to Orestes, but when he needed help at Troy he gave her to Neoptolemus instead.

Peleus appears and is told of his grandson's death. Neoptolemus was making a sacrifice when he was ambushed. Since he was a capable warrior, he was holding his own against his attackers until a voice echoed through the temple, urging the attackers on. They then killed him. The messenger attributes the voice to Apollo, and the ancient audience would believe him, since they knew the myth that claimed Apollo was responsible for Neoptolemus's death.

Thetis appears and orders Peleus to Delphi to bury their grandson, and then to join her in a sea cave and sport with her for eternity. She also predicts a happy ending for Andromache, who will continue her life married to the seer Helenus, another son of Priam. Her son by Neoptolemus will be the founder of the line of the Molossians.

This play was written during the earlier years of the Peloponnesian War. It contains anti-Spartan propaganda showing the men as duplicitous and cowardly and the women as shameless and self-centered. Andromache, like Medea, is a victim of Greek opportunism. This woman and an old man (Peleus) are the ones who show themselves as brave and moral. They are the new heroes. Euripides often shows the conventional heroes as corrupt and those normally thought weak as morally strong.

Most Euripidean plays have only one debate, but this one has two: between Hermione and Andromache and between Menelaus and Peleus. Both debates are lively. Peleus accuses Menelaus not only of waging a war for a whore, but also of taking credit for winning the war. He goes on to claim that generals often take the credit for what others have achieved. It is remarks like these which made Euripides unpopular in Athens, although the comment is suitably democratic.

There is a poignant scene in which Neoptolemus is carried onto the stage, to be wept over by his grandfather. The scene is rather like the one that ends *Hippolytus*. Thetis's promises are hardly enough to compensate for such a loss.

The play illustrates duplicity, treachery, and the precariousness of good fortune. A person should try to be as moral as possible; this way, at least, he dies with honor. If there is any flaw it is that Menelaus is too much of a villain. He has hardly any redeeming characteristics, except in responding to a daughter's plea for help. The daughter in this case is a rather spoiled princess with no sympathy for her enslaved rival, who was also a princess, or at least married to a prince. Menelaus does everything in excess and illustrates the passions which get most of the heroes in trouble. He articulates this trait well when he says to Andromache, "But don't forget, whatever a person most desires / becomes more important than any taking of Troy—he has to have it" (lines 368–69).

This is one of the four Euripidean plays which contains the maxim "Do not pronounce a person happy before the day he dies" (lines 100–102), which is our translation becomes: "call no woman happy until she's dead" (p. 6). The others are *Children of Heracles, Trojan Women,* and *Iphigenia at Aulis,* all plays about inordinate suffering. The same maxim is also found in Aeschylus's *Aga-*

memnon and three plays by Sophocles: *Oedipus Tyrannus, Women of Trachis,* and the lost *Tyndareus.*

Another lesson from this play is that for two women to share one man is a recipe for disaster. We saw this in Agamemnon's case with Cassandra, in Heracles' with Iole, and we now see it with Neoptolemus. The result in each case is fatal for the man.

The action takes place before the house of Neoptolemus. His body is carried onstage from the direction of Delphi. Menelaus and Orestes enter and exit from one route and Peleus from the other direction, which leads to his home. Thetis perhaps flies in on the *mēchanē* at the end to complete the picture of the mourning family (Neoptolemus was her grandson). She also complains about the pain that Achilles' death brought her, and she, as a goddess, had hoped to be free from pain. This is perhaps another lesson: suffering humanizes.

Hecuba

Euripides wrote this play early in the war years. Revenge is a theme which has a constant appeal, although it seems to me that he is more sympathetic to it in his earlier plays. I think he has more sympathy for Medea and Hecuba than for Dionysus, and that the bloodshed experienced during the Peloponnesian War (431–404) has led him to be even more circumspect about condoning vengeance. *Hecuba* dates from about 424 B.C. Like Medea and Alcmena (in *Children of Heracles*), Hecuba successfully inflicts a brutal vengeance.

From the very beginning, there are many exciting moments in this play. Polydorus, the youngest and last remaining son of Hecuba, appears as a ghost to deliver the prologue. He says that Hecuba entrusted him to Polymestor, the king of Thrace, during the Trojan War. He brought a sizable amount of gold with him. Polymestor waited to see how the war would go, and after the Trojans lost, he killed Polydorus and took the gold. Polydorus asked the gods to allow his mother to bury him, and his wish has been granted.

Hecuba is seen lying on the ground in front of the women's tent; she asks to be lifted. She has had a frightening dream about her children, Polydorus and Polyxena. The chorus tells Hecuba that Polyxena was promised as an offering to the dead Achilles, whose ghost had been seen demanding honor. With the plea that she had once saved his life, Hecuba begs Odysseus to spare her daughter. Odysseus admits that what she says is true, but all he owes her is her own life, nothing more. He is shown as a quibbling sophist, without mercy. Hecuba tells Polyxena to make an appeal, but she will not debase herself and says that she prefers death to an unhappy life. She is taken away, and the herald Talthybius later describes her death to Hecuba. Polyxena was about to be forcibly constrained, but she begs to be allowed to offer her life freely. Neoptolemus cuts her throat and offers her blood to Achilles.

When a body is brought in Hecuba thinks that it is Polyxena, but when she uncovers it, she discovers it is her son Polydorus. This is as devastating as in Sophocles' *Electra*, when Aegisthus uncovers a corpse that he thinks is Orestes but instead is his wife, Clytemnestra. In both cases it is a scene that carries a dramatic punch. On a lighter level, Admetus discovers that his wife, Alcestis, has returned to him when Heracles lifts the veil of the woman he has brought for Admetus's safekeeping. Unveilings are as important in Greek tragedy as verbal disclosures.

Hecuba is devastated and resolves to avenge herself. She sends for both Polymestor and Agamemnon. Agamemnon agrees to leave matters in her hands. When Polymestor arrives, Hecuba lures him and his sons into the women's tent, promising to deliver jewels to him personally and to tell him where the Trojan treasure is hidden. In the tent the women kill his sons and then blind him. Polymestor rushes out of the tent onto the stage, and a trial ensues with Agamemnon as judge. He is found guilty of treachery. He then predicts that Hecuba will be turned into a dog and buried on the shore. Cassandra and Agamemnon will both be killed by Clytemnestra. Agamemnon is infuriated and orders that he be abandoned on an island.

Throughout the play, Queen Hecuba, now a prisoner, learns how to beg. She wishes she had the gift of persuasion, a priceless power and the only power left to her. She tells Agamemnon that he owes her gratitude because he enjoys the favors of her daughter Cassandra. By the end of the play Polymestor crawls out of the tent, in the same abject position that Hecuba was at the beginning of the play. The prophecy reveals that Agamemnon will be the next to fall. This play also shows how suffering brutalizes. By the end of the play, we see Hecuba's moral debasement, comparable to her physical debasement at the beginning of the play.

This is a moving and dramatic play and shares much in common with other plays, not just the theme of vengeance. It is closest to *Trojan Women*. Many of the characters are the same, and both plays are set on the beach before the women's tent. Both contain the laments of the captive women and the sacrifice of a child. In each case the Greeks are shown to be more barbaric in their actions than their "barbarian" captives. They are also glib in their defense of their actions. Odysseus argues as speciously as Jason when he condemns barbarians who do not honor agreements (328–31). Polymestor, the army's ally and a Greek (Thracian), violates his commitment to Hecuba and murders her son. Odysseus himself hardly honors his own debt to Hecuba, so his argument appears doubly specious and ironic.

The vengeance on Polymestor is quite satisfying to an audience which has seen Hecuba suffer one tragedy and betrayal after another. Nevertheless, seen in the clear light of day, it is a brutal vengeance and more than an eye for an eye. Polymestor's children are innocent but must suffer for his betrayal. This is comparable to Medea's vengeance. The ending leaves us with a sour taste, but Euripides typically questions violence, however just it may be. When this play is staged it should respect this ambiguity. The audience should see the blinded father cradling the bleeding corpses of his children and ask if this brutality was justified. Agamemnon abandons Polymestor on a barren island for simply foretelling the future.

At the beginning, Polydorus appears flitting above his mother's head, so he may be flown in on the *mēchanē*. I saw an impressive production in Sicily (1998) with a powerful actress, Valeria Moriconi, whose voice was a voice from hell, and one shuddered at its dark vibrancy. That performance began with spirits floating out from caves in a cliff which symbolized Hades, until a black winged spirit summoned them all back.

The death of Polyxena and her brave attitude puts her in line with other heroines in Euripides' plays, such as Iphigenia and Macaria. It is the women and children now rather than the conventional heroes who show what virtue is. If they cannot live with honor, they die with it.

The Suppliant Women

This play is a distillation of lamentation. It shows the sufferings of those who are left behind after a war is over: the mothers and the children. This is Euripides' specialty: he is a master at conveying a victim's sorrow and the horrors of war's aftermath. This is yet another Theban play. Thebes is Athens's "other": a place where things go particularly wrong.

A bit of background is needed, even before the prologue. From Sophocles we know that Oedipus is the famous king of Thebes who married his mother and slew his father. He cursed his two sons, Eteocles and Polyneices. Eteocles would not share the rule of Thebes with his brother, so Polyneices went to Argos and asked the king, Adrastus, for help. Seven heroes on the Argive side fought seven Thebans at seven gates. All the attackers were slain. At the seventh gate Eteocles fought Polyneices, and both were killed, fulfilling their father's curse. Creon, the brother-in-law of Oedipus, became ruler and forbade the burial of the defeated enemies.

Aethra, the mother of Theseus, king of Athens, opens the play with a prayer to Demeter. A chorus of mothers of the Argive heroes defeated at Thebes appeal to her. They have come to the temple of Demeter in Eleusis to ask for help in regaining their sons' bodies so that they can bury them. Aethra says she pities them and has sent for her son. Theseus arrives and speaks with Adrastus, who leads the women. Theseus blames him for ignoring the omens which told him not to attack Thebes. Adrastus confesses that he erred but still appeals for help. Theseus refuses until Aethra tells him that Athens would gain honor if it would right this wrong. Theseus yields to his mother and says he will try persuasion first and resort to arms only if words fail.

A Theban herald arrives and defends the rule of one against what he calls mob rule. Theseus gives counterarguments in favor of democracy, the right of every man to speak freely and to be able to seek impartial justice. He claims that Athens is free from the violent abuses of tyrants. The herald tries a new approach and argues against war itself, saying, "When people vote on war, / no one thinks that he himself will die" (lines 481–82). Then he praises peace and its blessings, the arts, thriving children, and a flourishing economy. Theseus can hardly argue with this and he doesn't, but he does say that he upholds the law that all the Greeks support, namely, that the dead should be buried. He urges moderation because fortune changes.

Theseus musters his army, attacks, and wins. A messenger announces the victory. Theseus asks about the men who fell, whose bodies he has just rescued. Adrastus sings the praises of each and then asks for the bodies to be brought to the mothers, but Theseus advises against stirring up fresh sorrow. While the mothers are lamenting, suddenly Evadne is seen on top of a cliff over the pyre of her husband, Capaneus. Her father, Iphis, arrives, looking for his dead son and his daughter. Evadne calls to him, and when he sees her, he begs her to come down, but it is too late: she jumps onto her husband's pyre to join him in death.

The sons of the dead heroes bring the ashes of their fathers to their grandmothers and they weep together. The boys pledge vengeance. Athena appears and tells Theseus to exact a pledge from Adrastus that Argos will be Athens's ally for all-time. She also says that the boys will be successful in their attack on Thebes.

As typical of Euripides, the play ends on a sour note. Instead of heeding the anti-war lesson, another war is planned, and Athena abets it with a positive prediction of the outcome. Evadne in her mad suicide and search for personal glory is rather like the grandchildren who vow vengeance. They are young people who have learned nothing, and they do not think about the consequences of those who will suffer from their actions. More mothers and fathers will have to weep for the death of their children.

Parents say they are better off being childless rather than having to suffer the loss of a child (there was a similar chorus in *Medea*). The mothers speak of the hours they spent raising their children, tending them when they were sick, kissing them. Now they are alone. Things around their homes remind them of their children, but the rooms are empty; the parents now grow old alone, with no one to bury them. Each day's dawn for them means only another day for tears.

This is the litany of the bereaved parent, such as is found in many of Euripides' plays, for example, *Trojan Women* or *Iphigenia at Aulis*. In the latter, Euripides will give us the image of Clytemnestra walking through empty rooms and remembering her sacrificed Iphigenia. Fifteen out of the nineteen of Euripides' surviving plays feature the death of a child.

The set shows the temple of Demeter, which is symbolically important, since Demeter also lost a child. She is the epitome of the bereaved mother. Aethra is appealed to by the other mothers because, as a mother, she understands their sorrow. As so often in Greek tragedy a character is told to be merciful, because one never knows when one will need mercy oneself.

Staging Evadne's suicide is a challenge. She probably leapt from the roof of the *skēnē* so that she would land behind it. Her violent death would not be visible to the audience, following the Greek convention of not showing violence onstage, which certainly operates in the majority of Greek tragedies.

Capaneus's pyre can be imagined. Athena perhaps appears on the *mēchanē*. She resembles other gods in Euripides, showing herself no better than the mortals and encouraging their most bloodthirsty intentions. This play is the reverse of the *Oresteia*, which seeks to bring an end to violence. At the end of *Suppliants* we see the bloody cycle continuing. The mothers have two things to lament, not only the death of their children, but also their children's children carrying on this blood feud. This play is all the more powerful by showing just how seductive is the lust for war in spite of all the evidence of the suffering that it causes.

Electra

Although the theme of this play is the same as Aeschylus's *Choephoroi* and Sophocles' *Electra*, the main characters are presented very differently by Euripides. They are recognizable human beings and not very likable ones. Electra is a neurotic and Orestes is a coward.

The prologue is delivered by a farmer from Argos who has been assigned Electra as a wife. Orestes and Pylades appear, but when they see Electra coming they hide. Electra enters carrying a pitcher for water: she is dressed in rags and her hair is cut short like a slave's. These are signs of her self-imposed degradation. Orestes and Pylades come to the farmhouse and do not reveal their identity but claim to bring Electra news about Orestes. The farmer comes home and rebukes her for talking to strange men, but when he hears they are friends of Orestes, he invites them inside for a meal.

A neighboring peasant is summoned to bring food, and it is he who took the young Orestes to safety long ago. He now identifies Orestes from an old scar. After the recognition scene, the children plot. Orestes brutally kills Aegisthus from behind at a sacrifice. Electra revels over his corpse, which is brought onstage. Then she sends a message to her mother, saying she has just had a baby and asking her to perform a purification rite. The mother arrives. Electra and her mother debate, after which the children kill her in the house. Clytemnestra's brothers, the gods Castor and Pollux, appear and order Orestes to Athens to stand trial, and Electra into exile with Pylades as her husband.

Orestes sneaks back home, and Electra whines. This Orestes is weak, and Electra is tiresome and bloodthirsty. Orestes violates the law of guest respecting host by killing a man from behind who has invited him to a feast. Electra, after goading Orestes into the murder of Aegisthus, says that he should leave Clytemnestra to her, and she lures her mother to her death by a particularly loathsome trick, saying she has had a child simply because she knows her mother will respond. Her mother visits her out of consideration to perform a charitable action.

The play shows the diseased logic of revenge, something to be elaborated later in *Orestes*. Whether a god would command matricide is called into question. Orestes suggests that it was a fiend that spoke to him in the guise of Apollo. Castor and Pollux find fault with Apollo for this command.

In the debate with her mother, Electra complains not so much about the murder of her father as about the way she has been treated and deprived of her inheritance. Clytemnestra, after putting forward her reasons for killing Agamemnon, expresses regret and concern for her children. She says she saved them from Aegisthus. She asks whether, if Menelaus had been abducted, she would have had to sacrifice Orestes. This points out the double standard in favor of a male child.

Electra is psychologically complicated and seems preoccupied with sexual issues. This is perhaps partially caused by her self-imposed celibacy. Electra's farmer husband has not slept with her, saying that he respects her superior social status. Electra in her argument with her mother first condemns her for prettying herself when her husband was away from home. Electra has obviously not made that mistake herself. Orestes comments on how worn, ragged, and unkempt she looks. We know this appearance is cultivated: she refuses the offer of the chorus of young girls to lend her clothes to attend a festival. When she reviles Aegisthus's corpse, one might detect a note of envy as she condemns her mother's sexual relationship with him. All the men in this play seem weak beside the bloodthirsty Electra. We can imagine that Pylades could consider his marriage to her a death sentence.

Whereas Aeschylus and Sophocles set their plays on this theme in front of a palace in Argos, Euripides sets his in the countryside. He emphasizes the humble circumstances of Electra and her husband. Although we have no evidence which play came first, Sophocles' or Euripides' *Electra,* Euripides' sordid duo vividly contrast with the heroic pair in Sophocles' version.

Euripides' Electra rejects the Aeschylean recognition signs: a lock of hair ("How can a man's be the same as a woman's?"); a footprint (ditto); a piece of woven clothing ("I was too young to have done it and he would have outgrown it anyway"). This rejection does not, as is often supposed, merely mock the unlikely choice of tokens, but rather it indicates Electra's psychological inability to face the consequences of accepting them; as she says to the old man, they would indicate that Orestes has come in secret out of fear of Aegisthus, and this is incompatible with her view of Orestes as a fearless avenger.

The audience sees the farmer's hut, a suitably mean location for a sordid killing. The body of Aegisthus is brought onto the stage, but we never see the body of Clytemnestra. Castor and Pollux perhaps appear in the *mēchanē* at the end above the criminal duo.

Trojan Women

This is the greatest anti-war play ever written. From Aeschylus to Euripides there is a shift in focus. Aeschylus wrote with the glory of the Persian wars vividly in mind, but Euripides was overwhelmed by the horrors of the Peloponnesian War (431–404 B.C.), in which Greek fought Greek. The names of Marathon and Thermopylae are synonymous with Greek heroism, but the name of Melos is synonymous with the atrocity born of empire. Just before this play was produced (415 B.C.), the Athenians killed all the males and enslaved the women and children on Melos. This is vividly described by Thucydides, who reveals the Athenian *machtpolitik* (might makes right). In the same year the Athenians made the disastrous decision to invade Sicily, the first step toward their final defeat in 404 B.C. This play was strangely prophetic: a warning that was not heeded.

Though none of the other plays presented with *Trojan Women* has survived, the titles and some fragments of the two plays that precede it, *Alexander* and *Palamedes,* lead one to speculate that Euripides may have written a connected trilogy: each title suggests someone connected with Troy and the Trojan War. Even the satyr play that followed these tragedies, *Sisyphus,* might be connected to Odysseus, since Sisyphus has sometimes been mentioned in mythology as his father.

In a prologue, Poseidon reflects on the destruction of Troy, of which he was patron. He describes how the Trojan women will be taken to Greece as slaves. Athena asks Poseidon to join her in punishing the Greeks who had violated her temple. Poseidon agrees and says he will raise a storm the Greeks will

The Women of Troy. Translated by Kenneth McLeish. Directed by Annie Castledine. Poseidon (Leo Wringer, left) and Athene (Picka Vance) decide the fate of the Greeks at the beginning of the play. Royal National Theatre Production, Olivier Theatre, London (1995). Photo: Simon Annand. Used by permission.

not forget. Hecuba, the queen of Troy, is seen lying on the ground before the tents of the captives; she laments the loss of her family and city. The women appear, and a messenger comes to say that they have been allotted to various masters. Hecuba asks about her surviving daughters. Cassandra, driven mad by Apollo and condemned to prophesy the truth but not to be believed, has been chosen by Agamemnon for his bed. Andromache, the wife of Hector, the greatest hero at Troy and son of Hecuba and Priam, the king of Troy, is allotted to Neoptolemus, the son of Achilles, who killed Hector. Hecuba is given to Odysseus, whom she particularly hates. Andromache appears and tells Hecuba that her daughter Polyxena was sacrificed on the grave of Achilles to appease his spirit. Talthybius the herald arrives to tell Andromache that her son, Astyanax, is to be thrown from the walls of Troy. It would be a rare person in the audience who would remain dry-eyed when Andromache says good-bye to her son for the last time in a scene of close intimacy in spite of the public setting. This is one of the most moving scenes of Greek drama. It distills humanity's sorrows in the tears of a mother for her child.

There is brief comic relief when Menelaus meets Helen again, now a prisoner whom he has pledged to kill. Helen debates with Hecuba in an attempt to justify herself, even laying the blame for the war on Hecuba for not killing her son Paris in the first place. The audience had just seen *Alexander,* in which Hecuba and Priam, warned of the trouble their son will cause, expose their baby, who is called Alexander by the shepherds who save him. Paris survives, as exposed babies in drama often do, and, when grown up, is welcomed back as their son by Hecuba and Priam. Helen's accusations may have had a point. There are many reasons she should not be blamed, as the sophist Gorgias points out in his defense of her, a defense probably written about the same time as this play.

By the end of the scene with Helen and Menelaus, it is clear enough, if not explicitly stated, that she has won over her former husband. Hecuba may have won the argument on intellectual grounds, but Helen emerges unscathed because of the passion she can still provoke. Her argumentation is reminiscent of the sophists, something that Aristophanes satirized in *The Clouds:* arguing for the good or the true is irrelevant; it is only important that one argues well. Even Cassandra illustrates this skill in this play, and she almost convinces her mother that it is better to lose a war than win it. She claims that the Trojans never had to leave their homes, and they will inherit the glorious fame of defending their country, whereas many Greeks would have to die far from their loved ones, invading someone else's country for rather sordid reasons.

There is stark horror in the scene where the desperate Hecuba has to attend to the body of her grandson Astyanax. Talthybius carries Astyanax's corpse over to Hecuba for her and the other women to prepare for burial. He carries him on his father's shield, the very object that was to protect him. This makes the burial all the more pitiable.

Hecuba, who said earlier to Andromache that she should live, because "where there's life, there's hope" (line 633), now tries to kill herself by running into the flames of Troy. She is prevented from doing this by Greek soldiers. She joins the women in a final lamentation, weeping for their lost loved ones and the fall of Troy. Her plight frames the play, which ends as it begins, with her personal tragedy.

Hecuba, the former queen of Troy, is the pivotal figure. As her own tragedy unfolds, she has to face the murder of her daughter Polyxena; the rape of another daughter, Cassandra; the murder of her baby grandson by the Greek army; and her daughter-in-law dragged away, as she will be, into slavery. Hecuba at the end is pure Hecuba: suffering has burned away her impurities.

The Greeks are shown to be more barbaric than the defeated Trojans; they are cowards frightened of a child. They are afraid to leave a young boy alive in case he grows up to be an avenger. The shadow of Melos stretches over the play. This is Euripides at his greatest, savaging the conventional heroes and showing the reality and sordidness of war. Besides this, it is hardly just to destroy a country for the sake of a woman, as the historian Herodotus points out.

The message is as powerful as ever: earlier poets such as Homer, Aeschylus, and Sophocles focus on the glory of war, but Euripides shows us the suffering of women and children. For plays like this he was called the most tragic of the tragedians. This play is a play about the sorrow that comes from loss, particularly the loss that is irrevocable. In the Euripidean universe, chaos and malevolent gods rule and the human leaders imitate the brutality of the gods.

The Women of Troy. Translated by Kenneth McLeish. Directed by Annie Castledine. Hecuba (Rosemary Harris) and the chorus lament over the dead Astyanax, the child of Troy's greatest hero, Hector. Royal National Theatre Production, Olivier Theatre, London (1995). Photo: Simon Annand. Used by permission.

Man's only recourse is to make an alliance with other men: here, women with women. This alliance goes by the name of *philia*, or love.

The victims show a type of heroism in the way that they choose to live. This play is about grief, but it may offer a note of hope. Suffering burns away pettiness and purifies the soul. Perhaps the audience will experience a comparable transformation. The Greeks called that catharsis, and good art can bring about change.

This is a play for all time. It is a plea for peace and understanding, in addition to celebrating life and its passions. It shows that it is never too late to take a step toward the light of peace, away from the darkness of brutal war; death will have no dominion over the heroism of these women.

Trojan Women is like Aeschylus's *Prometheus Bound* in that one character is onstage throughout and others come and go. Both plays have been criticized for this and described as static, like their victimized heroes. But this staging can be seen as symbolic of the characters' capacity to endure and adds to their stature.

There has been criticism for the rather static plot; one disaster simply follows another. No major principles are set in conflict, as they were in *Antigone*. Euripides was experimenting with a new type of play where the emotions dictate the action. The fact that this play has been performed repeatedly over the centuries is proof enough of its greatness.

The play has to be seen for its tragic potential to be appreciated. There is an inner tempo and a shift of moods, from the light (the captured girls speculating on the relative merits of the places to which they may go; the debate between Helen and Hecuba) to the totally bleak (the burial of Astyanax; the final burning of Troy). One light after another is extinguished until all is darkness except for the fires of Troy in the background.

At the beginning of the play the gods probably speak from above the stage building. They argue, and Poseidon accuses Athena of leaping one way and then another in her loyalties. Hecuba echoes this by saying that Fate is like a madman, lurching now here, now there, and that happiness does not last. Hecuba probably lies before the door of the *skēnē* throughout the prologue. Astyanax's dead body may be carried in by Talthybius, since he says that he is bringing it to Hecuba for burial rites. Others come to and from the Greek camp by the *parodos* (entryway) on one side. The women probably come out from the center of the *skēnē*.

In a modern performance one might see flames in the background in the final scene or throughout, with them rising at the end. I think the wind should rise gradually throughout the play and be at its strongest when the women exit; Poseidon is fulfilling his promise.

Heracles

This play is an interesting study in the power of friendship. When the gods are not to be counted on, a reliable friend can be one's most valuable resource.

The play is set in Thebes. The prologue is delivered by Amphitryon, who is married to Alcmena. She was visited by Zeus, who fathered Heracles. Amphitryon tells us that Heracles is away performing his famous labors in the attempt to restore Amphitryon to his home in Argos. Amphitryon was banished and fled to Thebes. He is protecting Megara, Heracles' wife, and her children. They are under threat of death from Lycus, who has usurped the throne of Thebes. Megara would like to embrace death, but Amphitryon urges her to live. Just as Lycus is about to kill them, Heracles returns. He saves the day and kills Lycus. Then Iris (Hera's messenger) and Madness are seen on the top of the palace: Hera plans to drive Heracles mad in order to spite her faithless husband, Zeus. Heracles, while he is mad, kills his wife and children, but Amphitryon is saved because Athena intervenes by hurling a boulder at Heracles, knocking him unconscious. Amphitryon ties him to a pillar. The *ekkyklēma* rolls out to reveal Heracles just waking. Amphitryon tells him what happened and he decides to kill himself. Theseus, the king of Athens and good friend to Heracles, appears and talks Heracles into living. After all, Heracles had just rescued him from Hades. Heracles says the man who would prefer fortune or power to good friends is mad.

This play is unusual in many ways and at the same time shares many characteristics with other plays by Euripides. Its action is divided in two parts. The first is a conventional thriller, with the hero coming in the nick of time to rescue the damsel in distress and kill the villain. Then as the hero *becomes* the villain, we see Euripides' genius at work. Heracles becomes a parable for every man who is a helpless victim of fate. He is a guiltless Oedipus, condemned by the jealous whim of a goddess who becomes a symbol of all the irrational pow-

Heracles. Translated by Mary Yiosi. Directed by Andrei Serban. Lycus threatens Amphitryon, Heracles' human father (Zeus is his divine one). National Theatre of Northern Greece (2002). Photo: Paris Petridis. Used by permission.

ers that govern human beings. This is also a parable of the danger which lurks within, either in a human being alone or in a family.

The Heracles in this play is different from the one in *Women of Trachis,* where he has a different wife and appears hard and indifferent to human problems, and in *Alcestis,* where he is the typical drunken buffoon and strongman. Here is a loving father and devoted husband. We find a sympathetic hero who has just made the world a better place by doing away with some of its cruel and dangerous monsters. He is an innocent victim of a jealous goddess, Hera, and in this he resembles Hippolytus and Phaedra, who are both innocent victims of Aphrodite. Seneca has Juno (Latin for Hera) explicitly rage against Jove (Zeus) and his infidelities at the beginning of his play *Hercules Furens,* based on this one. But Euripides, by not having Hera appear, makes her even more ominous than the raging Juno that we see. Hera is like Zeus in *Prometheus Bound:* she sends lackeys to do her dirty work, which is all too effective at destroying this hero.

Just as Hippolytus shows himself better than the gods because he can forgive and they cannot, so in Euripides' play human friendship shows a humanity that is superior to the cruel whims of the gods. Friendship makes livable a life subject to unpredictable forces. Heracles, like so many other tragic heroes, illustrates that one cannot know whether human happiness will last until the day one dies. Heracles is also one of those humans who defines what gods should be ideally: he claims that a god to be truly godlike needs nothing. This is a variation on what Euripides said in the fragmentary play *Bellerophon:* "If the gods do anything shameful, they are not gods" (Diggle, *Fragmenta selecta,* 3.7, p. 100). He also rejects the tales of immoral actions on the part of the gods and amusingly rejects his own divine birth in the process. This is rational sophism and philosophy overriding mythology in a play that begins with a mythological scene.

The messenger speech describing Heracles' murder of his wife and children is extremely dramatic, as is the chorus that precedes it, telling of Heracles dancing to the tune of madness played on the *aulos* (the reeded oboe-like instrument used to accompany the tragic chorus). Some think that the chorus illustrates what it is describing by dancing in a comparably mad fashion.

This is an exciting play to stage. The palace of Thebes is visible, and Iris and Madness at one point appear on the roof or possibly fly onto the scene carried by the *mēchanē*. Madness argues with Iris, pointing out that what she is commanded to do is wrong; the minion shows herself more moral than the goddess in power (Hera) who ordered this. In other plays by Euripides, servants or slaves show themselves more moral than their masters.

Another gripping moment is the view of Heracles rolled out on the *ekkyklēma,* tied to a pillar and surrounded by the bodies of his children and wife. The final picture of Heracles, like the ending of *Women of Trachis* or *Ajax,* shows a defeated Superman. This emphasizes Euripides' lesson: even "super" people are subject to suffering and can be brought low. Human kindness is the medicine which will restore them.

Iphigenia among the Taurians

This play has a fairy-tale quality to it: the prince finds the princess and rescues her from her terrible fate. The princess also rescues the prince (something typically Euripidean). This is another of the plays which leads to New Comedy, with stories about the family, happy endings, and exciting adventures. Even Aristotle admired this plot. Shakespeare has similar comedies which feature the discovery of a long-lost relative.

The play begins with a prologue delivered by Iphigenia, who is living among the Taurians (in the Crimea, on the north coast of the Black Sea) and acting as a priestess to Artemis, after the goddess saved her at Aulis. She sprinkles water on all the Greeks who arrive, as a preliminary to their sacrifice to this goddess. She claims she loathes this duty, and she thinks that humans are blaming their own bloodthirsty desires on Artemis. Orestes and Pylades arrive but do not reveal their identities to Iphigenia. She has had a dream that Orestes is dead. Now she prepares the strangers for sacrifice, but discovering that they are Greek, she asks that one take a letter for her back to Argos. She says that it is for Orestes, her brother. Orestes says it will be very easy to deliver it, since he is standing before her. She believes him when he tells her things from their past. They are happily reunited and plan their escape.

Iphigenia tells Thoas the king that Orestes is polluted because of matricide and so is the statue of Artemis, which he has touched. She says that the statue (which Orestes has been commanded by Artemis to restore to Greece) must be purified with seawater. Thoas believes her. This is quite a comical scene, as Thoas remarks that no barbarian would commit an act so barbaric as matricide, and Iphigenia warns him to beware of Greeks. She, Orestes, and Pylades try to sail away, but rough seas are against them. A soldier runs back to Thoas to reveal the truth. Athena arrives to calm the seas (with Poseidon's help) and save them. She tells Thoas he has to obey the gods. He even has to release the captive Greek maidens who have been the chorus.

There are beautiful choral odes, one telling of the desire of the girls to escape and fly home, and others speaking of the Trojan War and telling myths associated with Iphigenia. These girls are loyal to Iphigenia and protect her even at the cost of their own lives.

This is a fantasy play filled with comedy and adventure. It is a delightful piece of entertainment. Perhaps it was meant to divert the Athenians from the heavier concerns of war. It was written approximately a year after *Trojan Women;* just as the second *Hippolytus* aimed at popularity rather than at "raising consciousness," so this play may have been written to amuse during times of stress.

Iphigenia is rational and questions a goddess who would ask for human sacrifice. This brings her in line with the servant in *Hippotytus*, Heracles, and Cadmus, who say that gods are not immoral, something refuted by the testimony of the plays themselves. It is another way that Euripides shows humans occasionally to be superior to the gods in virtue. Iphigenia might here shame the goddess into rethinking her brutality, since Athena at the end asks that rites be established at Halae which mimic human sacrifice but in fact only draw blood.

Iphigenia herself is concerned for her brother, as Orestes is concerned for Pylades; Orestes is willing to die so that Pylades could be free. He is as generous as Alcestis, who agreed to die for her husband, Admetus. But he is not so generous to foreigners. He readily suggests killing Thoas to help their escape. It is Iphigenia who says that he is a good man and that they should not do this. Helen and Menelaus are not so merciful in their escape (see *Helen,* discussed below); although they spared the king, they slew many of his followers.

Thoas himself, the barbarian king, shows that he is a fair man in his treatment of Iphigenia and that by sanctioning human sacrifice, he only wants to enforce what he thinks the goddess has ordered. He obeys Athena at the end and is horrified to hear of the misdeeds of the Greeks. Thoas is among the barbarians whom Euripides shows to be more civilized than many Greeks.

The play praises the mutual love and devotion that human beings have for one another. Orestes advises against heeding oracles and regrets the matricide, now understanding the horrific consequences of obeying Apollo. Iphigenia also decries bloody sacrifices. Once again it is the humans who are seen to be more generous and humane than the gods. It is typical of Euripides to make barbarians superior to Greeks and humans superior to gods in moral behavior. Euripides often favored the conventional underdog.

This play is staged in front of the temple of Artemis. At one point, Thoas conceals himself inside until his soldier summons him out. There are various entrances and exits. The temple walls are decorated with the bloody spoils of previous victims. Scene painting could do this. Athena probably appears on the *mēchanē* at the end to deliver her joint messages to Thoas and Orestes. Athena makes the humorous claim that a goddess can be heard at long distances to explain how Orestes on the ocean sailing to Greece can hear her as effectively as Thoas does. This could be anachronistically but effectively staged by having Athena use a cell phone.

Ion

Ion is often grouped with and dated close to *Iphigenia among the Taurians* and *Helen.* These plays have happy endings, and *Ion* is particularly close to Menander's type of New Comedy, which is based on recognitions and the discovery of long-lost family members.

Ion was born to Creusa, an Athenian princess who had been raped by Apollo. Creusa left Ion in the cave where she had been raped, but Apollo saved the child. On Apollo's order, Hermes delivered Ion to his temple at Delphi where he was brought up and is now a temple servant. Xuthus, the husband of Creusa and king of Athens, has come to Delphi to consult Apollo about his childlessness. All this is explained by Hermes in the prologue.

Ion appears and sings a beautiful song to greet the dawn. He tells how he cares for Apollo's temple. Creusa arrives in tears and pretends that she is seeking information about another woman who had been raped by Apollo who wants to know if her baby is still alive. Ion finds the question too rude to put to Apollo.

Xuthus consults Apollo's oracle and is told that the first person he will meet coming from the temple will be his son. (Apollo wants to conceal his own paternity.) It is Ion, who at first rebuffs this older man, thinking he is making a sexual advance when he grabs him. Later Ion accepts that Xuthus is his father.

When she hears this, Creusa is dismayed and plots with an old servant to poison Ion. A messenger describes how the old man put the poison in Ion's cup but because of a word of ill omen, the wine was poured on the ground. An unlucky bird drank the poison and died in agony. Ion noticed this and asked the old man who was trying to poison him, and the old man was forced to admit that it was Creusa.

Creusa clings to an altar to escape being killed by Ion. The priestess arrives with a cradle, saying it was the cradle in which she found Ion. Creusa recognizes the cradle and, without seeing its contents, she is able to identify the trinkets which she placed there with her baby. Ion is finally convinced that she is telling the truth and that she is his mother. She reveals that Apollo was his father. He is about to go off to confront the god, but Athena arrives as his representative, because, she says, Apollo was afraid he would be reproached if he came himself. Apollo, she explains, had said that Xuthus was the father in order to encourage Xuthus to adopt Ion as his son. Creusa will have more children, representing, in fact, some of the major tribes of Greece: Dorus giving his name to the Dorians and Achaeus to the Achaeans, just as Ion will give his name to the Ionians.

In spite of the happy ending, Euripides indicts a god for his callousness. The messenger in *Andromache* also criticized Apollo for allowing Neoptolemus to be killed in his shrine when he had appeared as a suppliant. Castor and Pollux at the end of *Electra* can barely restrain their criticism of Apollo, who commanded a son to kill his mother. Euripides often attacked oracles in general and Apollo in particular.

Ion shows an innocence which resembles that of Hippolytus, without however the fanaticism of the latter. He tells Xuthus that he would prefer to remain doing his duties in Delphi than to go to a city where, if his citizenship were suspect, he might not have freedom of speech. Freedom of speech was what characterized an Athenian citizen and democracy (this is a typical Euripidean anachronism).

Creusa weeps and complains, and her chorus, serving girls devoted to her, reinforces her self-pity. She exposed the child immediately after birth. Then when he returns as Xuthus's child (not realizing that he was in fact her own child), she tried to kill him because she felt that his presence might marginalize her: her husband has been able to have an heir without her. She confirms many of the misogynist remarks found in Euripidean plays. She lies, is a master at plots, and is ultimately violent. Perhaps we can forgive her because we see her as a woman who was genuinely wronged.

This play has more comic elements than many of the tragedies. There are realistic touches even in the midst of lyrical passages, such as when Ion says that he has constantly to drive the birds away from the temple because of the messes they make. The chorus at one point admires the scenery represented by the set. Euripides was the most down-to-earth of the three tragic playwrights. His characters speak colloquially. They also ask embarrassing questions of people in authority and, as we have seen, of the gods. There are humorous elements in this play, and it shares many of the characteristics of New Comedy which will be represented by Menander (342/41–293/89 B.C.). It is this type of comedy with mistaken identities and concealed births that will also inspire Shakespeare. New Comedy differs from Aristophanes' Old Comedy, which explicitly satirized and criticized real people, for example, the politician Cleon.

In the midst of the comedy, there are serious issues. This is a play that removes the flattering mask from Apollo and shows that his actions in many ways are worse than a human's. The question is raised of how should the gods expect good actions from humans if they themselves continually follow their passions with no ethical guidelines? Gods should set examples for men rather than commit the crimes they themselves forbid. Euripides seems to demand the same from the leaders of Athens: those in power should use that power with discretion and concern for those who are subject to that power. The humans in his plays are seen as superior to the gods when they forgive each other and finally reach an understanding based on compassion.

Euripides is investigating the gap between what seems to be and what is. We finally see Apollo's true nature: he is a philandering god without too much care for the humans he abuses. As Ion discovers Apollo's true nature for himself, he matures. Ion goes behind the appearance to the reality, and by the end of the play he finds out who he is.

There are beautiful descriptive passages of Delphi and its setting and also of the tapestries in the tent where Xuthus was going to celebrate finding his son. This tapestry showed the sky with its sun, moon, and stars. The description is so effective by itself that the audience can readily picture it in the imagination. I have seen the play staged with such a draping, but it did not increase the charm of the words.

The set shows the temple of Delphi. It is from there that the priestess will appear as Creusa is clinging to an altar. The altar, as in so many plays, is essential for the staging. Hermes can appear at the beginning on foot in front of the temple or possibly on the roof. Athena can also appear on the roof at the end. She does not sort things out so much as predict things to come. The Athenians in the audience delight in hearing both about their genealogy and their future.

Helen

Helen has many similarities to *Iphigenia among the Taurians*. Both plays show captive women in barbarian countries who are rescued at the end, through their own successful stratagems. Nothing is as it seems.

Helen, the wife of Menelaus of Sparta, gives the background and laments her captivity in Egypt. Hera was jealous of Aphrodite winning the beauty contest in which Paris was given Helen as his prize. Hera whisked Helen off to

Egypt to spite Aphrodite and sent a phantom to Troy in Helen's stead; so according to this play, the Trojan War was fought over an illusion. Proteus, the late king of Egypt, had promised to restore Helen to her husband. His son Theoclymenus, who is now king, wants Helen for himself. She has taken refuge at Proteus's tomb. Theoclymenus has a sister, Theonoe, who can foretell the future.

The Greek hero Teucer arrives in Egypt by chance and is shocked to see Helen, but he assumes it is simply someone who looks like her. He gives her news that the war at Troy is over and that the Greek fleet has been shipwrecked. He does not know where Menelaus is, but he tells her that Leda, Helen's mother, hung herself in shame over her daughter's supposed behavior. Her brothers, Castor and Pollux, have been transformed into stars. Helen tells Teucer to flee because Theoclymenus kills every Greek coming to his land. She laments and the chorus consoles her. She goes with the chorus into the palace.

Menelaus enters and begs the portress for help. He is in rags and weeps before her. She tells him to escape any way he can. Helen and Menelaus meet and there is a comic reunion in which Helen recognizes Menelaus, but he, who cannot believe this is the real Helen, tells her to take her hands off him. A servant appears to tell him that the phantom Helen vanished, but that, before doing this, she told the truth about the true and the false Helen. After hearing this Menelaus finally believes the real Helen's story.

The couple plots, and Menelaus, like Orestes in *Iphigenia among the Taurians,* is all for killing the barbarian king. Menelaus cannot figure out how to escape, but Helen comes up with a stratagem. She will tell Theoclymenus that her husband is dead and that she needs to make sacrifices in a ship at sea. Theonoe knows everything and is about to tell her brother, but both Helen and Menelaus plead with her. Helen makes the claim that the gods hate violence, which is rather incredible in the light of her own subsequent instigation of violent actions.

Theonoe gives in and the stratagem is successful. Menelaus and Helen kill most of the Egyptian sailors and escape. Theoclymenus is about to kill his sister for not warning him when Castor and Pollux appear and say he must forgive her and let Helen and Menelaus return home. Just as in the *Iphigenia among the Taurians,* divine intervention calms the barbarian king.

This is a light play with serious implications. It shows the conventional Greek heroes as deceptive and murderous, far less "civilized" than their "barbarian" hosts, or at least equal to them in their barbarous acts. Theoclymenus is not presented as a likable character, but both Menelaus and Helen gain audience sympathy (particularly since they are Greek). If one looks at their actions, however, one could make a case against them. Helen is vain, treacherous, and (like Electra) a moaner. Both Helen and Iphigenia in *Iphigenia among the Taurians* use the excuse of religious obligations to further their deceptions.

Menelaus seems ridiculous, first appearing in rags and weeping before a portress. This is rather like Agamemnon envying the happiness of his slave at the beginning of the *Iphigenia at Aulis*. How the great have fallen! This illustrates yet again the transience of happiness, power, and prosperity. When Menelaus has to argue his case in front of Theonoe, he says that heroes do not cry and that this is why he will not resort to tears. Yet the audience has just seen him debasing himself before a portress.

The character who comes off best in this play is the servant who is willing to risk his life to save Theonoe. The next best are the two barbarians, Theonoe and Theoclymenus.

There are many comic moments and a happy ending. Nevertheless, modern audiences are left with a sour taste, realizing how many Egyptian lives it cost to secure the lives of two Greeks. The ancient audience was probably not as sensitive to these issues but instead went along with Helen's claim for the superiority of the Greek over the barbarian, among whom, as she says, "all are slaves but one." (That one is the king.) One reason the Greeks feel superior is because they have expelled their tyrants and have established democracy. This is obviously an anachronistic comment in the play, since Greece at the time of the Trojan War still had its kings. Perhaps these kings were somewhat democratic. We certainly saw this in Aeschylus's *Suppliant Women,* in which the king has to consult his people over the decision to take in the suppliants.

In *Helen,* the chorus members express a wish to fly back to Greece, like the chorus in the *Iphigenia among the Taurians.* They are Helen's allies, although like the chorus in *Electra,* they tell the protagonist that enough weeping is enough. Helen weeps more than any female character in Greek tragedy; most of her tears are for dramatic effect.

The set includes a palace with a central door, and there is a tomb where Helen takes refuge. Castor and Pollux probably fly in on the *mēchanē.* The messenger speech at the end describing the initial deception and the escape is particularly vivid.

The contrast between appearance and reality was a popular philosophical issue of the day. Drama itself is an illusion like the false Helen and, like her, can influence history.

Phoenician Women

This play alludes to most of the stories told about Oedipus and his sons. As transmitted in the manuscripts, it is Euripides' longest play, with 1,766 lines, but many of these lines are later additions to the original text. For example, the ending from line 1,582 was probably added by a writer who wanted to include allusions to Sophocles' *Antigone* and *Oedipus at Colonus.* This play was popular in antiquity, and this may explain why there were so many additions: more at each performance.

As the play opens, Jocasta reviews the history of the house of Oedipus as revealed in Sophocles' *Oedipus Tyrannus* and Aeschylus's *Seven against Thebes.* Polyneices is returning to attack his own city. Jocasta has asked for a truce to try to reconcile the brothers. Antigone and her tutor appear on the roof, and he points out some of the heroes who have come to attack the city. He tells her to return inside before people begin to gossip at seeing a young girl in public. The chorus of Phoenician maidens (distant relatives of the Thebans) enters; they were on their way to Delphi but were detained because of the war. Polyneices enters fearfully. His mother comes out and is glad to see him. He tells her how horrible it is to live in exile; one loses freedom of speech, and one is forced to adapt one's ways to suit others. He says a penniless man has no friends. He is reluctant to bring war against his own country, but he claims he must satisfy his sense of justice. He is clearly Jocasta's favorite son, and she is desperate to reconcile him with his brother.

Eteocles enters and argues that might makes right and calls tyranny a god, and it is obvious that this is the god he worships. Jocasta argues for equality between relatives, cities, and allies. She says that justice entails sharing, as the day shares with the night. She also questions the value of wealth: one only needs so much, and great wealth is unreliable. She criticizes both her sons for bringing the city into danger.

Teiresias responds to a summons and tells Creon that his son Menoeceus must be sacrificed if Ares is to be on the side of Thebes; his life will pay for the death of the dragon that Cadmus slew. Creon objects vigorously, but Menoeceus has heard the oracle and, contrary to his father's will, decides to give his life for his city. A messenger describes his heroic death and also the fights of the heroes at six gates. Polyneices and Eteocles are about to fight at the seventh, but Jocasta rushes to the field with Antigone to try to save them. She is too late, arriving only to see their last moments.

As he dies, Eteocles looks at Jocasta with love, and Polyneices bids her farewell, begging her and his sister to bury him. Jocasta takes a sword from them and thrusts it into her own throat: she follows them in death. Oedipus is told about this and Antigone joins him in mourning. In the ending that was written later, Creon exiles Oedipus, because Teiresias told him that Oedipus and his seed were the source of sorrow for the city. Creon orders Antigone into the house, but Antigone says that she will go with her father and that she will bury her brother (it is rather difficult to do both at once, particularly if she is caught and imprisoned or executed for doing the latter).

I titled a review of this play "Mother Knows Best." Jocasta is the one who makes the most sense in this play, as she argues for peace and an equal division of rule. She says nothing justifies putting one's country in danger. She respects the common good and loves her sons. If the sons had followed the mother, there would not have been a tragedy.

This play shows why each son fought. Other accounts simply show the sons fighting as a result of their father's curse, and they try to avoid it. Here we see the psychological reasons behind their fight and why they are so eager for it. Euripides is the master of psychology and realism. He also understands a mother's love: once her sons die, she has no further reason to live. One might argue that Antigone and Ismene were reason enough, but her sorrow by the end of the play is shown to be overwhelming. Reason governs no one's actions in the play. Passion is the real winner.

Both sons are deftly portrayed, and their arguments reveal their true personalities. They care more for their own lusts, one for wealth and the other for power, than for the common good. By contrast, Menoeceus, instead of putting his city at risk, gives his life to save it. He is the true hero. He is superior to his father, Creon, who says that if it comes to a choice between his child or his country, he would choose his child. This is the reverse of the claim made by the Sophoclean Creon in *Antigone*. Euripides makes Menoeceus, a child, ethically superior to his father, the ruler.

Euripides also differs from Sophocles because both Jocasta and Oedipus are alive when their sons die. This vividly shows the psychological effects of their suffering after the loss of their children. Euripides often highlights the pathetic in his plays, as he does here. The scene between Jocasta and her son is truly moving.

Oedipus is a pale reflection of the Sophoclean hero. He only appears at the end as a witness of further horrors and because of the consequences of his curse. He is described as having tried to kill himself. He is not successful even in this. The Sophoclean Oedipus would have been, if that had been his choice. Sophocles creates Oedipus as a hero; Euripides creates Oedipus as a broken man. Sophocles' Oedipus was all the stronger for choosing to live after the reasons for living seemed to have vanished.

This play is staged in front of the palace. One direction leads to the battlefield and the other may lead to Argos; it is from this direction that Polyneices would enter. The tutor and Antigone view the army from the palace roof. The messenger speech is particularly gripping for its graphic description not only of the fight between Polyneices and Eteocles, but also of their deaths

Orestes. Translated by K. H. Myris. Directed by Stavros Tsakiris. Orestes (Yannis Vouros) is condemned to death because he killed his mother. He and his sister Electra (Aglaia Pappa) plot his escape. Theatre of Kalamata, Greece (2002). Courtesy of Hellenic Festival S. A.

in their mother's arms. Jocasta's suicide follows the logic of her heart and moves anyone hearing the account.

Orestes

Orestes reflects the chaos described by Thucydides in his account of the Peloponnesian War. It shows what murderous alliances can do. Orestes, Electra, and Pylades will stop at nothing, and what they call friendship is perverted loyalty. This play is a parody of heroism and *philia* (friendship).

Electra begins by complaining (this is an Electra we know). She speaks of her sufferings and those of Orestes. After he killed their mother, following Apollo's command, he has been pursued by the Furies, who in this play are only in his mind. Electra has become his nursemaid. She says that the people of Argos are voting on Orestes' and Electra's fate, and it is likely that the sentence will be death. Helen enters and is shown to be as vain and insensitive as ever. She asks Electra to carry an offering (a lock of her own hair) to the grave of the mother she helped murder. Electra refuses. Hermione, Helen's daughter, is chosen instead. When Helen leaves, Electra comments on how neatly she cut her hair so that her beauty would not be marred. The chorus enters and Electra tells them to be quiet and not to disturb Orestes. Orestes awakes and Electra tends him. He has a seizure and imagines he can see the Furies.

Menelaus, Helen's husband, returns from Troy and asks for Orestes. Orestes admits his crime to Menelaus and says that he suffers from a guilty conscience (this is a "scientific" answer, rather than the typical mythological response, which would be to attribute his suffering to the vengeance of his mother's Furies). Tyndareus, Helen's and Clytemnestra's mortal father (Zeus was their divine father), appears and argues with Orestes. He goes to the trial and helps convince the people to vote for Orestes' and Electra's death. After he has left, Orestes asks Menelaus to commit a crime to help him, just as Agamemnon committed crimes for him. Menelaus says he would help if he could, but since he has no army, it would be useless for him to oppose the decision of the people of Argos.

Pylades comes on the scene and offers Orestes and Electra his full support, even if it costs his life: he becomes their partner in crime. A peasant friendly to Orestes arrives to tell about the decision condemning them to death. They will at least be allowed to kill themselves. Orestes and Electra despair, but Pylades has a plan: murder Helen. Electra adds her suggestion to take Hermione hostage. Helen is heard screaming inside, and Electra urges Orestes on, rather as she does in Sophocles' *Electra* when Orestes is killing their mother. Hermione is taken hostage. Orestes waylays Helen's servant, a Phrygian, plays with him mercilessly, and threatens his life if he does not fall into line. The Phrygian's part contains a wonderful lyric solo sung in broken Greek describing his terror. His "messenger speech," describing what happened to Helen, is also in faulty Greek for humorous effect: "laughing at the colonial." The Greeks consider anyone who does not speak Greek "barbarian"—they say "ba ba" instead of making sense. Imperialists often construe the colonial as barbarians, just as the British did the Irish, even in their textbooks. One suspects that Euripides has more sympathy for this Phrygian than for the brutal Orestes.

Menelaus appears, and the group threatens to kill Hermione if he does not do what they ask, namely to give Orestes the throne of Argos. Apollo appears to sort things out and tells Orestes that he (Orestes) will marry Hermione, the girl "on whose neck you hold a knife" (line 1627), and Pylades will get Electra. Helen is safe and now is a star in the sky like her brothers, Castor and Pollux. Orestes is to reign in Argos. Orestes then greets Apollo. Although Orestes admits that what Apollo said came to pass, nevertheless he was afraid: Orestes thought that perhaps, instead of Apollo, he had he heard the voice of a vengeful demon (*alastor*, line 1669, a doubt he also expressed in *Electra*). He concludes with the reassuring "All's well that ends well."

This strange play is a black comedy. One might see the ending as a happy one, but it is the result of one crime after another. The play was performed in 408 B.C., just four years before the end of the war and about two years before Euripides' own death. It shows a war-weariness which has gone beyond tragedy. Now Euripides' response seems to be ghastly laughter. As Athol Fugard said of Beckett's humor, "Smile, and then wipe the blood off your mouth" (*Notebooks*, p. 67).

Orestes may have been Euripides' last play before he left Athens in self-imposed exile to go to the court of Archelaus in Macedonia. It shows graphically his disillusion with a political process based on might making right.

It is amusing that the chorus wakes Orestes up with its entry. This is another Euripidean metatheatrical touch. Electra is furious at it for making so much noise. This touch of comic realism is typically Euripidean and is a parody of stage conventions.

Aeschylus's *Oresteia* saw the law court established for the first time when Orestes was put on trial. In *Orestes*, courts are already in existence. This anachronism raises another question, which in fact Tyndareus asks: why didn't Orestes leave Clytemnestra to the courts?

The Helen we see in this play we have met already in *Trojan Women*. Menelaus is like her in that he does what suits him. Nevertheless, his argument makes sense. He does not have his army and is not able to oppose the Argives; he is also not willing to take risks, and certainly is not willing to commit crimes as Pylades does for his friends.

Orestes, Pylades, and Electra are a murderous trio. In other plays they express some doubts about the dilemma that Apollo's command imposed on them; here they are willing to commit even worse crimes, such as killing Helen for the gratuitous pleasure of doing it. Hermione is wholly innocent and shows herself ready to argue on their behalf, and yet they are ready to slit her throat to benefit themselves. As a final crime, Orestes tells his sister to set fire to the palace. We remember Orestes in *Iphigenia among the Taurians* suggesting they murder Thoas. He has not changed much from that play to this one. It is a logical conclusion to the Aeschylean Orestes asking Pylades in *Choephoroi* whether he should murder his mother. Euripides always takes the next step in his plays to underline inherent violence in a person's character. In this way he gets the audience to question its own role in using or advocating (sometimes voting for) violence. It is still a useful question.

The messenger who comes to tell them about the Argive decision claims that he may be poor, but he will act nobly. He tried to support Orestes. Both he and Hermione come off best in this play: a peasant and a young woman, typical heroes in Euripides. The adult characters who are noble by birth are hopelessly corrupt.

There is a lot of exciting action. At the end, while standing on the roof of the palace, Orestes holds Hermione prisoner. Pylades and Electra waving their torches resemble Furies, while Menelaus looks on helplessly. We are reminded of Jason looking at Medea, holding his two dead sons. Medea, like the three here, is in the position of a god at the end of the play. Apollo functions as a friend to the criminals; one can almost call them a murderous foursome. He is their dragon-drawn chariot (Medea's getaway car) and their means of escape.

One way of staging this is to have it all presented as Orestes' dream, namely the wandering fantasy of an insane person. One production set it in a hospital.

I have seen various ways that Apollo can be played. In one production he was a robot whose electronic voice got stuck; in another he was a game show host: "And for your prize, Orestes, you get Hermione! And Argos!" It is not one of Apollo's best moments. But in Euripides, Apollo rarely has a good one.

Iphigenia at Aulis

This play was produced posthumously in 405 B.C. by Euripides' son, along with *Bacchae,* and *Alcmaeon at Corinth* (which has not survived). In each of these plays parents either kill (*Iphigenia, Bacchae*) or threaten their children (*Alcmaeon*). This is another anti-war play. Like *Trojan Women,* it can deeply move audiences.

It begins in the darkness just before dawn. Agamemnon is speaking with his old slave, and he gives background for the Trojan War. Helen's suitors were pledged to fight against anyone who would take her from her rightful husband. Paris, the prince of Troy, took her from Menelaus. The Greek fleet has gathered at Aulis with the various leaders pledged to give their support to their Commander in Chief Agamemnon, Menelaus's elder brother. The fleet is detained by a lack of wind. Calchas has told Agamemnon, in the presence of Menelaus and Odysseus, that Artemis demands the life of Iphigenia. At first Agamemnon accedes to this request. He makes up the spurious excuse of marriage to Achilles to lure Iphigenia to Aulis. However, he changes his mind and asks the servant to deliver a letter to Argos to tell Iphigenia not to come. The servant leaves and is stopped by Menelaus, who has been eavesdropping. Menelaus takes the letter and confronts Agamemnon. He accuses him of being after power and not caring for the people, and Agamemnon in turn accuses him of being uxorious, mad for a wife who is not worth it. The arrival of Iphigenia is announced. Now it is Menelaus's turn to change his mind, and he tells Agamemnon not to sacrifice his daughter. Agamemnon says he will no longer fight with fate but will sacrifice her. In a semi-comic scene with Achilles, Clytemnestra and Achilles find out they were duped.

Clytemnestra confronts Agamemnon, who tries to deny the deception but finally confesses. Iphigenia pleads for her life. Achilles says he will give his life for Iphigenia; he reports that his men threw stones at him for trying to defend her. She changes her mind and says that she will give her life to Greece, claiming that ten thousand women's lives are not worth one man's, and furthermore that Artemis has commanded this. She goes off to her death. In an ending which was clearly written by a much later writer, a messenger tells Clytemnestra that Iphigenia was saved by Artemis, who substituted a deer for her.

War has been a timeless concern for man; one questions its goals and the price one pays for them. War and its consequences intrigued Euripides. He questions its abuses. This play is symbolic of all the young people who are needlessly sacrificed in wars, not only as the victims of attacks, but also as the soldiers who are ordered to fight.

Homer extols the glories of battle and the honor of the hero, but Euripides shows the heroism of the victim, which more often than not is futile. The old heroes are unheroic, and in the very first scene in this play we see Agamemnon envying the happiness of his own slave. This play is his tragedy also, if we accept his expressed love for his child as genuine.

The heroism and idealism of Iphigenia point out the corruption of the leaders. Menelaus unmasks Agamemnon and Agamemnon does the same for his brother. Just as in the argument between Pheres and Admetus in *Alcestis*, the men are shown to be inferior to a woman, and in this case a child.

Achilles, by contrast with Iphigenia, is vain and self-serving: he says that he would have lent his name to the ruse if he had been consulted in the first place. Because he was not consulted, his honor, or self-pride, had been damaged.

Clytemnestra calls the sacrifice murder and we believe her. It is possible that in antiquity there was more sympathy for Agamemnon. After all, a father for the most part had power of life and death over his children, and girl babies were more likely to be exposed in some wild place and left to die than boy babies.

None of the characters is wholly villainous or wholly heroic. Even Iphigenia develops gradually. First she prays for life at any cost. At the end, however, she makes her heroic choice, and Aristotle blames Euripides for this abrupt change, which he considers a flaw in the plot and characterization. However, Menelaus too changes his mind abruptly and so does Agamemnon, but that does not seem to bother Aristotle. One only needs to see the play, or indeed the film by Cacoyannis, to be convinced of the tragic logic. Aristotle was a philosopher not a playwright, and I think he is wrong here.

Iphigenia's nobility is timeless and is made more believable because she matures throughout the course of the play. By asking her mother to forgive her father she resembles Euripides' Hippolytus, who forgave his father for causing his death. She puts into practice *philia*, a cross between love and duty, in this case loyalty to her father.

The choruses in this play seem not as relevant as they are in earlier plays. Some choruses are purely descriptive (the first one describes the fleet). Others are reflective (about the wildness of love). Others offer mythological interludes (a description of the marriage of Peleus and Thetis).

The set shows Agamemnon's tent, before which most of the action takes place. We are to imagine the beach at Aulis, as it is described in the first chorus. One direction leads to Argos and the other to the beach.

There are interesting roles for both men and women. I would suggest omitting the ending, which I consider spurious and which I believe undercuts the tragedy. Just as there are two versions of Helen in Euripides' plays (one as unfaithful and one as virtuous), so I suspect there are two versions of the Iphigenia myth. Euripides refers to the substituted deer in *Iphigenia among the Taurians,* but I think *Iphigenia at Aulis* is a different type of play. To underline his anti-war point, I think it probable that Euripides intended that his heroine should die.

It is very likely that Euripides died before he finished the play. In addition to the ending, which, as said earlier, is certainly by a much later writer, other parts of the play may have been written by his son, shortly after his death, or by later producers in the following century.

Bacchae

Bacchae of 405 B.C. (with *Iphigenia at Aulis*), performed posthumously a year before the end of the Peloponnesian War, shows similarities to *Hippolytus* of 428 B.C., performed near the beginning of the war. Both Dionysus and Aphrodite take vengeance on humans who have denied them worship.

In the prologue Dionysus tells the audience he has returned to his birthplace, Thebes, to assert his divinity, which has been questioned. He has driven the women mad and sent them to the mountains. He has taken human form in the guise of a priest and leads a band of Asian bacchantes. Pentheus, the young king, enters, claiming that the women have left the city and have gone to the mountains, where they take part in what he suspects are lewd orgies. Although his grandfather Cadmus and the prophet Teiresias advise him to welcome the new god, he tries to imprison the priest (Dionysus), who escapes from his bondage and causes the palace to collapse. A messenger tells Pentheus about the supernatural power of the women on the mountainside.

Teiresias, Cadmus, the bacchants, and even the ecstatic women represent different types of worshippers of Dionysus. Teiresias is the sophist prophet who sees Dionysus as the god of wine, essential for man. Cadmus sees his worship as bringing the family benefits. After all, he claims, it can't hurt to be related to a god. Cadmus represents the attitude toward religion that asks: What can it do for me? It reflects a more practical and utilitarian point of view. The bacchants are those who worship the god with their bodies, souls, and hearts, in contrast to the more rational Teiresias and Cadmus. The ecstatic women are like members of cults: madly and blindly following their leaders. One thinks of all fanatic and charismatic leaders for whom their followers will kill: the bin Ladens and the Hitlers (where the political becomes a religion). Finally there is the disillusioned worshiper: Agave, whom suffering awakes to a tragic anagnorisis, or gained knowledge. She will henceforth avoid the worship of Dionysus.

Dionysus gets the king under his spell and dresses him like a woman, a disguise which is meant to enable him to spy on the bacchantes. Dionysus seats him in a tree and then points him out to the women: they tear down the tree and dismember him. His mother, Agave, brings home his head, boasting that she has slain a lion. Cadmus restores her slowly to sanity. Dionysus tells them they got what they deserved. Cadmus complains that gods should not equal men in their passions.

After comic tragedies, such as *Iphigenia among the Taurians* and *Helen, Bacchae* was a return to a more traditional type of tragedy. It has puzzled audiences and scholars, who have been divided in their opinion about whether this is an affirmation of religious faith or rather an attack on religion. I believe it contains elements of both.

Dionysus is a god to be reckoned with. He is a god of the theater, transformation, wine, and freedom. He is a democrat and appeals to the people. Everyone must make his or her peace with Dionysus, by a synthesis rather than an expulsion; otherwise one can be literally blown or torn apart. The collapse of the palace is a warning to Pentheus and prefigures his own dismemberment.

Pentheus is secretly fascinated by what he claims is repulsive and agrees to be dressed by Dionysus as a woman. Dionysus gains his power over Pentheus by playing on his own inner desires. Dionysus is a director who stages "The Death of Pentheus."

One of the conflicts in the play is between wild nature and the civilized life of the city. The women abandon their duties at home and take to the mountains. Pentheus wants to control the wild forces that are disrupting his city and that exist inside himself. His suppression of both results only in disaster.

Dionysus is called both most gentle toward men and most fierce. He is like an animal with his tame and wild side. Somehow a thriving city (*polis*) has to tame and integrate Dionysus. Theater itself is a way of integrating the passions into the life of the city. If they are repressed they will explode, as does the palace itself. Hippolytus and Pentheus are both dismembered for not worshiping a god of passion; they have to realize that this god is in themselves. These two young boys also violate the Greek maxim, "Nothing in excess." So do these gods of excess, Aphrodite and Dionysus. They are far worse in their vengeful passions and immoral actions than their human victims. Just as in *Hippolytus,* the humans learn from their suffering and show compassion to each other. Not so the relentless god.

There is probably some political allusion also. In Athens at this time there were some who were out for power and were not willing to settle for peace when it was offered. So also there were opportunistic individuals out for self-promotion. One can easily trace these figures in *Bacchae*. After the war Athens will be dismembered as dramatically as Pentheus.

There is a play on the meaning of wisdom, and knowledge is contrasted with skill, and wisdom with book learning. The sophist is the master of skills but the philosopher of wisdom. At the beginning of the play, Dionysus in the guise of his priest appears to be wise, particularly in his answers to Pentheus. This scene is rather like the one between Teiresias and Oedipus. Dionysus accuses Pentheus of ignorance, as Teiresias does Oedipus. Dionysus says: you do not know what life you are leading, what you are doing, nor who you are. This triple accusation is rather like Sophocles' Teiresias telling Oedipus that he is blind in his ears, mind, and eyes. By the end of the plays both gain tragic wisdom and insight. Pentheus repents at the end, but it is too late. Learning too late is another frequent theme in Greek tragedy.

Dionysus on his lowest level acts like the bull with which he is identified. He is skillful in his brutal vengeance but hardly wise. Pentheus must also learn wisdom and restraint, but the lesson is fatal for him. One has the feeling that at the end of the play Dionysus has learned nothing; their gain in wisdom makes the humans superior to the god.

I think that in production it is very important not to make Pentheus into a villain. He is one of many children who are victims in Euripides. He should be played by a young actor, an adolescent who is the victim of his own drives. A modern audience usually sympathizes with Dionysus, because it sees him abused at the beginning of the play. But, like Medea and also Aphrodite in *Hippolytus*, the god goes too far and destroys the innocent as well as the guilty.

The staging shows a palace, and one exit leads to the mountains, the other to the city. The distinction could reflect the polarities of the wild and the civilized, the fierce and the mild, the country and the city, and the dual nature of Dionysus.

The destruction of the palace poses a problem. In the ancient performance it may have been simply left to the audience's imagination. Dionysus is the god of theater and imagination, so he may create the illusion for the chorus, which then dances in response. The audience members may see the destruction in their minds as they hear the words. In modern productions, I have seen the palace literally fall apart during the earthquake speech. A director can also suggest this by sound and lighting alone.

Dionysus appears first as a man addressing the audience in front of the palace. At the end he appears in all his divinity, probably elevated on the roof of the *skēnē*. One may represent him at the beginning as a young unbearded boy and at the end as a bearded man.

The chorus is hardly the ideal spectator. It glories in vengeance. The cos-

Bacchae. The chorus of Bacchantes sing and dance in honor of their god Dionysus. Epidaurus, Greece (1962). Photo: Gjon Mili/Timepix. Used by permission.

tuming should convey the "asiatic" and barbarian look. The music, with drums, should add to the drama. There should be a strong element of ritual conveyed by the chorus and the choral music.

This play is one of the most touching tragedies written by Euripides. The audience feels profound sympathy for Agave, and her role is one of the great ones for a skilled actress. The moment when she recognizes her son's head is a moment of inexpressible horror. The best performance I have seen of this is by a Japanese actress, Shiraishi Kayoko, who expressed her intense grief through silence.

The actor playing Pentheus should be young. This was a naïve boy who simply was out of his depth. One of the most poignant parts of the drama is the messenger's description of how he touches his mother's cheek and begs her to recognize him and not kill him. Dionysus's vengeance goes too far, and part of the tragedy of this play is seeing how people are made to suffer much more than they deserve. Would a just god have gone as far as this? Would a just and almighty god tolerate the existence of the atrocities we see committed everyday in the world?

Cyclops

This is the only complete satyr play that survives. The language of satyr plays is closer to tragedy than comedy, and yet these plays make tragic themes comic. Satyrs are followers of Dionysus, the god of theater. Their costumes feature horses' tails dangling from behind and phalluses in front (erect for the young and dangling for Silenus, their aged leader, often called their father).

In the prologue, Silenus explains that he and his satyrs once went searching for Dionysus when they heard that he was kidnapped by pirates. A storm blew them off course into the land of the Cyclopes in Sicily, near Etna. Now they are slaves to Polyphemus, a huge one-eyed Cyclops who eats men.

Odysseus shows up and negotiates with Silenus for food. He produces some wine given to him by Maron, the son of Dionysus. The chorus of satyrs arrives, driving the sheep home and performing a lively kind of dance which is traditionally associated with satyr plays. Polyphemus comes home and traps Odysseus and his men, threatening to eat them. Odysseus offers him some wine, and in return the Cyclops agrees to eat him last.

Odysseus conceives the plan he used in Homer's *Odyssey*. After the Cyclops has eaten some of the men and fallen into a drunken sleep, he puts out the Cyclops's eye with a long stake, sharpened at the end. When the Cyclops is blind, the survivors escape. He screams, but when asked by the chorus leader who hurt him, he answers "No One," because "No One" was the name Odysseus gave him when he was asked for it. Then Odysseus reveals his true name as he is sailing away. Polyphemus says that an old oracle predicting this fate has been fulfilled and goes off to find a boulder to throw at Odysseus's ship. Odysseus escapes, taking the satyrs with him.

This is an amusing reworking of the epic story. In the original there were no satyrs. There are several jokes as Silenus steals sips of wine at the same time that Polyphemus is drinking. As they both get drunk, Polyphemus becomes amorous and exits with Silenus, who complains that he is about to be raped.

Polyphemus appears as a blasphemous buffoon, criticizing Odysseus for the Trojan War. He nevertheless says that he himself is a god and that he worships only his own belly ("the greatest god of all" [line 335]). Here the Cyclops is certainly a man-eater, but this Odysseus is a cruel, devious trickster. These two deserve each other.

Comedy generally mocks what tragedy takes seriously: gods, nobles, and other forces that one fears (such as death in *Alcestis*). Laughter empowers a person to make light of superior forces.

There are delightful parodies of heroic attitudes found in tragedy: Odysseus pompously asserts, "If we have to die, we should die nobly" (line 201). This humorously echoes Sophocles' Ajax and other characters in Euripides, such as Macaria (*Children of Heracles*) or Polyxena (*Hecuba*). Odysseus is pretentious and claims that the Cyclops should be grateful because he and the Greeks saved Greece, including the shrines of Sicily, from the barbarians. This is particularly amusing in that there were Greek-Sicilian wars at the same time as the Greek-Persian War. We also remember how Odysseus came up with the stratagem of the Trojan horse. He could achieve by cunning what Achilles could with strength. From his speech here, we would think he was the bravest of the brave. He was certainly brave in Homer's epic when defending his men or his own home. But *Cyclops* is obviously parodying the hero.

There are metatheatrical moments, such as when Odysseus describes the horrors he saw in the Cyclops's cave as things that people do in stories but not

Cyclops. Translated by K. H.
Myris. Directed by Yannis Rigas.
Odysseus tries to outsmart
the Cyclops, and offers him
wine. A satyr watches. National
Theatre of Northern Greece
(2001). Photo: Nicos Pantis.
Used by permission.

in actual life. He then describes the violence in graphic detail. This is a host who eats the guests rather than serves them food.

There is also a parody of a wedding hymn, such as we find in Sappho. The chorus praises Polyphemus as if he were a handsome bridegroom: "Blessed the groom, blessed the bride." (The chorus in 495–502 and 511–18 describes scenes of lovemaking reminiscent of Sappho's odes to the bride and groom; see *Poetarum Lesbiorum Fragmenta*, no. 112, 9 App., p. 89.) Silenus is the unlucky "bride."

The satyrs are true to their nature, lustful and cowardly. When Odysseus needs help in blinding the Cyclops, they give none.

Odysseus reasons like a sophist, those popular teachers who sell their talents, claiming they could teach a person how to win an argument regardless of the truth. Odysseus's heroic posturing in front of the Cyclops is typical of this type of rhetoric. Odysseus tries to put himself forward as a representative of civilization and regards the Cyclops as a barbarian—but they are equal in their barbarous acts. I am sure the ancient audience would be on the side of Odysseus, as it would be on the side of Helen and Menelaus in their confrontation with Theoclymenus.

The setting is a cliff and a cave, like the setting for Sophocles' *Philoctetes*. This rugged setting suits the barbarism depicted. The Cyclops probably had a large mask with one eye, but the audience has to imagine that he is a giant.

Given the theatrical setting, the action must take place outdoors, so Odysseus and his men are not trapped inside the cave, barricaded by a boulder, as in the *Odyssey*. Odysseus has to be able to enter and exit freely, and yet he still needs to blind Polyphemus so that he can escape with impunity. This might be solved by some use of the *ekkyklēma*, which would allow the audience to view the blinded Cyclops in his cave.

Rhesus

This play, if it is by Euripides, may be the earliest of Euripides' plays. Some say it is post-Euripidean by an unknown fourth-century writer. It lacks a conventional prologue (though the original prologue may have been lost) and plunges us into the drama *in medias res*. The action all takes place at night. It is the shortest tragedy we have and the only one whose plot comes directly from Homer, namely book 10 of the *Iliad*.

The chorus leader tells Hector, the main hero of the Trojans, that there is activity by the Greek ships. Hector immediately leaps to the conclusion that the Greeks are fleeing and decides that the Trojans should attack. Aeneas restrains him and says they should first send a scout to find out what is happening. They ask for volunteers and Dolon comes forward. He asks for the horses of Achilles as his reward if successful. He boasts about the men he will kill. A shepherd comes to tell Hector the news that Rhesus, the Thracian king and Trojan ally, has arrived. Hector rudely tells him he should have come earlier, and not simply in the tenth year. Rhesus says that his kingdom had been attacked and he had to defend himself. He boasts that he will end the war in one day.

Two Greek heroes, Odysseus and Diomedes, enter the camp stealthily. They have gained the password from Dolon, whom they have killed. Athena directs them to Rhesus, so that they can kill him. They also want to kill Hector, but she forbids them.

After they have gone off, Paris, the Trojan hero who kidnapped Helen, appears. Athena pretends that she is Aphrodite, his patron goddess, and assures him that all is well. The Greeks kill Rhesus and escape. The Thracians think the Trojans have betrayed them, for the sake of Rhesus's horses and treasure. The Muse, Rhesus's mother, appears. She says that Odysseus did the foul deed with the help of Athena. She laments her child, another *mater dolorosa* in Euripides' pantheon, and foretells that he will become a prophetic spirit. Hector is all for attacking and believes this will be his lucky day.

This play contrasts the clever man with the strong man: in the Trojan camp Aeneas advises Hector to be more cautious, and in the Greek camp, Odysseus advises Diomedes. The "strong men" are boasters and pay for it. We know from the *Iliad* that Hector will be killed by Achilles.

Rhesus thought he could win the war by himself, but his wealth and power turn out to be useless to him. Dolon spoke proudly about his victory in advance. Boasting is hazardous to one's health in this play, as in most of Greek tragedy.

There is much deception. The root of Dolon's name means "deception," and he conceals himself in the skin of a wolf. He is outwitted and slain like an animal. Odysseus and Athena are a pair full of lies and deceit. But deception is more successful than force in this play.

The lamentation by the Muse is moving. She claims that Thetis will have more to mourn when she loses her son Achilles. At least the Muse's son will become an underground spirit. She points out it is better to be childless, to escape the risk of mourning lost children.

There are many characters and the action is exciting. There is no one great acting role, except perhaps the Muse with her lamentation. The night setting is perfect for the various stratagems. The staging would surely utilize the convention used in Peter Shaffer's *Black Comedy* and require the audience to imagine it is all taking place in the dark. Hypothetically it could have begun at early dawn, in a type of darkness, and as the sun came up, the theatrical convention would be accepted (the light imagined as darkness).

The staging probably features a tent and the entrance to it. The Muse may appear on top of this stage building at the end. The only females in this play are goddesses.

Performance Tradition

There were regular revivals of Euripides' work after 386 B.C. The Romans prized Euripides. Ennius (239–169 B.C.) adapted *Andromache, Hecuba, Iphigenia at Aulis, Medea;* Pacuvius (ca. 220–130 B.C.) adapted *Antiope;* and Accius (170–?86 B.C.) adapted *Alcestis, Bacchae, Hecuba, Medea,* and *Trojan Women.*

Half of the plays by Seneca (?1–65) are based wholly or partly on Euripides: *Hercules Furens, Trojan Women, Phoenician Women, Medea,* and *Phaedra.* Ovid (Publius Ovidius Naso, 43 B.C.–A.D. 17) wrote a *Medea,* from which two lines survive. Euripides became known in the West mainly through Latin translations and came to Shakespeare via Seneca. Jasper Heywood was the first translator of Seneca into English, and his versions were available from the second half of the sixteenth century on.

Medea

In *Medea,* Seneca transforms his heroine into the witch who is popular in many later representations, including opera. Euripides emphasized Medea's human aspect, and her magical powers were secondary. As Seneca's play begins, Medea is not seen mourning but calling for vengeance. The nurse tries to tell her she is powerless, but she counters: "I shall become Medea" (lines 171–72).

Jason tells Medea he saved her life, because Creon wanted her executed. Medea invites Jason to flee with her. He refuses. She asks for her children, but Jason refuses them also, so she plans her revenge.

The nurse then gives a graphic account of Medea's magic: she mixes herbs, snakes, and other foul creatures, even her own blood, into a boiling cauldron. She summons all the spirits of the underworld. She applies the resulting poison to a dress and diadem for Creusa, Jason's new bride, and sends the gifts to the princess with the children. When the children return, she kills one of them as an offering for her dead brother. She takes the living one to the roof, along with the corpse. Jason returns with soldiers and pleads for her to spare the life of their remaining son. She takes her time and plays with Jason, relishing his pain. Then she plunges her dagger into the child and flies away in her dragon-drawn chariot. This Medea needs no Aegeus for a refuge in Athens. Jason's final words are, "Show that wherever you go, there are no gods" (line 1027). Medea is proof that the gods do not exist (if they would tolerate such injustice).

One of the earliest versions of Greek tragedy translated into English is by Lady Jane Lumley, of Euripides' *Iphigeneia in Aulis,* around 1560, at about the same time as Jasper Heywood's translations of Seneca. In France, La Péruse along with Pierre Corneille did versions of *Médée* in 1635.

I have located fifty operas based on or including the myth of Medea (including a modern musical): eleven come from the seventeenth century, nineteen from the eighteenth century, four from the nineteenth century, and sixteen, plus many revivals, from the twentieth century. The ages of absolutism (seventeenth century) and imperialism (nineteenth century) seem less prepared to sanction a rebellious Medea. The eighteenth and twentieth centuries have been more faithful to the original Euripidean text, with its powerful Medea who, after she achieves her vengeance, gloats from her dragon chariot with impunity at Jason's impotence. She is most popular in the twentieth century; operas such as Rolf Liebermann's *Freispruch für Medea* (1995) and Michael John LaChiusa's *Marie Christine* (1999) and books such as Christa Wolf's *Medea Stimmen* (1998) show her as an appealing heroine for our time and represent her faithfully in her complex, passionate totality.

When women's rights are taken seriously (eighteenth and twentieth centuries), Medea is a tragic and powerful heroine who achieves a successful vengeance and escapes with impunity: even the titles celebrate her bloody victory, for example, Giuseppe Moneta's *La vendetta di Medea* (1787). When women's rights are not an issue or are not taken seriously (seventeenth and nineteenth centuries), operas about Medea are fewer, and in those there are she is usually either weak and submissive and commits no crime or is punished for her violent acts. This is not to say that there are no exceptions to such claims; I only propose that the majority of the evidence points in this direction. Medea in opera is a barometer of sexual politics.

The eighteenth century produced treatises such as Jean Jacques Rousseau's *Discours sur l'origine et les fondements de l'inégalité parmi les hommes* (1755); this debate was over universal equality. Pierre Augustin Caron de Beaumarchais wrote subversively in *Le mariage de Figaro* (1784); Mozart's opera derived from this (1786) includes the victories of the valet over his master and women over men. Napoleon said words that suggest that this work was the first stone flung in the French Revolution. In the twentieth century women finally gained the vote: 1920 in the United States and 1945 in France. Fifth-century Athens, eighteenth-century France, and twentieth-century Greece have been cultures when democracy was either practiced—although with limitations which excluded women and minorities—or discussed as an ideal to be achieved.

In the seventeenth century, art pursued the bizarre and exceptional; music also showed freedom in its use of modes and dissonance without the regularized adherence to major and minor keys which would take place in the eighteenth century. In the nineteenth century, romantic independence was stressed. One might think that Medea would be popular in these centuries, but the emphasis on individualism did not extend to females as independent, unconventional, and successful in crime as she was, and the statistics of operas written about her support this. The eighteenth and twentieth centuries were periods large enough in their universalizing concepts to contain even Medea.

The most well-known operas on Medea are Marc-Antoine Charpentier's *Médée* in 1693, with the text by Thomas Corneille, Pierre's younger brother; Georg Anton Benda's *Medea* in 1775; Maria Luigi Carlo Zanobi Salvator Cherubini's *Médée* in 1797; and Mikis Theodorakis *Medea* in 1991.

Mikis Theodorakis's opera *Medea* is based on a translation of Euripides, word for word, into modern Greek. Theodorakis suggests in his opera the sufferings of the Greek nation in both victories and defeats. Understanding the tragedy of vengeance, having lived through a bloody civil war, he shows the sufferings on both sides. Although the words are from Euripides, through his music Theodorakis allows us to understand and sympathize with Jason more. At the same time he celebrates Medea in all her glorious tragedy. She destroys herself by killing those she loves, her children. The civil war in Greece in which child might oppose father forced many a mother into tragic choices.

In 1882 Franz Grillparzer wrote a dramatic trilogy on the story of Jason and the Argonauts (*Das goldene Vlies*), and the final section was *Medea*. This shows Jason and Medea arriving at Corinth and asking for refuge. According to this story, Jason grew up in Corinth. He gathered his Argonauts there before setting out to win the Golden Fleece and was regarded as a hero. Now as a suppliant, Jason lies to Creon, saying that they have committed no crimes. Creon's daughter Creusa is a gentle, innocent girl who tries to teach Medea how to become a civilized Greek girl. In this version, it is clear that both Medea and Jason are responsible for the death of her brother and father in Colchis, and Pelias in Iolcus.

Messengers come and say that because of the crimes at Iolcus, the king must exile both Jason and Medea. The king gives up only Medea. Medea sends Creusa a jeweled chalice with a lid that sets her on fire when she opens it. Medea kills her children and flees. The king is spared, and he exiles Jason because he brought disaster on his daughter. This account shows that Medea's crime arises from her love of Jason; Jason is even more culpable than Euripides showed him. He rejects Medea mainly because he considers her a barbarian. He is punished and Medea escapes, with no Aegeus to help, nor a dragon chariot. Grillparzer also needed no chorus to provide commentary. Reinhardt staged his production of this in 1909.

The American poet Robinson Jeffers wrote a poetic, abbreviated, and dramatically viable version for Judith Anderson who starred in the 1946–47 performance. In 1982 it was revived at the Cort Theatre in New York with Anderson playing the nurse, and Zoe Caldwell, Medea to great acclaim for her animalistic and passionate performance. She won a Tony for it. In 1974, at the Little Theatre in New York, Eugenie Leontovich directed and adapted Robinson Jeffers's version of *Medea,* which she called *Medea and Jason.*

Jean Anouilh wrote a version (1946) in which Medea is shown as an outcast, living in a caravan with her nurse. She begs Creon to kill her, and when he refuses because he has promised Jason not to, she accuses him of being too old to rule. Jason appears, and their dialogue is as much concerned about their former love as Medea's present hate and Jason's present indifference. He says that he will never love anyone as he loved Medea, but he wants a chance at a normal life and happiness, rather than their former life of wandering, danger, and crime. He blames those crimes on Medea, as does Creon.

Jason also accuses Medea of having an affair with a young shepherd from Naxos, who she then betrayed to Jason so that he could kill him. She said she had had the affair because she had anticipated Jason's leaving her and wanted to leave him before he left her, but she found she could not. (Sophisticated sexual nuances particularly characterize modern versions of Greek tragedy by the French.) Anouilh's Oedipus had many affairs with the pretty slaves that Jocasta sent him, but he always returned to the warm place he felt safe (to Jocasta). The nurse says that Jason is not worthy of Medea's hate, because she already preferred sleeping alone.

Medea asks Jason if he ever considered that she might have liked to lead a life of normal, peaceful happiness with him herself. She also asks him if he would believe her if she said that she wanted to begin again? He answers "No." He thinks a life of compromise and restraint is not for her.

Medea sends her poisoned robe to the princess. Jason arrives with armed men merely to see the caravan (set on fire by Medea) and have her tell him that she has killed the children before she stabs herself. This is a modernized, romanticized, and rather melodramatic view of Medea. She resembles Anouilh's *Antigone* in being an immature girl who needlessly martyrs herself.

Robert Wilson's *Deafman Glance* (1970), based on *Medea,* lasts several hours and shows a mother approaching her children (on an upper floor, presumably a bedroom) with a glass of milk and then a knife. She takes the milk from an icebox in what is probably a kitchen. At the end she washes the knife in a sink on the lower floor. This version was made into a film. I find the absence of both words and Jason weakens it as a version of Medea. As a meditation on the power of women and on mothers who have the dual capability of nourishing or killing it is strong. When it was performed as a play in Delphi, Wilson played the role of a father, possibly Jason, performing actions which were parallel to those by the African-American actress who played the mother, or Medea. The production took over two hours.

In 1973 Minos Volonakis's performance of his adaptation of *Medea* came to Uptown's Circle in the Square (New York), with Irene Papas delivering a powerful performance as Medea. The performance had a strong feminist slant, and much sympathy was evoked for Medea. It was staged with masks and costumes evocative of antiquity. Ritual and passion characterized the performance.

Andrei Serban and Elizabeth Swados's production of *The Greek Trilogy* (1974) includes *Medea,* Sophocles' *Electra,* and *Trojan Women.* He had a live snake twining around Aegisthus's arms in *Electra.* The audience members were part in some performances of the action as they moved from room to room to see various tableaux. Swados composed the piece in Greek, Latin, and other languages so that the audience will not understand the language, but will concentrate on the emotions and the visual action instead. This is one reason Stravinsky gave for having his *Oedipus Rex* translated into Latin. Serban shows Medea as a chained prisoner, and uttering incantations out of Seneca. *Trojan Women* features a Helen raped by a bear.

José Triana wrote *Medea in the Mirror*, based on Euripides' play, in 1960, a year after the Cuban revolution. This play was banned in Cuba after the first performance. It features voodoo magic and Cuban music, accented by drums. A black Medea (Maria) is in love with Jason (Julio), a charming seductive Cuban of mixed blood. Julio abandons Maria with her two children to marry the daughter of a white man, Perico Piedra Fina (Creon), a successful businessman.

Maria takes vengeance on the wealthy landowner and his daughter by sending her poisoned wine. By looking at herself in the mirror, the violent, vengeful Medea confronts the loving Medea, and wins. Her mother's ghost hands Maria a doll, and a witch doctor gives her a long dagger. She slays both Jason and her children in effigy. The final scene shows us Jason rushing to kill Medea, but she is hoisted high by the chorus and she declares herself God. She needs only the protection of her people, who ban together to protect their leader.

In 1977, Dario Fo and Franca Rame's *Medea* takes the feminist view that the killing of the children is symbolic and an act of liberation. The brevity of this play (a few pages) facilitates all the characters being played by one woman, and the first was Franca Rame herself.

Yukio Ninagawa's production of *Medea* (1978, 1984, and 1993) followed Euripides' original text while using elements from the Japanese dramatic tradition. He claimed that he was making a statement for the independence of women. His stylized version with a male actor (Hira Mikijiro) playing Medea is more powerful than many Western versions. This is in the *onnagata* (a male actor playing a female) tradition of Kabuki. Kabuki, like Noh drama, follows ancient Greek tragedy in having male actors play female roles. The play begins with a shredding of the text, and the floating white papers suggest the cherry blossoms that are so often used in Kabuki to suggest the transient beauty of life.

The costuming is stylized and draws on Kabuki. The actor playing Medea has crystal drops that adorn her eyes like dangling necklaces of tears. The elaborate makeup which is familiar from Kabuki makes the faces resemble masks, but at the same time they retain an emotive quality.

Music is used to characterize various scenes. When Medea resolves to kill the children "La Folía" is heard, a melody used by many composers, including Bach and Scarlatti. The title appropriately means "madness." Grétry used it in his opera *L'amant jaloux,* "The Jealous Lover," a title that could apply to Medea. Ninagawa's *Medea* concludes with a popular Japanese melody strummed by the chorus on Japanese samisens (stringed instruments). Music by Mikami, a popular artist, adds lyrics and music familiar to moderns. He mingles this modern sound with that of a temple gong. He also adds wooden clappers to punctuate the action, as they were used in traditional theater. Both Creon and Jason strut around the stage like Japanese shoguns. The children play with their mother and with each other. They are dressed in white, a color which is often associated by the Japanese with death. They gain genuine sympathy from the audience.

When Medea has finally decided to kill the children, "she" exits with a sword held high over her head, to the strains of "La Folía." There is a majestic dignity to her. At the end, Medea's exit in the dragon chariot is truly spectacular. In the Greek play she has been compared to the god or goddess who appears "in the machine." Here she is like the transformed hero or heroine in Noh drama and Kabuki who becomes a demon. She grimaces above the stage with truly diabolic power. Her laugh is deadly in its bitterness. At the very end, "La Folía" is drowned out by the sounds of the samisen. The Japanese element is dominant.

This is an exercise in stylized drama firmly rooted in Japanese theater. There are gestures borrowed from that tradition, such as covering the face with long sleeves and rocking the body to symbolize weeping. The stylization does not diminish audience involvement or catharsis, and soon into the drama one accepts the conventions. One realizes the power of the fundamental myth to stir emotions. This is by far one of the best renditions of *Medea* in our time. It captures not only the sacred ritual of ancient performance but also the inherent drama of the myth.

Heiner Müller in his *Medeamaterial* (1983) sets his play in the aftermath of World War II (this was well performed by Theodoros Terzopoulos in Greece and America in 1988). It includes sections called *Medea: Verkommenes Ufer, Medeamaterial,* and *Landschaft mit Argonauten.* The first section speaks of a lake near Strasbourg and its pollution. The second part, in monologue form, allows Medea to berate Jason and to recount her vengeance. The last portion shows the aftermath and destruction of the world: the wood from the Argo that crushes Jason's head is the world striking back at us, "the theatre of death" (*Hamlet-Machine,* p. 125). This reworked play is a play of despair. It speaks of colonialism, and the colonized fighting back. Heiner Müller has explicitly claimed that he had British and European imperialism in mind: "The end signifies the threshold where myth turns into history: Jason is slain by his boat

. . . European history began with colonization. . . . that the vehicle of colonization strikes the colonizer dead anticipates the end of it" (*Hamlet-Machine*,
p. 124).

Müller's play is also about man's general rape of the earth, polluting and
destroying it: eventually man will be the victim of the earth he mutilated. This
is also the story of Medea. It is very apt, because it will be the children of the
violators that will be destroyed: future generations. This is the world we are
living in, deadly, infested with pollutants, its ozone layer peeled off.

Euripides gave us some hope. He shows the horror of terrorism, the killing
of the innocent, but there is a part of us that applauds Medea fighting back.
It is tragedy, but one thinks that a future is possible. Not so with Müller's version, nor with Terzopoulos's interpretation. His stage is littered with debris,
and man is part of it. Part of the pollution comes from technology: a television
runs with no picture but occasional static. The actors are dressed in rags and
are filthy: they are walking trash. Actors and actresses endlessly repeat their
motions in a compulsive way. Distinctions are blurred; Medea's lines are given
to Jason and vice versa. Gender again is fluid, and identities are elided. This is
a deconstructed landscape: signifier represents signifier in endless regression:
man represents the dead and vice versa. We hear the "Blue Danube Waltz," an
idyllic recollection that mocks the reality. Heavy-metal rock music invades at
one point. Then there is the sound of an airplane flying overhead while rolls
of film drop from the sky (modern bird droppings?).

Jason sucks at a balloon-breast, and as it bursts over him, covering him
with milk, he basks for a moment in symbiotic ecstasy. Medea compulsively
alternates between striking her breast and fondling it. She wears the poisoned
bridal dress as if it were a straitjacket, and this will be her gift (in German
"Gift" means "poison") to the new princess. Repetition. Repetition. Shoes are
endlessly polished.

The young bride contrasts with the old Medea; images of sexuality and
fertility are conveyed by a young girl who beats a sheaf of wheat between her
legs while the old Medea can barely raise her head from the mud: fertility followed by futility.

Identity finally becomes another disposable item. We see a picture of
Heiner Müller, and we get the feeling that no originals are left. There are only
copies and repetitions. This is despair, without even the catharsis of agony.
Medea asks her nurse as Jason appears, "Nurse, do you know this man?"
(*Hamlet-Machine*, p. 133). Even *his* original is lost. There is no future; we, like
Jason, have murdered it through neglect and indifference: our own demise is
imminent. Terzopoulos has shown us the devastated landscape of our present
and our future. Man is reduced to landfill, and the earth to debris.

Terzopoulos has brought ritualized movement to a peak. Medea beats herself and the ground continually as she draws the analogy between the pain of childbirth and the struggle to grow the grain, repeated actions to further the human race in its endless cycle of birth and death.

Tony Harrison's *Medea: A Sex War Opera* (1985) shows that men as well as women kill children out of vengeance. So far this libretto has not been set to music.

Harrison elaborates on how Medea has been misunderstood:

> Men's hatred had to undermine
> > MEDEA's status as divine
> > and to reduce her
> > to a half-crazed children-slayer
> > making a monster of MEDEA
> > like the Medusa. (*Dramatic Verse*, p. 432)

Tony Harrison concentrates on the sex war and shows that the blame should be shared with the men. He contrasts Medea with Heracles, who in mythology was also a monster, a father who slew his own children; nevertheless his general reputation was one of a hero.

Heracles could not kill his wife to avenge himself because she sent him a poisoned cloak, not unlike the gift Medea sent which eliminates her rival. The cloak in Heracles' case was the ultimate embrace of the wife, woman-mother. He asked to be burned in a pyre, a burning externalization of his own passion, which Lichas says was his only master, the only monster he could not slay. But this pyre also freed him from the embrace of the mother. He would not be buried in earth, her ultimate imprisonment. He says, "At last in death I shall be free / of enfolding Femininity" (*Dramatic Verse*, p. 438).

Harrison unmasks the attempted validation of power behind words, as Euripides did earlier, by showing how men make myths to justify their abuse of women. Harrison feathers his magpie nest of Medeas with mixed languages and mixed versions, having the children vary from two to fourteen. Medea is executed in his opera, and Heracles is killed by Deianira in a way that parallels Creusa's death: the passion that obsessed them in life eats them alive as they don Nessus's cloak and Medea's coronet and robes. The cap used for Medea's electrocution is the bowl she mixes her poisons in, so no one goes free in this final version, which defines but does not resolve the sex war. Headlines conclude the libretto, speaking first of mothers who slew their children, then fathers.

Not only is Harrison's *Medea* a compendium of former *Medea*s, it also adds characters, such as Heracles and Butes, the beekeeper, Argonauts from the original voyage. Here they represent, along with Jason, three approaches to women. Butes loves one woman, has had a happy marriage, and longs to rejoin his wife in death.

Harrison's Heracles for the most part loathes women and will die at their hands. Jason loves women but mixes one too many into his marital scheme. All three perish either actually or spiritually at the hands of women. Since Medea is electrocuted at the hands of men, at least there is some equality here, sparing one the resentment felt when Medea goes free in Euripides' play. But this loses the awesomeness of the Euripidean ending, which allows the murderess not only success but impunity.

Snakes represent both life and death in Harrison's libretto, paralleling the writhing fire and the dragoness with her sibilants. Harrison directs at one point,

The text for the DRAGONESS uses the Greek, Latin and French texts . . . but given a more 'snake-like' setting. Another ancient aspect of the 'female' like the GODDESS, and should have some musical connection with those linked 3 voices. The 20 voices are one continuous voice, writhing, squirming, fierce, fiery, threatening, ever-wakeful, coiling, and unwinding, making sudden darts with its heads . . . the separate words should be considered its 'vertebrae', the total sound its continuous glide. (*Dramatic Verse*, pp. 401–402)

Harrison has written an opera libretto which delineates polarities or oppositions set up in conjunction with the logic of parallels: life and death, male and female, all juxtaposed against the universal, the character, the person, and the particular. Euripides wrote an acutely accurate psychological portrait of a woman who understands the inner workings of men. When her external world is threatened she takes vengeance in a devastatingly internal way (with all the psychological acuity she has mastered), and she destroys her enemy's external power as he had destroyed hers. Her inner world is destroyed also by her external weapon, and she says, "forget your children for this short day, / but mourn them for eternity" (*Med.* lines 1248–49). Jason's princess and realm was "other" and external, but the children are self and internal. The price of her external victory as hero and wife was her destruction as internal woman and mother, an ironic affirmation of self by validation of the mask.

Harrison, as Euripides, universalizes Medea's story by showing her conflict with Jason as the eternal conflict between men and women, which in antiquity, and in particular fifth-century Athens, entailed a conflict between a public and a private life. Boundaries are blurred, and women now fight in public as men fight in private. The implications suggested by Euripides are fully developed. Harrison has created a play which looks gender issues directly in the face.

Medea is also used in the colonial context when the colonized want to protest against an oppressive regime. It shows the victim successfully fighting back. In South Africa, Guy Butler's *Demea* (1990) shows Medea as a black princess, abandoned by the Englishman, Jason. This play also deals with the racial issues of apartheid.

Demea, an anagram for Medea, is a Tembu princess, with Captain Jonas Barker (Jason) as an officer from the Peninsular Wars; since 1815, he has been an adventurer-trader in South Africa. Jonas is leaving Demea to join an all-white trek led by a Boer leader named Kroon (meaning "crown," while suggesting "Creon"). Demea makes alliances with tribes that are roughly equivalent to the Xhosas and the Zulus. Rather than side with the whites who have betrayed her, Demea makes sure her black allies have the gunpowder. The latter win. Kroon kills her sons, and Jonas ends up being flogged by a runaway slave who had often been flogged by the whites.

Alistair Elliot's translation of *Medea* was performed in 1994 at the Longacre Theatre in New York. Medea is a challenging role to say the least, and one can understand why an actress like Diana Rigg would want to attempt it. She had established herself as a Shakespearean actress, and, having already played the title role in Tony Harrison's *Phaedra Britannica,* she wanted to add another Euripidean heroine to her credits. She seemed perfect for the role of Medea, since she had played such assertive, aggressive women as Lady Macbeth and Regan. She had in Jonathan Kent a director who had proved himself in other modern classics (e.g., Ibsen's *When We Dead Awaken*) and as a designer Peter J. Davison, who engineered a brilliant set that can be played like a musical instrument. There was also an outstanding chorus of three women, who restore to the modern stage the ancient technique of dancing in accompaniment to their own songs.

But Rigg just does not bring this performance off. She plays Medea too much like Emma Peel of *The Avengers.* She speaks her lines so quickly that even with her impeccable enunciation, much is lost. She is fashionable and cool, with sporadic outbursts of rage, more like a petulant member of Parliament than a passionate woman scorned. She also gets a lot of laughs, and when she is described as weeping, she is in fact dry-eyed. In the final scene she is presented stationary before a rolling backdrop to simulate flying, and here one sees her as the figurehead of a ship, a mythical icon, and that is consistent with the rest of her performance. Her hairstyle and dress (classic, for all occasions) put her again in the "impeccable" category. She blazes with anger, which might please feminists, but what of passion and grief? She plays Hillary Clinton, not Medea.

Alistair Elliot reduces Euripides to Rigg's size. He takes out mythological references, except for the minimum. Ino is cited as a parallel to Medea for killing her children, but the chorus reiterates the feature that distinguishes the two: "Medea is not mad" (p. 62). He also adds his own turn of phrase, like Creon saying, "You sour faced-women, squalling at your husband" (p. 30). Medea describes a man's freedom, "A man who's tired of what he gets at home / Goes out—and gives his heart a holiday" (p. 29). This is in contrast to a woman who is tied to one man: no holidays for her. The chorus also says, "You lost the husband from your bed, / And now you lose the bed" (p. 35), to describe her exile after divorce. This is Euripides reduced to the lowest colloquial denominator.

We moderns thrive on violence, so Kent does not disappoint us. He shows us bloodied, screaming children just before they are killed by Medea. A woman behind me gasped and started to sob (she did better than Rigg). These glimpses of violence are obviously meant to titillate modern sensibilities. We are not spared the display of the dead bodies just because we have seen the nightmare premonition. The only thing we are deprived of is the dragon-drawn chariot (there must be some budgetary restrictions on a production made for export).

This production is admirable in having its chorus dressed in black garb, reminiscent of victimized women in many societies. The brown and black dress of the nurse continues the theme. The chorus women can remind us of Bosnian women, Palestinian women, or the many Irish women who put on black to mourn their parents, their children, and their mates destroyed in the deadly conflict that still rages in the North, a legacy of imperialism. Medea is a symbol for one who fights back and is willing to pay the price, no matter what, as long as her enemies will not laugh at her. She is a freedom fighter and a heroine. The chorus members are those who do not make that choice. They are the victims. They show horror and sorrow during the messenger speech recording the offstage deaths of Creon and his daughter. Rigg-Medea relishes every word with an unmoving body, reclining as she faces the messenger (back to the audience), revealing her pleasure only in a finger tapped on her shoulder and her rapt attention.

The set by Peter J. Davison consists of large coruscating panels which resemble the rusting plates on an old battleship. They are banged to emphasize moments and statements: Creon's order of banishment or Medea's accusations. She bangs the plates loudly, while Jason only hits them lightly as he tries to defend himself; perhaps he realizes how hollow his excuses are by comparison with Medea's claims. The panels clang open and shut, as if they formed the walls of a giant prison. Medea is first seen in the alcove formed by one, and in the final climactic scene where she flies off with her children's bodies, she is revealed by the plates crashing down. This is a prison escape to end all escapes.

Both Euripides in his play and the director of this production show us the mix of earth, air, fire, and water, as if Medea were the fifth element. She is a type of chthonic goddess: she crossed water to come to Greece, burns the princess with her fire, and escapes in the air. The play begins and ends with birds that shriek, comparable to Mnouchkine's dogs that ended the acts of *Les Atrides* or to the ominous birds in Cacoyannis's *Trojan Trilogy*. Medea flies like a bird at the end. Water is made visible by a pool on the stage, and at times its ripples are projected onto the brazen walls. Medea and the chorus wash their hands in it. The women have access to this purification. We hear of the fire in the messenger's speech. Further, Elliot's Medea tells Aegeus to "Swear by this dust of Earth, by Helios the sun" (p. 45), translating Euripides' "Swear by the plain of Earth, and Helios." Earth, air, fire, and water are well represented in this production.

Probably Kent has seen *Dream of Passion*, Jules Dassin's reworking of the Medea myth, and Pier Paolo Pasolini's *Medea* or has simply made the same choices. Medea's sanity or insanity is a big issue in the former film, so this play is clear about Medea being sane. The chorus reiterates it with anaphoric overkill. Kent dresses the children in white just as Pasolini dresses them in his film and crowns them with a wreath (Iphigenia in Cacoyannis's film is also so attired in victim chic).

Kent has Jason and the messenger appear with nearly shaved heads but sporting ponytails in back. They could be drug dealers. Creon and Aegeus have more conventional hairstyles. I can understand giving Jason a bit of stylish punk, a touch of the eternal egoistic adolescent, but why the messenger?

The oppressor cannot oppress forever. Lessons are learned and tables are turned (see Frantz Fanon's study of this phenomenon in *The Wretched of the Earth* and Edward Said's in his *Culture and Imperialism*). Many who have reworked this play tap into some of its elemental power. *Medea*'s elemental tragic messages are elided in this production which can be called the Masterpiece Theatre *Medea*. One cannot applaud Diana Rigg for a passionate performance, particularly if one has seen Judith Anderson or Irene Papas. Rigg is terminally stylish. The barbarian Medea has become a posh Londoner.

The Irish use Greek tragedy to express their political concerns in the second half of the twentieth century. Instead of *Oedipus* or the *Oresteia*, dealing with identity or the establishment of a law court, they gravitate toward Euripides' plays, particularly *Medea* and *Trojan Women*. They appropriate the tragedies introduced by the colonizer and use them as intellectual weapons to protest injustices.

Brendan Kennelly has written a brilliant *Medea* (1988). We can see Jason as Cromwell in his play. Jason is cut from the British mold, using self-righteous words that suit Cromwell. Medea is the colonized victim who fights back. Medea is Ireland.

Kennelly's *Medea* has feminist overtones, and we see the rage of woman toward man: Medea calls them "the horny despots of our bodies" (p. 25). Medea gave everything to Jason, but he was unworthy because he lied and cheated; he did not keep his oaths. In vengeance she killed her own children.

Another theme that sets Kennelly's *Medea* clearly in Ireland is that of exile: "Exile is the worst form of living death" (p. 17). Many Irish were exiled because their land was confiscated or because they were convicted of crimes; others left because of their poverty, simply in order to survive.

Kennelly expatiates on prayer. Jason tells Medea: "Pray to make sense of the swirling world." She answers:

> Your prayer for sense—
> the commonest of common sense—
> is an insult. Prayer is not
> a way of coping with fools.
> Prayer is for dealing with the injustice caused by fools . . .
> Prayer, my plausible friend, is
> anger at what is, and a longing
> for what should be.
> Prayer is a bomb at the door of your house. (p. 42)

Prayer returns us to the Irish question. Prayer can lead to acts. As the nurse says, "Medea knows the meaning of prayer. / She knows the meaning of revenge" (p. 23).

Marina Carr's *By the Bog of Cats* (1999, following Euripides' *Medea*) conveys well the Irish Midlands with their land struggles through its sparkling dialogue. Carr makes Hester (Medea) strong and Carthage (Jason) weak and dependent. Hester is an Irish gypsy, an outsider who loves the bog and practices magic. Her husband is leaving her to marry the daughter of the land-owner Xavier (Creon). Both Carthage and Xavier are concerned about property and station.

Carr adds an element of incest. There is a suggestion that Xavier was involved with his daughter, in addition to Hester's mother. This rampant sexuality is typical of many rural areas in Ireland, where jokes abound about the similar appearance of the children.

Hester burns down her house, which Carthage wanted to turn over to his new bride along with her land. Hester also kills her daughter, Josie, along with herself: Josie begs her mother to take her with her when her mother tells her she will be leaving. Hester kills Josie to keep them together for eternity: this is their escape to freedom. Carr often populates her plays with ghosts. Hester also does not kill the new bride. She feels that if her husband, Carthage, has to live with his new bride, who is somewhat of a simpleton, that is punishment enough.

This play does not give Medea the majesty that Euripides gave to her. She does not take her vengeance and escape to a better life, in the sense that we generally understand life. But this Medea gains in the spiritual and emotional love she shows for her daughter; in Carr's hands suicide becomes an affirmative act. It allows Hester to escape her sordid reality along with her daughter, and in the Irish landscape we assume we have not heard the last from them. This countryside is populated by ghosts and wandering divinities.

My *Medea, Queen of Colchester* (Sledgehammer Theatre, 2003, directed by Kirsten Brandt) has an entirely male cast and features a colored South African drag queen who used to run drugs with James Eliot (a Jason stand-in). They have become partners in every sense. She raises James's two sons after his wife died in an accident. The play opens with James preparing to marry Athena, the daughter of Michael Creontos, a casino owner in Las Vegas who is dying of cancer. James assures Medea that this is just a marriage of expediency, and that Medea is and will be his only true love. Michael asks Medea to leave because he is afraid of her: he knows her reputation as a sangoma (witch). Medea meets Edward Jameson, who will help her escape to Cuba. She plans her revenge and kills Athena, Athena's father, and James's children. James goes mad at the end of the play, but the audience does not know whether this is permanent. He will suffer more if he is sane and remembers. The choruses have the Euripidean messages delivered in the form of rap songs. Issues of colonialism, gender, and gay rights all factor into this plot.

There are several films about Medea. Pier Paolo Pasolini's *Medea* (1967) dealt with the myth behind the play in psychological and anthropological terms. Pasolini points out the universals behind the myth, showing us woman as a conduit to the gods and a source of the earth's fertility, stable and unmoving, versus man the mover, the traveler, the opportunistic hunter, the capitalist, and the thankless adolescent who does not realize his dependence on his mother.

Here Medea is a priestess in her eastern home but helps Jason steal the fleece. We have allusions to Jason's mythological past, and the centaur who educated him appears in the form of a man toward the end: a mythological childhood must cede to the realities of adulthood. There are two versions of Creon's daughter's death: the mythical one, with her perishing miserably after she puts on Medea's deadly gifts, and the modern one, with her committing suicide, presumably out of sympathy for Medea and possibly all suffering women. Medea is grounded to the earth and is also a gifted priestess. She evokes the sun to help her and to return to her powers which had left her when she followed Jason. Jason, on the other hand, is an opportunist, willing to pillage, raid, and make the best of any situation as long as he benefits. Pasolini has many shots which transform Maria Callas (who plays Medea) into a princess in a Renaissance painting. He also consciously plays into her known image as a diva in opera.

This differs from Jules Dassin's version in *Dream of Passion* (1978), which shows Melina Mercouri as Maia, an aging actress who wants to play Medea before she dies. She meets a woman, Brenda, who is in prison for killing her children because her husband was unfaithful. It also shows Brenda as essentially mad. There is a transfer of identities, as in Bergman's film *Persona* (alluded to in this film). Maia's performance of Medea gains from her added understanding. This film is rather naïve. It lacks the strength of Euripides' original, which shows that Medea killed her children not simply out of jealousy, but because of the diminution of her honor and status after she had sacrificed everything for her husband.

Lars von Trier's *Medea* (1988) taps into the psychological and mythical heritage. This Medea enlists her older child to help her kill his younger brother; he then freely offers himself for execution. Medea escapes with Aegeus, who appears in a boat at the end. The opening scene showed her emerging from the water. This suggests that she is an elemental spirit of nature, rather like Kennelly's representation of her.

Hippolytus

Phaedra is as popular as Medea as a subject for modern versions. In his *Phaedra,* Seneca has Phaedra directly proposition Hippolytus: verbal sparring replaces Phaedra's eavesdropping. When Hippolytus draws his sword on her, she says this is what she has prayed for, to die at his hands with her honor intact. Hippolytus hurls the sword away and flees. When Theseus appears, the sword is used as evidence of Hippolytus's violent intentions. Here father does not confront son. He condemns his son *in absentia* on the basis of Phaedra's testimony.

Seneca seems to be reconstructing Euripides' earlier version of *Hippolytus,* where Phaedra remains throughout the play. She is clearly at fault. There are no goddesses to give her an excuse. It is this version that will inspire Racine. Seneca also delivers what seems to be critical judgment of the rulers of Rome when the chorus says that evil men are in power and idiots are promoted; virtue is neglected. The use of Greek tragedy as political commentary once more can be traced to the ancients.

The description of Hippolytus's death is horrific. A tidal wave arises, and the bull is given grotesque details, with eyes that change color and a roar that

makes the sea itself bellow. Hippolytus confronts the monster with stoic heroism: "My father has tamed such bulls as you our line does not give way to the
bellow of empty threats" (*Seneca, the Tragedies*, p. 122). He is dragged by the
reins, and his head is dashed on the rocks. The fields are spattered with his
blood. Brambles and stones maim his face and his beauty. A tree trunk impales
him in the groin, but thorns and trees continue to tear him.

When Phaedra hears of Theseus's curse fulfilled, she confesses her guilt,
and Hippolytus's sword delivers the death she longed for as she plunges the
sword in her own breast. Seneca's Theseus does not beg forgiveness from his
son. In fact, he bids his tears not to flow as he reassembles the pieces of his
son's body and laments his lost beauty. The play ends with Theseus's curse on
Phaedra, thus contrasting with the humanity in the ending of Euripides' play.

Racine (1639–99) reached the acme of his career with his *Andromaque*
(1667), *Iphigénie en Aulide* (1674; fragmentary, published posthumously in
1747), and *Phèdre* (1677); like Euripides he enjoyed representing passionate
women and the destructiveness of love.

This *Phèdre* is clearly based on Seneca. Racine adds a love interest for Hippolyte in the form of Aricie, and in his preface he says that he did this because
he had to take away from the perfection that ancient philosophers accorded
the original Hippolytus. A director should be faithful to Racine and the modern taste that enjoys this addition and hardly regards Hippolytus's love for
Aricie as a fault.

Racine outdoes even Seneca in baroque effects. Racine's messenger scene
is gory and horrible to its last detail. Groans surge from the earth and the
ocean. A seething tidal wave vomits a monster with horns and scales—half-
bull, half-dragon—infecting the air as it spews fire, blood, and smoke. Hippolyte wounds it, and his terrified horses stampede. Hippolyte is tangled in
the reins and dragged until "his body was a single wound" (*Racine*, p. 222). He
is discovered by the trail of blood and the parts of his body scattered on the
bloody path. He is unrecognizable to both lover and father.

Thésée begins to be suspicious when he sees Aricie cradling Hippolyte's
remains but begs Phèdre not to enlighten him, since that might increase his
suffering. Phèdre will not spare him. She says she took poison rather than use
a sword because she wants time to tell him the truth. She admits her guilt, and
in so doing implicates Thésée. This violence is the worst of all. Thésée the
ruler has lost face: he speaks like an imperial ruler and says stiffly he will go
to mingle his tears with the blood of his unfortunate son and give him due
honors. He also says he will adopt Aricie as his child. He is too busy making
arrangements to mourn onstage like Euripides' Theseus. We see a royal *déli-
catesse* in Phèdre, who acts like a gentle noblewoman. Thésée exercises his
royal prerogative, concealing his human side under the mask of king.

Ted Hughes translated Racine's *Phèdre* in 1998, where it was performed at the Albery Theatre in London; it starred Diana Rigg of *Avengers* and *Medea* fame. Overacting characterized her entire performance and an overactive fog machine duplicated the excess. One entered the theater with fog oozing over the seats as a foghorn moaned in the background. The fog never completely dispersed, and this made it difficult to see the actors. Rigg played Phèdre as a jaded demimonde rather than as a young woman victimized by love. This is performing against the text.

In the London production the fog was used to create effects. To the left of the stage, presumably representing the shore that could be seen from the windows of the palace, we see the bull and hear its bellows. Television and graphic films have created a taste for visual renditions of violence, and the staging of this play does not disappoint. Euripides and the other ancient Greeks relied on the words for their effects.

The best part of the play is found in the words of the translation by the former poet laureate Ted Hughes. With assonance and graphic images, his lyrics tap into the vitality of the myth with lines such as Phèdre's "I am not one of those women who manage their infidelity with a polished smile and a stone heart" (p. 43), or Theseus's "My very fame blazes with shame" (p. 79).

Racine, combining Euripides with Seneca, gives us a love interest for Hippolytus in a young princess. So why is he punished by Aphrodite for ignoring her? In the London production, a huge statue of Aphrodite looms overhead and dominates the part of the set on the right, the palace. So the director Jonathan Kent restored the controlling love goddess that Racine eliminated.

This Hippolytus is totally innocent; we are not even allowed the scene of reconciliation and forgiveness between a flawed father and an intransigent son, as Euripides shows us. In Racine the good is all good and the wicked, wicked. This follows Seneca. Euripides was by contrast a master of ambiguity and of the mixture of good and evil which characterizes most human beings.

Phaedra illuminates not only the theater but also the modern screen in two film versions, one American and one Greek. Eugene O'Neill's *Desire under the Elms* was adapted by Irwin Shaw as a film directed by Delbert Mann in 1958. In 1962 Jules Dassin produced *Phaedra*, his own adaptation (with Margarita Liberaki) of Euripides' play. Eugene O'Neill translated and adapted both Euripides (in *Desire under the Elms*, 1925, which reworks *Hippolytus*) and Aeschylus (in *Mourning Becomes Electra*, 1931, a reworking of the *Oresteia*). O'Neill finally wrote the tragedy of his own family in *Long Day's Journey into Night*, performed after his death in 1956, in which two sons are torn apart by a vain, avaricious father and a drug-addicted mother. This play won the Pulitzer Prize. In the earlier plays he was simply rehearsing, with the help of Greek tragedy, for his own masterpiece. Both *Desire under the Elms* and *Phaedra* fea-

ture Anthony Perkins as the Hippolytus figure. His persona as a sexually ambiguous adolescent captures the essence of Euripides' conception. The arrogant absolutism of youth is destroyed by a world demanding compromise; we
need only compare Pentheus of Euripides' *Bacchae*.

These productions feature tyrannical, insensitive fathers. In Euripides'
play Theseus mocks his son and does not listen to him. In O'Neill, we find
comparable scenes between the father, Ephraim Cabot, and his three sons,
Simeon, Peter, and Eben. After Eben's mother dies, Ephraim takes a young wife
named Abbie; Eben is rightly suspicious of the new woman's interest in inher-
iting the farm when his father dies. The farm had been his mother's property,
and Eben feels his father stole it from his mother. Abbie is told by Ephraim
that she will only inherit if she produces a son for him, which she sets about
doing with the help of her stepson Eben.

Clearly O'Neill wanted to reinforce the basic sexual tension of the Greek
original with the American obsession for owning property (cf. Arthur Miller's
similar attack in *Death of a Salesman*). This parallels the more broadly political
themes of the Irish adaptations of Greek tragedy. Not coincidentally, in *Long
Day's Journey into Night*, O'Neill attributes his father's avarice to his Irish immigrant background, where everything is sacrificed to win property, since this
was relatively impossible in the old country.

Though an emotional involvement was not her initial intention, Abbie
falls in love with Eben and he responds. After their son is born, Ephraim tells
Eben that he is now cut out of his inheritance, and with her new son Abbie
has triumphed. Eben believes his father and rages at Abbie, who says she will
do anything to regain his love. She kills the baby, thinking this will win Eben
back. Eben is horrified when he finds out and reports her to the authorities.
He then has second thoughts, realizing how much Abbie loves him. He surrenders himself, saying both he and Abbie planned the murder.

The play that begins with the sons admiring the land ends with the local
officials admiring it. The land is constantly before our eyes in the film, and it
is seen as beautiful, seductive, and constraining. Close-ups try, sometimes
successfully, to convey the psychological details of the characters. Nevertheless
the film loses the nuances of the play and lacks the immediate danger and
excitement that one finds in a theater, with live actors and actresses addressing
a live audience. A darkened room with screen figures cannot reproduce this
type of interactive excitement.

The film based on this play explains much that O'Neill left purposely
vague. The young wife now becomes Italian to accommodate Sophia Loren in
the role. The brothers, also fine actors, have larger parts than in the stage play,
and a whole sequence is added to show how they have married and have become successful in the West after they left home in protest when their father

returned with a young bride. Eben had bought out their shares of the farm and provided them with the stake money to go West. With its gold and land California beckoned, and they wanted to try their luck.

In O'Neill's play, Abbie is jealous of Minnie, a woman of easy virtue who lives nearby. Eben regularly visits Minnie and seeks comfort in her arms. He learns that she had similarly welcomed his brother and father. When he discovers this, in the film he prudishly abandons her, but in the stage play he is more accepting. Eben lifts his arms up to the night sky and describes what he likes in Minnie in a dialect called "Down East," or more colloquially "Emmet," and O'Neill reproduces its musicality:

> Waal—thar's a star, an' somewhar's they's him,
> an' here's me, an' thar's Min up the road—in the
> same night. What if I does kiss her? She's like t'night,
> she's soft 'n' wa'm, her eyes kin wink like a star, her
> mouth's wa'm, her arms're wa'm, she smells like a wa'm plowed field, she's
> purty . . . Ay-eh! By God A'mighty
> she's purty, an' I don't give a damn how many sins
> she's sinned afore mine or who she's sinned 'em with,
> my sin's as purty as any one on 'em! (*Complete Plays*, 1:326)

Min becomes the earth and the heaven and the night, binding the two, Eben and Min, together: she is warm and pretty. The film eliminates this. A film rarely presents poetry literally unless it has someone reciting it: it often works through sight or musical sound rather than words. In the film we see a beautiful night and Eben insulting Min. Eben's insensitive rejection in the film brings him even closer to Hippolytus.

As we progress in time, we seem more influenced by the secular: O'Neill eliminated gods and ghosts from his play. He did not use Euripides' Aphrodite and Artemis, though he did add the ghost of Eben's mother to haunt the house. The elms themselves seem to replicate her, and O'Neill's stage directions are poetically explicit: "Two enormous elms are on each side of the house. They bend their trailing branches down over the roof. They appear to protect and at the same time subdue. There is a sinister maternity in their aspect, a crushing, jealous absorption. They have developed from their intimate contact with the life of man in the house an appalling humanness. They brood oppressively over the house. They are like exhausted women resting their sagging breasts and hands and hair on its roof, and when it rains their tears trickle down monotonously and rot on the shingles" (p. 318). It is difficult, perhaps impossible, to translate this language into film. O'Neill's oppressive and beloved mother appears in many forms. The gigantic tree and dim lighting in the film make a good attempt to convey this mystery, but they ultimately fail: no camera can equal the human imagination as evoked by suggestive words.

In the play it seems that the spirit of the mother lingers on as if to take vengeance on Ephraim and perhaps to encourage her son to take his part in that vengeance. She becomes Aphrodite and may likewise involve an innocent person in her revenge. Ephraim goes to the barn to sleep in the warm hay to escape her ghostly chill. It is during one of these "escapes" that Eben and Abbie first make love. The film shows Ephraim going to the barn, but there is little said about the spirit in the house. We see a storm and dark skies outside, so the room where Eben and Abbie make love appears to be a warm shelter; imagination must link this warmth to that felt by the dead mother for her son.

We have a passionate Phaedra, a brutal Theseus, and a Hippolytus who misunderstands Phaedra's passion. So far so good, but passion is reciprocated with tragic consequences. We do not see the lovers die, but it is likely that Abbie and Eben will be hanged. The spirit of the mother has seemed to encourage their passion, and in this she functions somewhat as Aphrodite, but the fatal decision is the lovers' own. We see again how decisions operate on two levels, the supernatural and the human, and in this *Desire under the Elms* resembles *Hippolytus*.

The universe shatters and chaos reigns. The one spot of warmth is the reconciliation of the lovers with each other. The lovers have a tragic anagnorisis, or recognition, tragic because it comes too late. In both *Hippolytus* and *Desire under the Elms*, forgiveness for what cannot be forgiven shows us a glimmer of humanity in a dark universe.

The modern play and film are both centered on property and the lust for property as much as the lust for the flesh. O'Neill came from an immigrant Irish Catholic family that had to struggle financially. Land was prized. In the play, the old man says that he wants to keep hold of his land even when he is dead. That is another reason why he is adamant in having only his own children inherit. He seems indifferent as to which son it is, as long as it is the "child of his loins," that is, his genetic offspring, so he indulges his young wife and chooses her son as his heir. Eben lusts for the property initially, but he refocuses his desire on Abbie, at first a rival for the property but then his ally in trying to secure it for themselves and their heirs.

Euripides' Hippolytus is singularly unconcerned with power or property and, like Ion in his play, explains that a life of freedom without care is worth more than one with the constraints that such responsibility would bring. Phaedra is a typical Euripidean heroine, dedicated to securing her good name. Also typical of Euripides, Phaedra's vengeance goes too far—Euripides' play is about passion and honor. Obsession with property is found only in O'Neill's play, which makes it less heroic.

T. C. Murray wrote *Autumn Fire* in 1924 in Ireland about the same time that O'Neill was writing his *Desire under the Elms*. Ellen is an additional character, an Electra figure who is overly attached to her father and is supposed to inherit the house. She is a bitter child who is behind the disasters that strike her family and engulf her father, Owen, and brother, Michael, and her school friend Nance. Nance comes into an inheritance and returns to her mother. Owen falls in love with Nance. Michael is also taken with her, but she falls for the more vibrant Owen. She marries him, but he becomes an invalid after an accident and takes to his bed. Owen was about to leave his farm to Nance, but jealousy causes him to revise this decision. Ellen fans the flame of jealousy and suspicion in her father about Nance and Michael. It is decided that Michael should leave to avoid temptation, on the advice of a priest. Finally, Owen finds Nance kissing Michael and will not be convinced that it was an innocent kiss of farewell. Owen is lost in bitterness, and we see him saying the rosary at the end, believing God alone is trustworthy.

Everyone's life is destroyed by Ellen's bitter warnings, good intentioned as she might have been (which is doubtful: she wanted the property and exclusive rights to her father). This play is rather like a Hardy novel; things get worse and worse. Like *Othello* it shows the disastrous effects of jealousy. It eliminates the gods, but it shows how one cannot escape one's fate, particularly if that fate is written in one's own nature. Heraclitus said that character is destiny. This play shows *Oedipus* without Delphi calling the shots. There is no chorus, either. It is a well-made play but no masterpiece. It is also a good actor's vehicle.

Just after Eugene O'Neill's *Desire under the Elms,* H. D. (Hilda Doolittle), in addition to her many poems on classical themes, devised her translation and adaptation of Euripides' *Hippolytus: Hippolytus Temporizes* (1927). She cuts freely but remains faithful to the original plot. People have characterized her drama as commentary in action. She not only devises her own poetic realization, but also adds extended stage instructions and commentary on the text.

Jules Dassin's *Phaedra* (1962) continues the theme of obsession with wealth. His film speaks of a Greek ship owner, and it is difficult not to think of this character as a version of Onassis. Phaedra, played by Melina Mercouri, is intent on securing a good name and an inheritance for her son.

In this film, Phaedra is married to a tycoon named Thanos, which bears the ominous etymological suggestion of death in Greek; the name also suggests Theseus, not only with the "th" component, but also with the fact that Theseus visited Hades. Thanos turns out to be fatal for both his workers and his son. He causes his son's death, not only by his curse and by sending him into exile, but also by giving him a fast car which he drives off a cliff.

In Dassin's film, Phaedra has a sister, and the two have married men like their father, wealthy, but not as wealthy as he is. Phaedra's husband has a former wife, "the English woman," by whom he had a son who is studying art in London. It was an inspired idea to choose an English woman as the equivalent of Hippolytus's Amazon mother. This modern Hippolytus is associated with the effete and over-cultivated. (One might compare the Alan Bates character in the film version of Kazantzakis's *Zorba the Greek*.) The sexual ambivalence suggested by the choice of Anthony Perkins for the Hippolytus figure adds to the characterization. The young man who refuses the advances of the overwhelming maternal figure might not be interested in women at all.

Phaedra is sent to bring the son back to Greece. She fears for her own young son; perhaps his inheritance will go instead to the English woman's offspring. Phaedra seduces her son's rival, Alexis, and forbids him to come back. Thanos insists, however, that this son should return, and he arranges a marriage between Alexis and Herse, Phaedra's niece. Phaedra seems to have fallen more desperately in love and cannot tolerate the thought of Alexis married to her niece, so she goes to Thanos and tells him the truth. Thanos curses Alexis and sends him away. Alexis does the same to Phaedra: he tells her he wants her to die. She kills herself. He races along the cliffs in his Aston Martin sports car until he is forced off the road by a large truck (the bull from the modern sea that makes Hippolytus's chariot useless). His car flies off the cliff, and his body is torn by the rocks like the body of Hippolytus.

The father is remote, cruel, and uncomprehending. In this film the son avoids sex until he is seduced. As in O'Neill's *Desire under the Elms*, the son is won over and the seduction is successful. Sex once again figures in the modern adaptation of a classic.

Dassin's film offers a wide-angle view of Euripides' play: instead of just the elite, we see the workers. The major tragedy comes when a ship named *Phaedra* sinks off the coast of Norway with hundreds of employees killed. Wives and mothers throng Thanos's office in hopes of learning about the fate of their loved ones. The jet-set tragedy of an unfaithful wife shrinks by comparison. Dassin lets us see the exploitation of the worker, and he weaves a tale out of the juxtaposition of the ship owners on the one hand and their employees on the other. As O'Neill added an antimaterialist theme to his adaptation of *Hippolytus*, so Dassin adds a socialist, if not actually communist theme: ownership of private property corrupts, and the concentration of huge wealth in the hands of a few Greek ship owners corrupts absolutely. Only the idle rich have the leisure to pursue their incestuous passions; the workers are too busy earning a living. (In the witch-hunt waged in the 1950s against communists, Dassin was blacklisted by the Un-American Activities Committee.)

In these modern reworkings of Euripides, the moral issues are influenced by the material issues. The desire for wealth and power corrupts the protagonists as much as their physical passion impels them to break the laws of society. In Euripides and O'Neill there are touches of humanity that redeem the inhumanity, but in Dassin we search for redemption in vain.

Desire under the Elms is very much a filmed play. The set hardly changes, and the audience is as trapped by the house and land as the house itself is trapped by the elms. In contrast to Euripides' play and *Desire under the Elms,* which shows a unity of place, Dassin's film *Phaedra* ranges wide; the characters change location frequently, as one might expect of the jet set. We are whisked away from a Greek island to London to Paris and back to the island. Instead of citizens of a Greek polis, we meet Eurotrash; their morals are as changeable as their locations. Virtue, or lack of it, becomes a fashion statement.

Grand gestures abound. A yacht is strewn with flowers from a helicopter; Thanos gives Phaedra a valuable ring, which she throws in the Thames as an offering to Aphrodite. It is as if she has extinguished her love for Thanos as she invokes Aphrodite's flame, which indeed will be given to her in excess. The photography is superb, and the symbols of both flame and water are combined when Phaedra and Alexis make love in an apartment in Paris. It rains outside, as if in anticipation of the tears that this love will cause. The blazing fireplace reflects the passionate, destructive flames that consume the lovers and many around them. Note that Phaedra, whose name means "the shining one," has a rival named Herse, "dew." Herse is truly refreshing, but she does not share Phaedra's exciting and passionate fire. In the final scenes, Phaedra takes a fatal drink, and Alexis's own flame will be extinguished in the ocean after his fall.

We know Greek tragedy had music, and it is a great loss that we only have fragmentary evidence of it. In *Phaedra* we hear the music of Mikis Theodorakis, which augments the poetry: "Rhodostamo" (Rose-water) tells of one lover offering honey and the other offering poison. Phaedra says the song is "about love and death like all Greek songs." *Desire under the Elms* has music by Elmer Bernstein, which captures the passionate feeling of the American South, although O'Neill's play is set in New England amid the rocky fields of New Hampshire or Vermont.

Both the music and the cinematic images bring the ancient poetry to life again, in spite of a certain lowering of the stature of the ancient characters. Nevertheless, certain important social issues are addressed. Dassin's version expands Phaedra's personal tragedy: the duty of an executive officer to his workers is more important than that of a wife to her husband.

Brian Friel's *Living Quarters, after Hippolytus* (1977) can be read as a political parable, full of sound and fury signifying despair. In this play, we are conscious of the Irish republic's problems, since the hero of the play, Commandant Frank Butler, is in the Irish army. He lives in a remote part of County Donegal, Ireland.

Friel often visits the classics in his plays. Not only does he make the Irish characters polylingual, including Greek and Latin in their repertoire in *Translations,* but he also uses myths and classical allusions freely in other plays.

Translations ends with Hugh O'Donnell's quotation from book 1 of Virgil's *Aeneid:* the analogy is drawn between Ireland as Carthage and England as invading imperialist Rome. *The Gentle Island* (1971) might be considered even closer to *Hippolytus* than *Living Quarters*. Sarah falsely incriminates Shane, who has rejected her advances. She gets her father to avenge her honor by killing Shane. *Wonderful Tennessee* (1993) also has classical references and contains a not-so-veiled allusion to Dionysian *sparagmos,* or rending of a victim.

Living Quarters has a dreamlike quality as Frank Butler's family reconstructs the circumstances around his death. The play opens with Butler returning to his family after a successful tour of duty in the Middle East, presumably in a United Nations operation, with his hoped for promotion imminent and a wife (thirty years younger) waiting for him. Also awaiting his arrival are his children by his former wife, dead after a long bout with crippling arthritis: Ben, Helen, Miriam, and Tina.

Friel organizes his play around a narrator, called Sir, who also acts like a stage manager. He consults a ledger, which is the "written word" that may be rearranged but not deleted. This narrator can be seen as God, as Fate, as History, or as the collective will of the people involved: "And in their imagination, out of some deep psychic necessity, they have conceived me—the ultimate arbiter, the powerful and impartial referee, the final adjudicator" (pp. 177–78).

Some see Sir as a Greek chorus. The sisters and priest can also be seen to function as a Greek chorus, witnessing and commenting on events. They act at times as if they were sources of objective truth. Unlike in Euripides, the characters in this play know the plot of their lives; we, the audience, must wait until it unfolds. The action does not occur chronologically but like flower petals falling one after another, until we are left to view an empty stalk.

One specific day is described, "as if it were a feast laid out for consumption or a trap waiting to spring" (p. 177), an allusion to the trap of *La machine infernale,* Jean Cocteau's account of Oedipus, who is caught in a trap which he cannot escape. Greek tragedy operates with these two seemingly contradictory assumptions: there is an overriding notion of fate, yet man remains responsible for his choices. We get the same feeling in Friel's play, which also observes the ancient unities as described by Aristotle: one place, one day, one theme.

When direct speech is used it can become a violent speech act. Anna, the young second wife of Frank, addresses him and the sisters: "I had an affair with your son, Ben—with your brother, Ben! An affair—an affair—d'you hear!" (p. 202). This is the climax of the cadenza, but it is ignored when first heard. The words gradually seep into the characters' psyches and they lead, like Phaedra's false accusation, to death. In this case the accusation is all too true. Anna's confession is like Phaedra's letter, but it kills the father rather than Hippolytus. Even Sir points out that the affair could have remained secret, and "Frank's life would have stayed reasonably intact" (p. 207). We remember Racine's Thésée not wanting to be "enlightened." This avoidance is another typically Irish solution.

The father is as remote and unavailable as Theseus: both go on "campaigns." Miriam, one of the daughters, points out her father's faults: "He's set in his ways and damned selfish and bossy" (p. 189). She notes, speaking of her mother, "That this bloody wet hole ruined her health and that he [her husband and their father] wouldn't accept a transfer" (p. 189). One is reminded of O'Neill's *Long Day's Journey into Night*, where the husband (the author's father) destroys his wife (the author's mother) through his remoteness, enhanced by drink.

Frank admits his faults of failed intimacy to Helen, another daughter, "What has a lifetime in the army done to me? Wondering have I carried over into this life the too rigid military discipline that—that the domestic life must have been bruised, damaged, by the stern attitudes that are necessary over— I suppose what I'm saying is that I'm not unaware of certain shortcomings in my relationships wth your mother and with Ben; and indeed with you" (p. 194).

Anna is not overcome by passion as is Phaedra, and the gods are conspicuously absent as causal agents. It is true that she did not spend much time with Frank before he had to leave. They were married for five months but had only spent ten days together. For Anna, this was indicative of how much time Frank was ready to devote to the family. Yet one cannot help thinking that Anna could have contrived her escape in a less destructive manner. She seems indifferent to any meaningful relationship. For in telling his father, she is perhaps, as Ben says, "a heartless bitch" (p. 236). Careless, cruel Anna is armed with the missiles of her words. Euripides was more sympathetic to Phaedra.

There is very little suggestion of sex, and the only allusion the audience is given is in a few words, referring to "our attempt at a love affair" (p. 219). The fact that Anna and Ben have had a physical relationship is a change from the original play, but the mutual emotions seem superficial by comparison. It is obvious that Ben is more involved with the memory of his mother than with any living woman. Perhaps this parallels Hippolytus's rejection of women.

Physical violence occurs with the commandant shooting himself after hearing about his wife's affair with his son. He does not bother to curse Ben but instead turns a gun on himself. He is driven by guilt and the sense that life holds nothing further for him, in spite of his promotion. Like Agamemnon, he is a man with victories in the outside world, returning home to be destroyed by his own family. A stage direction conveys the violent act: "Then a single revolver shot off" (p. 242). No blood is described, and the priest will not even admit it is suicide since this would prevent burial in sanctified ground: "There was never any doubt in my mind that it was an unfortunate accident" (p. 243). Friel taps into a rich dramatic heritage: with the single shot, Hedda Gabler or Konstantin Gavrilovitch in *The Seagull*, come to mind; Ophelia offers a parallel for the lie enabling burial in sanctified ground.

And the rest is silence. When Frank goes off the stage to kill himself, the stage directions say, "He stops and looks around at the others—all isolated, all cocooned in their private thoughts. He opens his mouth as if he is about to address them, but they are so remote from him that he decides against it" (p. 241).

Violence is applied to time as the story leaps forward and backward. We learn about the family and that Frank's stubbornness in refusing to move his family to more comfortable quarters may have added to his first wife's illness. Frank felt he had finally achieved happiness with his young new bride. The shattering of this illusion is fatal for him.

In Friel's play Phaedra and Hippolytus do not die; they just fade away. After Frank shoots himself, Ben leaves for Scotland and is seen back in Ballybeg, drunk. The two unmarried sisters immigrate to England, where they live separate lives; thus Friel shows the disintegration and alienation of a family. One might compare *Dancing at Lughnasa*, 1990, and even the stories of Joyce which end in emigration: the characters leave Ireland but cannot escape their Irishness.

Anna, the young wife, goes to California where she finds a roommate and travels, leading an anaesthetized life. Clearly there has been no passion in the relations between Ben and Anna. Anna commits a type of incestuous adultery out of loneliness and boredom; Ben, because of an ill-defined revenge.

Ben blamed his father for his mother's death, and his father had hit him during "hostilities" which Ben will not forget. Like Ireland, he nurses his grudges. As Heaney claims in *The Cure at Troy*, some fall in love with the wound. Ben says of his father, "The day she died I called him a murderer" (p. 212). Ben is regarded as a failure; as Miriam says, "He's a wastrel—a spoiled mother's boy" (p. 187). But until his mother's death Ben was the golden boy, enrolled as a medical student at University College, Dublin. After her death he dropped out of school and developed a stammer.

At the same time Ben loved his father. He tells the narrator that he would have liked to say to his father, "I always loved him and always hated her [Anna]—he was always my hero. And even though it wouldn't have been the truth, it wouldn't have been a lie either: no, no; no lie" (p. 245). It is typical that they could not have communicated while Frank lived.

Ben's violent revenge was to make love to the young wife he hated and to cause his father's death by this shame and loss. This is a drama between father and son. By his actions in this play, Hippolytus becomes Oedipus.

Frank, the soldier, at the end lodges "a formal protest . . . And I am fully aware that protesting at this stage is pointless—pointless . . . it does seem spiteful that these fulfillments should be snatched away from me—and in a particularly wounding manner. Yes, I think that is unfair. Yes, that is unjust. And that is why I make this formal protest, Sir. Against an injustice done to me. Because I have been treated unfairly, Sir—that is all" (p. 240–41). We think of Job futilely indicting God; we also think of the Irish rehearsing their wounds. The formalism of anguish is musically repetitious here. There is a ritualistic aspect to this; gods breathe in Friel's plays and are invoked in various ways.

The play does not end with the forgiveness between father and son, as does Euripides', although at one point there is an abortive attempt. Ben says, "But what I want to tell you, Father, and what I want you to know is that I—" Frank (leaving), "Some other time." Then Ben congratulates his father, and "suddenly Frank opens his arms and embraces Ben warmly, and says, 'Ben! Thank you, son'" (p. 228). This formal shriveled exchange is typical of Frank.

No one in the family can fully tolerate the happiness and success of another. In a strange and haunting way this becomes a parable of Ireland that uses the inner strife and betrayal which occurs within the family itself. Violence here is verbal and internal, and in this we see a return to Euripides. Nevertheless, this Hippolytus (Ben) was as guilty as Phaedra (Anna) of the act which destroys his father. In this case the father instead of his son is Aphrodite's victim.

Euripides left us in Theseus a hero with a sterile past; Friel gives us a Hippolytus and a Phaedra with useless futures. The nexus is clear. It is not simply the external enemy that one can blame. Friel uses the power of Greek myth, reinforced by the authority of the character Sir, to represent the seemingly inescapable tragedy of Irish political and family life. Enemies in the family and in oneself can be the deadliest.

Sarah Kane wrote *Phaedra's Love* (1996) as bitter satire directed against the British royal family. It shows a decadent Hippolytus who sleeps not only with his mother-in-law but also with his sister. Phaedra dies in shame, accusing him of rape. He is finally killed violently by a crowd (including his father) in a *sparagmos* worthy of Dionysus. The stage directions are as follows: "Man 1 pulls down Hippolytus' trousers. Woman 2 cuts off his genitals. They are thrown onto the fire. The children cheer. A child pulls them out of the fire and throws them at another child, who screams and runs away. Much laughter. Someone retrieves them and they are thrown to a dog" (p. 101). Theseus arrives home to witness and hasten his unloved son's death: "He takes the knife and cuts Hippolytus from groin to chest" (p. 101). Theseus himself turns Hippolytus over to the people who are screaming for his flesh: "Hippolytus' bowels are torn out and thrown onto the fire as he is kicked and stoned and spat on" (p. 101). Theseus then rapes and kills his own daughter and finally cuts his own throat. The final image is of the mangled Hippolytus opening his eyes to see "vultures" and concluding, "If there could have been more moments like this" (p. 103). He luxuriates in finally feeling something. The anti-royalist sentiments degenerate into farce.

As tragedy is engulfed by grotesque comedy, this play becomes one violent act. Nor is the violence simply verbal; it is physically performed. In spite of horrendous violence explicitly enacted onstage, one is impressed with Hippolytus's apathy. Gone is any concern about shame or guilt. The change from Euripides is obvious, and this most modern of our variations on the theme of Phaedra and Hippolytus numbs the audience rather than offering it the rich emotions evoked by ancient tragedy. This escalation makes one fear the next performance. The Phaedra-Hippolytus theme has evolved from individual suffering to political farce and simply rehashing news from a scandal sheet; much is lost at this end of this spectrum. Violence has replaced tragedy.

Charles Mee has a new version of Euripides' *Hippolytus* which he combined with Racine's *Phèdre, True Love*. It was performed at the Zipper (it was a formerly Zipper factory) in New York in 2001, directed by Daniel Fish. A wife falls in love with her stepson and fireworks result. There is a meditation on a father molesting his daughter, an electronic masturbation with car cables, and a lemon pie ground by an actor into an audience member's crotch.

There is also text from Andy Warhol, the *Jerry Springer Show*, and the trial of the Menendes brothers. Along with Mee's *Big Love* (based on Aeschylus's *Suppliant Women*) and *First Love,* this is a stylized, avant-garde meditation on gender relations. On his website (http://www.panix.com/~meejr/html/big_love.html), Mee describes his plays as "broken, jagged, filled with sharp edges, filled with things that take sudden turns, clinging to each other, smash up, veer off in sickening turns. That feels good to me, it feels like my life." He says honestly about his versions of the Greeks: "Recently, I have come again and again to take the text of a classic Greek play, smash it to ruins, and then atop its ruined structure of plot and character, write a new play, with all-new language, characters of today speaking like people of today, set in the America of my time—so that America today lies, as it were, in a bed of ancient ruins." In these plays Seneca meets Heiner Müller in America, with a bit of spice added from Mee's breakfast.

Hercules

Seneca's *Hercules Furens* has many elements that are different from Euripides' *Hercules*. It begins with a jealous Juno wanting vengeance on Jupiter for his philandering and the visible symbol of this philandering, Heracles. Juno feels that Heracles has met every task with ease, and that he seemed to be looking forward to the next labor so that he could gain more glory. He corroborates this when he appears. So she says she will make him destroy himself. This is consistent with the psychological acuity for which Seneca is known.

Lycus has usurped the throne of Thebes, and he wants Megara, Hercules' wife and the daughter of the last king, to make his rule secure by becoming his wife. Megara blames Lycus for killing her father and brothers. Lycus woos her by pointing out that after a person is victorious one forgets the war waged to bring that victory about. Victim must be reconciled with victor. She pleads for death, and he finally is about to kill her and her family when Hercules returns with Cerberus and Theseus and kills Lycus. Hercules boasts inordinately, as if he were a figure out of *Alcestis* or a satyr play. The sky darkens and his boasting and blasphemy increase. He brutally kills his children and his wife: all of this is vividly described by Amphitryon, Heracles' human father. Heracles tries to kill himself, but both his father and Theseus persuade him to live. Amphitryon even has a drawn sword and threatens suicide. Hercules gives in and lives but longs for Hades as soon as possible. He says there is nowhere he can hide from himself and his guilt. Even Hades knows him and his crimes now. Hercules becomes an angst-ridden everyman, fit for stoic salvation. This is another Senecan *Lehrstück*, "a play that teaches" (a term used by Brecht), filled with lessons for living life well. It has some dire warnings for rulers abusing their power. One thinks of Nero, to whom Seneca was tutor.

Heiner Müller wrote three different plays on the myth of Heracles: *Heracles 5* (1966); *Heracles 2, or The Hydra* (1972), and *Heracles 13, after Euripides* (1991). In the first play he shows Heracles as a disgruntled hero and as an example of the evils of the "personality cult," which colored the political world of the Germany he knew. It deals with the cleansing of the stables of Augeus. The "shit" becomes a metaphor for the human condition. *Heracles 2, or The Hydra* is written in a type of nightmare monologue and offers added commentary to *Zement*, Fyodor Gladkov's novel about the Russian Civil War of 1919–20. *Heracles 13, after Euripides* freely adapts the story of Heracles. Theodoros Terzopoulos directed Heiner Müller's *Herakles* in 1997 in Greece, with his group called Attis. The play was performed in an empty square room with a ring of round lights around the bottom. The drama centers on the actors, two women and three men. Müller's *Herakles 5* shows the task of cleaning the Augeian stables, which in Herakles' hands becomes destructive. He has no concern for how many of the cattle are killed. He ignores Augeias's protests. In *Herakles 2*, Herakles struggles with the Hydra and then with his madness when he believes he has become the Hydra. In *Herakles 13* we see his madness leads him to kill his own family. The acting is brilliant and can only be created by people who have undergone the most rigorous training.

There is much repetition, and lines are delivered by the actors and actresses interchangeably, mainly for the sound of their voices rather than because of their gender. Music is used extensively, both in pure rhythm that corresponds to a heartbeat or a machine and in fragments from Livio Tragtenberg's *Othello*. The actors create their own orchestra. The sound of their stamping continues even when the lights go out: the audience can feel the danger. One sees all moving like machines to a beat, and then one actor starts to go faster and seems to end cataclysmically in a heart attack. The ghost in the machine has a stranglehold on man. Herakles dared too much and had to be taught that he was human and had limitations.

Terzopoulos has said, "Even for theatre, man is tragic, because the war with the gods is lost" (personal interview in my *Ancient Sun*, p. 168). Here we see the tragedy of Herakles, defeated by the gods and himself. Man, the powerful, technological wizard who invents the bomb, explodes from within. And the moral? The Hydra is us. The many-headed Attis group holds up the mirror for us to see our own reflection.

Trojan Women

Seneca's *Trojan Women* depicts each death with the usual attention to bloody detail for which Seneca is known. Hecuba describes the death of Priam at the hands of Pyrrhus, Achilles' son. Pyrrhus demands the sacrifice of Polyxena on his father's tomb. At first Agamemnon opposes him, having learned some restraint from his war experience. He points out the atrocity of human sacrifice. Pyrrhus taunts him about his sacrifice of Iphigenia and the crimes in his own family. Calchas the prophet, however, corroborates Pyrrhus's request and says that the gods demand two sacrifices, Polyxena and Astyanax: Hector's son must also be thrown from Troy's towers for the fleet to sail back to Greece. The chorus undercuts all this by saying that ghosts do not exist and that Achilles' request is a fiction.

Ulysses plays a cat-and-mouse game with Andromache, who had been warned by her dead husband in a dream to hide their son. Her own anxiety gives her away. Ulysses says they will raze the tomb where the boy is hidden and scatter Hector's ashes to the winds. Andromache sees she has lost, and Ulysses gloats in his sadistic victory. Astyanax is seized and the messenger tells us that he bravely leapt off the walls by himself. Polyxena is led by Helen to a mock marriage with Achilles, to be slain in her bridal gown over his grave. She dies without complaining or flinching. Seneca's victims show Stoical bravery.

Hecuba is left alone mourning her dead, in contrast to Euripides' Hecuba, who joined with the chorus in a communal lament. The gods at the beginning were eliminated: cruelty is shown to be a human specialty. Odysseus threatens torture. Even the chorus' vision of the places they will go is as bleak as can be; there is no Athens or other location that is a desired haven. This is consistent with Stoic pessimism.

Euripides' *Trojan Women* is particularly apt for social protest. Franz Werfel's *Die Troerinnen* (1915) decried the horrors of World War I; a production of *Trojan Women* was mounted in Oxford to coincide with a conference of the League of Nations in 1919.

Jean-Paul Sartre's *Les Troyennes* (directed by Michael Cacoyannis at the Palais de Chaillot in 1965) is an anti-war play that protested abuses in Algeria. One can identify the Algerians with the Trojan women and all of mankind with the victors and victims. It showed the misery of the war, and at this time Sartre even encouraged French troops to desert. Sartre says, "The gods will perish with the humans; and this common death is the lesson of the tragedy" (*Sartre on Theatre*, p. 315).

Sartre updated the context and wrote in his own philosophy. Sartre shows the gods as being as malicious as in Euripides' plays, but he goes further. Hecuba finally reaches the conclusion that the gods are not only unreliable but evil: she calls them "filthy."

Sexual allusions are also explicit; Helen is referred to as a whore, and Clytemnestra is regarded as equally faithless. Sartre, in notes, calls Andromache "a little Bourgeoise."

Helen's main argument, first put forward by Euripides but developed at length by Sartre, is that if she had not sacrificed her chastity in obedience to a god, Greece itself would have been invaded. Sartre recognizes the imperialists' love of land.

Sartre tried to modernize and yet retain the ritual quality, so he wrote his text in verse. His language is often colloquial. His characters are modern, with modern complexes. He writes about Cassandra's erotic perversity in her enthusiasm for entering into a sexual relationship with Agamemnon, realizing it will cause his death.

Sartre says his play ends in total nihilism. The gods are not there for man, and man is abandoned to the contemplation of his mortality. It is just this mortality that makes war so futile for everyone. While the insights may be applauded, this is a play that deals more with ideas than with suffering human beings.

Suzuki's *Trojan Women* (1974) bemoans the disaster of Hiroshima. Euripides appears to be Suzuki's favorite of the ancient Greek tragedians; his acute psychological commentary and social criticism seem appropriate for the issues that Suzuki deals with. *Trojan Women* is a study in suffering. A woman who has survived a catastrophe (Hiroshima?) imagines herself as Hecuba, and the drama unfolds. The original actress, Kayoko Shiraishi, played Cassandra also, and her transformation before our eyes from aged queen to young maiden is spectacular and thoroughly convincing.

Another variation by Suzuki is to show not only Andromache's child killed, but the entire chorus put to the sword. This play indicts the arrogance of the conqueror and shows how in wars the women and the children are the real ones who suffer: they survive only to mourn. Hecuba at the end returns to her role as a modern woman who has lost everything. She carries a bag with all that is left of her world. She finds Priam's shoe and a tin can, which she throws away, and when it falls she asks in Japanese: "Did you hear? The last sound of Troy."

The stage backdrop consists of brightly colored fishnets, and the suggestion is of the tangle that exists in the human mind, as in society. Samurai soldiers goose-step onto the stage, standing in for the ancient Greeks. Their arrogant swagger and cruelty increase our sympathy for the abused women. A Japanese bodhisattva (enlightened saint or god equivalent; a being destined for Buddhahood who chooses to remain in this imperfect world for the sake of suffering beings), Jizo, is introduced. He stands on the stage motionless until Andromache pelts him with a flower, blaming him for not protecting the innocent, particularly children. He doubles over in agony. She tries to help Hecuba, who refuses to leave her reverie. Hecuba collapses and presumably dies. Andromache, who has been raped by the soldiers, leaves the stage to the sounds of the pop song "I Want You to Love Me Tonight."

In 1978 Edward Bond directed his *The Woman* at the Olivier, National Theatre, London. It is his version of *Trojan Women* and focuses on Hecuba, her suffering and final death. Hecuba was brilliantly and passionately played by Yvonne Bryceland. Bond keeps the sharp edges of Greek tragedy and a dramatic integrity, but he changes the original myth in many places. Heros is married to Ismene, and he is leader of the Greeks. He is a self-serving politician, typical of most war leaders. Priam is dead and Hecuba rules in his place, five years into the Trojan War. The war seems to have been fought to get possession of a statue of Athena. Ismene becomes a type of surrogate Helen, held hostage by Hecuba at Ismene's own request. She was bringing a peace offering in return for the statue, and she knows that the Greeks will not keep their word. Several characters in the play refer to propensity for lying. Hecuba says, "This is one of those times when a pinch of truth will bring out the full flavor of our lies" (p. 30). Ismene says, "I am a Greek—and speak the truth as far as I can" (p. 52).

Hecuba's son (called Son) takes over, brutally imprisons Ismene, and keeps Hecuba under guard in her palace. Son is killed by an angry crowd when, like Julius Caesar, he speaks to them from the top of steps, "Trojans! Goddess! Friends!" and the crowd answers, "Death!" (p. 49).

Ismene keeps preaching peace (like a Tokyo Rose or Lord Haw Haw with their broadcasts), so she is tried as a traitor when the Greeks get their hands on her. They immure her (like her sister Antigone), but because she wears her jewels, soldiers release her after Troy is taken. They steal her jewelry but let her live. When Astyanax (here the son of Cassandra) is executed, Hecuba blinds herself in one eye and covers the other (an Oedipus, not wanting to look at her world).

Both Ismene and Hecuba live protected by villagers on an island where they were washed up after a storm destroyed their ship. Man (a Greek slave who worked in the silver mines) escapes to the island on a ship with Greeks who want Hecuba and Ismene to come to Athens and also to find the statue. This is rather like the Greeks coming to find Philoctetes on Lemnos and to bring him and his bow to Troy. Hecuba refuses to return and the Greeks leave empty-handed.

Man is sheltered by the islanders. He becomes Ismene's lover. Ismene pretends she has lost her memory, but she remembers as needed. Heros returns and wants to bring Ismene back with him. Hecuba declares a race between Man and Heros and says that the winner will find the statue. Man returns to his house and gets his sword. At the end of the race he kills Heros. Nestor sails back to Greece. Hecuba is killed by a waterspout, impaled against a fence. Man lives with Ismene, and in a way, she is his prize.

Bond shows us the corruption of those who give in to the lust for power. Ismene says, "You only need leaders to lead you astray! The good shepherd leads his sheep to the butcher!" (p. 44). Hecuba confronts Heros: "No one would license so much murder and not know the answer" (p. 59). Hecuba taunts him by saying he must know how to tell between right and wrong. Heros answers: "Troy would have done the same!" Hecuba replies: "Troy would have been wrong!" (p. 59). Heros also says, "A leader really needs only one virtue—restraint—but many vices. A good ruler knows how to hate. He even knows the limits of restraint. From time to time he surrenders it to anger. How else can he make the people afraid?" (pp. 91–92). The Roman historian Tacitus described fear as the perfect tool for ruling people and the army as the key to power. Bond speaks of the *Pax Athenaea*, recalling the *Pax Romana*, and the *Pax Americana*, all euphemisms for imperialism. As Tacitus says, "They make a desert, and they call it peace" (*Agricola* 30.5).

Bond shows how the poor are exploited, as Man was to help Athens build its city. He also shows the suffering of women in war. They see the truth behind war: how ultimately it gains nothing but death. He shows the warmth of one person caring for another, Euripides' *philia*, or love for another. This is an effective and moving play. A seasoned playwright often writes a better play than a professional poet, particularly when that playwright is somewhat a poet himself, like Bond, O'Neill, Fugard, and Friel. This is true for the ancient Greek authors. Bond is poetic, for instance, has Cassandra express her suffering when she is told her son will die by saying, "The world is cruel. If the whole sky was a cloth, and I wrapped it round my wound, the blood would soak through in one moment" (p. 61). (Bond substituted Cassandra for Andromache whose son, Astyanax, was killed in Euripides' *Trojan Women*.)

Brendan Kennelly's *Trojan Women* (1993) is filled with poetic meditations. It celebrates women and develops a theme of the sea as parallel to them, with its mystery and wildness. His poetry can be beautiful: "The day wears pain like a black jewel" (p. 28). Sometimes it stops the action and becomes a philosophical meditation: when Poseidon asks Athena if he is to let the ships flounder, she answers, "I want them to know that home / is what is always in the mind and always out of reach" (p. 11).

The language is sexually explicit. Hecuba speaks like a marine trooper, calling Helen a "cunt" and saying, "I am not a fuck" (pp. 59, 74). This mixes the language of Greek comedy with tragedy.

Kennelly has wonderful maxims, such as "Freedom is like health—you never know it until you've lost it" (p. 8). He also has that wonderful statement so appropriate for Ireland, "There's nothing more dangerous for a winner than one seed of hope in the heart of the loser" (p. 71). This refers to history and colonialism. We find mystery and poetry here, and Hecuba reaches a true epiphany, seeing God in her suffering: "I heard the music of our hearts / I knew the everlasting beauty of the song of earth and heaven. I kissed God's hand! I am real. I am so real / I am not afraid to look into the eyes of God" (pp. 69–70).

We see the Catholic God and a Christian transfiguration which is also faithful to the Greek claim that the gods teach man through suffering. There are references to song and magic: "Beware the song of Helen's beauty. . . . I've seen the very air seduced / by magical ripples of her sweet manipulating voice. / Her voice is her best song, song of beauty, song of hell!" (p. 75). There is more hope than in the original play: "The living must forget the dead . . . Let the dead rest in peace. In peace let the dead rot" (p. 74). This applies to Ireland. There is also rhyme in the poetry: "Dance like the happy light, let earth and heaven sing / here where I make this bright and fiery ring" (p. 22).

Kennelly plays on the image of Paris as a firebrand. He knows his mythology, as this was Hecuba's dream. It is also poetically suggestive: the fire of passion brought about the torching of Troy.

Hecuba is called a wave of the sea, and the image comes from Yeats's "Fid-

dler of Dooney," where people dance "like a wave of the sea." Kennelly celebrates Hecuba's freedom when he says that she is a "natural, fearless wave of
the sea" (p. 79). Who can enslave a wave of the sea?

The play ends in hope. "The waves are free. The war is over. The war begins—for me!" (p. 79). We know that Hecuba will prevail. As for Ireland, freedom is her battle cry. This play celebrates women and Ireland, as Kennelly has
done in all his versions of Greek tragedy.

Aidan Carl Mathews's unpublished play *Trojans* (1994) is set in Germany
after World War II. This is a witty meditation. Astyanax dies, but hardly in the
way that builds up suspense. Hecuba asks where he is and she is told he is dead.
The women, mainly secretaries of the Reich Chancellery, at the end assume
the pose of statues, and they are equally lifeless. Even though some are said to
die and others live, one does not really care. There is little characterization
which could create audience sympathy.

This is more about German history than Irish history, yet some of the
abuse of the women was certainly comparable to what happened to the Irish,
including genocide. The gods are eliminated, but God appears. There is wordplay: "I have an urgent disappointment somewhere else"; "My friends call me
Mene. My enemies call me Laus." . . . "My name is none of your business."
"None-of-your-business is a very long name. May I call you None?" There is
anachronistic wit: "My German is eighteenth century"; "We can see *Gone with
the Wind* at the Parnassus." We are reminded that here are Catholics: "You were
a priest"; "The priest will melt the jewellery of the slaughtered into a new chalice"; "I do not want to be safe in the arms of Jesus. I want to be safe in the arms
of my husband." Wine as part of Catholicism is illustrated when Cassandra
drinks from a wine bottle and says, "Let this chalice never pass from me."

There are allusions to justice or injustice: "Spoken like a true Social Democrat"; "Will you tell the segregated nigger regiments about Thomas Jefferson?
Will you tell them about his hundred and eighty slaves?"

Sex is explicit; contrary to the Greek original, Menelaus and Helen make
love in front of the others. Cassandra speaks of Agamemnon's bath as "a bath
in a brothel, with his cock sticking up out of the suds like a periscope." There
are Irish references to sex: Menelaus says he enlisted "to get drunk. To get laid.
Bushmills and pussy."

There are poetic and philosophical observations: "Animals die of grief,
but a human being goes on grieving until she dies." While Joyce says, "History
is a nightmare from which I'm trying to wake," Mathews says, "History is a
fucking forced march. They don't want to be History." There are many literary
allusions: "For wonders are many and none is more wonderful than sham,"
which reworks Antigone's, "There are many wonders in the world, but none

more than man." Cassandra has her litanies and prayers. There is little poetry or song and much violence. Repetition assumes the quality of a litany: "They know about blood. There is nothing to be said about it. There is nothing to be said for it. There is nothing to be said." There are no nobles. Even the gods are people: Poseidon is a submarine veteran. There is little music and no poetry. This is a play of ideas and witticisms with hardly any dramatic drive.

Charles Mee's *Trojan Women: A Love Story* is based on both Euripides and Berlioz. It was directed by Tina Landau and produced by the En Garde Arts in New York in 1996. It "incorporates shards of our contemporary world, to lie, as in a bed or ruins, within the frame of the classical world." It is a collage, like other versions by Mee of the classics. It shows victimized women, Polyxena killed and Hecuba telling Aeneas to exact vengeance. It includes the story of the ape buried in a pit which was told also in Mee's *Agamemnon* to illustrate the perverse acts of war. The second part features Dido and Aeneas. Aeneas tells Dido his plans to leave, and she drowns him in a hot tub. The chorus concludes, "But if you'll let me love you it's for sure I'm gonna love you all the way" (http://www.panix.com/~meejr/html/trojan.html). This is another Mee meditation on the vicissitudes of love, which owes very little to the ancient stories invoked in the titles. But it does owe much to modern violence and the taste of audiences for viewing it.

In 2000 my version of Euripides' *Trojan Women* was performed at the Globe Theatres, directed by Seret Scott. It is faithful to the original but puts it in a modern setting, with images reminiscent of all wars in our time. It begins with a phone conversation between the two gods, Poseidon and Athena. Athena's callous decision to take vengeance on the Greeks after supporting them shows the unreliability of the gods. They also want to teach mortals a lesson: "People are mad to fight wars. Everyone thinks he'll never die; it's always the other person. But the winner today is the loser tomorrow, and everyone loses eventually. Death comes soon enough" (*TW* lines 95–97)

The interlude between Menelaus and Helen develops an element of comedy which was already there in the original. Helen is seen to be a symbol that men need for fighting wars. She says to Menelaus:

It seems your mind's made up. You will still think me guilty no matter what I say. You forget that I was only a young girl when I married you, Menelaus! You needed an excuse for war, and there I was! We all know about war, don't we? Winners never think of what it is to be a loser until they lose. The winners also like to have excuses, and that's where I come in. Blame it on the woman: anyone will do. We'll call it "Operation Helen." (unpublished version)

Hecuba makes a journey through suffering to anagnorisis, or personal insight:

The Trojan Women. Adapted by Marianne McDonald. Directed by Seret Scott. Helen (Celeste Ciulla) tries to seduce Menelaus (John Campion) into forgiving her for running off with the Trojan Prince, Paris, and causing the Trojan War. Old Globe Theatre, San Diego, California (2000). Photo: Craig Schwartz. Used by permission.

Oh, trembling legs, trembling body,
Carry me a little further.
It won't be much longer.

Suffering has burned me like the city.
Tempered me like steel.
I am pure
Nothing more to lose.
Nothing to hope for.
I want nothing.
I have nothing to fear.
Hecuba is now finally Hecuba.

This is a work for the millennium, directed by a woman and adapted by a woman, and its message is peace and a celebration of the women who are always the victims in every war.

The Trojan Women. Adapted by Marianne McDonald. Directed by Seret Scott. Trojan women try to comfort their queen Hecuba (Randy Danson) who has been told her grandchild, Astyanax, must die. Chorus (left to right): Eleanor O'Brien, D'Vorah Bailey, Tami Mansfield, Michele Vazquez and Rosina Reynolds. Old Globe Theatre, San Diego, California (2000). Photo: Craig Schwartz. Used by permission.

Phoenician Women

Seneca's *Phoenissae* is fragmentary. Some think that this is intentional, but there are elements which are difficult to reconcile. In the first part Antigone is seen with her father, and she tells him she will never leave him. In the second part she appears at her mother's side on the battlefield. The most obvious explanation is that this was unfinished. There are only a little over 660 lines, whereas all the other plays have over 1000.

The first portion seems based on *Oedipus at Colonus.* It consists of Oedipus's long lamentation over his life, displaying Seneca's rhetorical skill. Antigone tries to keep her father from despairing. When a messenger arrives to ask Oedipus to persuade his sons to give up their fight, he refuses; instead, he spurs them on to their own destruction, rather like Tantalus did in *Thyestes.*

Jocasta in the second part arrives while Eteocles and Polyneices, her sons, are still alive, unlike what happens in Euripides' *Phoenician Women*. She gets Polyneices to remove his helmet and tells him to attack another city to win glory, but not his fatherland. He argues that his brother was supposed to share the throne and asks how will his brother pay for his crime. Jocasta answers, "by ruling." Eteocles seems equally defensive of the kingship. He says it is worth any crime to retain it. That is where the fragments break off. There are no Phoenician women to give choral commentary. I think it is unstageable in this form but that it offers a scaffolding for some clever adaptor to fill in the blanks.

Alcestis

Alcestis has particular appeal in the twentieth century. T. S. Eliot's *The Cocktail Party* (1949) is based on *Alcestis*. It is a witty reconstruction of someone coming back from death, in the guise of a failed marriage, and another choosing death as a form of self-revelation. An unidentified guest, who turns out to be a therapist named Reilly, helps people gain insight into themselves. It is tempting to identify Reilly with death, and in this case death as the definer. The Apollo stand-in seems to be a gossip named Julia, always willing to deliver oracular pieces of information. Heracles seems to be Alexander (whose name means "defender of men"); he is always traveling to foreign countries and has a skill with food and wines that comes from deep appreciation, not unlike Heracles' own. All three of the semi-divine figures (really, Alex and Julia) work out the fates of the others. They chant blessings: "May the holy ones watch over the roof" and in the other, "Bless the road" (p. 369). Reilly concludes: "Go in peace. And work out your salvation with diligence" (p. 357).

The play begins and ends with a cocktail party: Edward Chamberlayne as Admetus is ever the good host. Lavinia Chamberlayne (the Alcestis stand-in) has left her husband, but Admetus carries on with a party. An unidentified guest says that he will return her to him.

Edward Chamberlayne is having an affair with a young woman called Celia Coplestone; his wife, Lavinia, also has a lover, a young man called Peter Quilpe. After the first cocktail party, Edward breaks off with Celia. Peter goes off to Hollywood to become a screenwriter. Reilly reconciles Lavinia and Edward by having them face up to who they are. As in *Alcestis*, the wife is returned to the husband. Their choice is an ordinary one of marriage, elevated by the self-knowledge which comes from the rather painful confrontations engineered by Reilly.

Celia, on the other hand, opts for the extraordinary life and becomes a nurse in "Kinkanja." She is crucified near an anthill. She becomes a type of saint who finds "something given and taken, in a lifetime's death in love, /

Ardour and selflessness and self-surrender" (a quote from Eliot's "The Dry Salvages," from *Four Quartets*, in *Complete Poems and Plays*, p. 136). In her vocation she found what before was merely an empty longing. In this play, compassion is a key to each person's salvation.

Eliot's religious associations replace Euripides' mythical ones. There are no saints in Euripides' play. Nevertheless, just as Admetus had his mask removed, so does Chamberlayne. Both, we assume, will lead better lives from their insights and come to appreciate wives that they formerly undervalued.

Thornton Wilder wrote an excellent tetralogy: *The Alcestiad, or A Life in the Sun, with A Satyr Play, The Drunken Sisters.* It was first staged in Edinburgh in 1955 and directed on a monumental scale (as the Wilders claimed to its detriment) by Tyrone Guthrie. The three acts observe the unities of one day each. The first shows the marriage of Alcestis, in spite of her desire to serve Apollo. She is finally convinced of Admetus's love and so is willing to become his wife. Four herdsmen have joined the household, and one of them is Apollo in disguise, serving a year's time because of some transgression.

The second act (twelve years later) shows one of the herdsmen fatally wounding Admetus in a quarrel. A messenger arrives from Delphi saying that someone can die in his place. Alcestis agrees to die although many others volunteer, including the herdsman who was responsible for wounding Admetus. Alcestis says it must be out of love not expiation, and so she dies. Hercules visits and finally learns that it is Alcestis who has died. He said that she forgave him long ago when he tried to violate her, yet stopped. For both Admetus and Alcestis, Hercules goes to Hades and returns her to her husband.

The third act (twelve years later) shows the city afflicted by a tyrant who has enslaved Alcestis and killed her husband and two of her children. The third son, Epimenes (whose name means "the one who remained"), returns with a friend and tries to kill the tyrant, but is prevented by his mother after she recognizes who he is. She quotes Admetus: "the murderer cuts the sinews of his own heart" (p. 92). The tyrant loses his own daughter in the plague; he decides to return to his own kingdom because he sees this one is cursed. Apollo returns to lead Alcestis to what seems to be the Elysian fields: "into my grove." It is not a grave: "You will not have that ending. You are the first of a great number that will not have that ending" (p. 96). It seems that Apollo was sending a message that man must learn. The last bitterness of death is "the despair that one has not lived . . . her [the tyrant's daughter] life is vain and empty until you give it a meaning" (p. 95). Each person has to work this out for himself. Alcestis finally asks about her life: "All the thousands of days . . . and the world of cares. . . . And whom do I thank for all the happiness?" Apollo answers, "Friends do not ask one another that question. Those who have loved one another do not ask one another that question" (pp. 96–97).

Wilder's satyr play shows how Apollo made the Fates drunk so that if they did not guess his riddle, he could save Admetus's life. He wins, but the Fates then said someone would have to die in his place. And so the tragedy began.

Wilder has been faithful to the myth in its broad outlines but has changed the details (for instance, Wilder adds four shepherds and a disguised Apollo). He brings in other myths, such as the story of the Fates, a plague that he seems to have borrowed from the *Iliad* or *Oedipus,* and Epimenes, returning like Orestes for vengeance. His play teaches that man must learn from suffering: he must learn to lead each day as if it were his last and give his life meaning. This is the same lesson that Wilder taught in *Our Town* and in *The Skin of Our Teeth.*

Wilder wanted his play to be staged simply. He used masks that kept the chin and the mouth free. The stage was to show Admetus's palace. There was supposed to be a grove with running water that was the mouth to Hades, possibly in the orchestral pit. Wilder gave elaborate staging and costuming suggestions. Apollo, when he appears as Apollo and not in disguise, "is dressed in a long dark cloak, with hood, of dark blue. From time to time on a gesture his cloak falls apart, and the light falls upon his costume of glittering gold. In this treatment Apollo moves about among the actors invisible to all except Death" (p. 12).

Ted Hughes wrote a version of *Alcestis* in 1998. Northern Boardsides (Halifax) did a performance in 2000, with Barrie Rutter directing. The acting was superlative, and the comic elements were fully developed.

This tells the story of Alcestis in a new poetic version and adds interludes involving Heracles' labors and the release of Prometheus. This, in my opinion, shows that Hughes did not trust the original *Alcestis* as he should have. Hughes includes the labor describing the taming of the horses of Diomedes, and yet Heracles goes off to do just that at the end of the play. He claims when he predicts his earlier victory that "I see into the future" (p. 54). Hughes also omits Heracles' final labor of bringing Cerberus, the hound of hell, back. Hughes has a strange mixture of Greek and Latin versions of names; for example, he calls Asclepius, Aesculapius (the Latin spelling), but he uses the Greek version for Heracles (not Hercules) and Admetos (not Admetus).

There are many poetic asides, besides insights that we imagine come from Hughes's own life, for instance when the chorus says:

Never say marriage
Brings more happiness to those who marry
Than it brings pain.
Think of all the marriages you have known.
And now—look at this one. (pp. 16–17).

Hughes was married to two women who committed suicide, so this story was one with which he was familiar, although those women did not commit suicide out of love. It is as if before he died Hughes rewrote his marriages as he wished they would have been: he makes Alcestis truly admirable, and Admetos repents. Hughes also is faithful to the original in making Admetos a complainer who is chided by his father and later by the chorus. In the original, Admetos is found weeping more than any male character in all of Euripides' plays.

Hughes also reinterpreted Admetos's violent denunciation of his father in psychologically apt terms:

Chorus 1:
   Grief has made him mad.
   He doesn't know what he is saying.

Chorus 2:
   The Admetos that brought Alcestis to the grave
   Is like the body of a rat
   Trapped with bones and sinews in the trap.
   He is trying to chew it off—the whole body.
   Admetos is trying to gnaw himself
   Free from Admetos. Admetos
   Is spitting out the torn flesh and the blood
   Of Admetos. (p. 47)

One sees a brilliant poet at work. Death says, for instance:

What you call death
Is simply my natural power,
The pull of my gravity. And life
Is a brief weightlessness—an aberration
From the status quo—which is me. (p. 6)

The entire play is a happy one and can be summed up by Alcestis's message to us, "Don't waste the sun. Be happy" (p. 19). It shows death defining life, and we should not waste our moments on earth. We also get to see the nobility of Admetus, more than in the original: Heracles says, "There is nobody to touch him / For loyal friendship, for kingly behaviour" (p. 66). This shows a man repenting from a mistake. One lesson from Hughes's version is that one should not waste life mourning, but should instead turn a bad experience to good use. Admetos learns through his suffering, and one thinks that Hughes understood this well.

The final recognition scene, if I dare say so, I find even more dramatic than the original. The recognition scene is drawn out, and the suspense pays off in the audience's joyful reaction to Admetos regaining his wife. Admetos's final words are

> Throughout my kingdom
> Let all give thanks.
> Let all rejoice—
> Dancing, music, feasting, bonfires.
> We have taken the full measure of grief
> And now we have found happiness even greater.
> We have found it and recognized it. (p. 83)

This is a message that all of Greek tragedy tries to teach. Medea is a woman very different from Alcestis. They both inflict pain on their husbands in different ways and for different reasons. The chorus describes Alcestis: "No woman ever loved a man / As she has loved Admetos" (p. 11).

My version of *Alcestis*, *The Ally Way*, was directed by Seret Scott in New York in 2002. It shows Adrian, a philandering African-American secretary of state, disillusioned with his job. His wife, Alysin, takes a bullet meant for him in an assassination attempt. She is saved by a visiting brain surgeon from South Africa. He is a vital force like Heracles. Alysin finally forgives her husband when he agrees to practice law and leave his government position. He will also give up philandering because he realizes at last how much Alysin means to him. The play features misogynist comments from literature and handbooks for the good wife but finally emerges in praise of the heroic Alysin, much as Euripides intended for Alcestis.

Iphigenia among the Taurians

Goethe (1749–1832) wrote two versions of *Iphigenia among the Taurians* (1779, in prose, and 1787, in verse). It is a play in five acts that celebrates the heroine Iphigenia, who wins Thoas over to "humanity." Iphigenia is made a priestess for the Taurians, saved from death by Diana (the Latinized Artemis). Thoas stops human sacrifice and proposes to her. When his offer is rejected, he reinstitutes human sacrifice. Orestes and Pylades are captured and they are condemned to be sacrificed. Through exchange of information and recognition of scars, Iphigenia is convinced Orestes is her brother. At first she agrees to lie for them so that they can escape, but finally she tells the truth and throws herself on Thoas's mercy. He reluctantly acts the gentleman and lets them go, providing they do not take the statue of the goddess with them. It turns out that it was only misinterpreting the oracle that led them to think that the statue was indicated when a sister's return was mentioned (at first they thought it was Diana who was to return to her brother Apollo). Instead it was Iphigenia who was supposed to return to her brother Orestes and Greece. This happy ending, complete with belief in humanity and generosity, particularly coming from a woman, is very much in line with Goethe's other plays.

This is a combination of Racine's *Phèdre* (with a love interest like Aricie for Hippolyte in the genial Thoas), Sophocles' *Antigone* (the dilemma of representing family over obeying the authority of the government), and Sophocles' *Philoctetes* (the dilemma of lying for expediency). However, there is more excitement and tension in Euripides' *Iphigenia among the Taurians*. We do not have a captive chorus in Goethe's play with whom we sympathize, nor the intervention of a god at the end. God is now found in the human spirit. Guymond de la Touche's version of *Iphigenia among the Taurians* (1757) was adapted by Nicolas-François Guillard into a libretto for the opera by C. W. Gluck in 1779, the same year as Goethe's first version.

Ion

August W. Schlegel (the older brother of Friedrich Schlegel, who commented on Greek literature) was the famous translator of all of Shakespeare's plays into German. He adapted Euripides' *Ion,* and it was produced in 1803 at Weimar. He brought the poetry and the genius needed in rendering the ancient Greeks.

Hilda Doolittle's *Ion, A Play after Euripides* was written in 1937. It is another poetical rendering. She makes it into a rather mystical parable, with Creusa as the virgin mother and Apollo an uneasy "Holy Ghost." The ancient Greeks descended from this union (the Ionians) are considered by Doolittle the bearers of "a new culture, of an aesthetic drive and concentrated spiritual force, not to be reckoned with, in terms of any then known values. . . . For this new culture was content, as no culture had been before, or has since been frankly with one and but one supreme quality, perfection" (p. 112). She calls the Italian Renaissance a faint imitation (p. 113). She goes on to say, "Greece is indeed the tree-of-life, the ever-present stream, the spring of living water" (p. 133).

As might be expected from such hagiographic writing, she elides anything from Euripides that might be messy or might conflict with her beliefs in the glory of Greece. Therefore Ion simply drives the birds away at the beginning: he does not complain about the messes that they make. There is no criticism of anyone, including Apollo. He is basically seen as a god who moves in strange ways, the only possible mate for her heroine, Kreousa, who is said to choose him (an interesting interpretation of rape). Kreousa is not seen as a potential Medea who attempts to kill an innocent child out of jealousy and vindictiveness. Doolittle passes over her wrongdoing by saying in this case that the goddess took over the human being. So Euripides' sharp edges are filed away and neither Delphi's god or the "goddess" Kreousa is censured.

Much of the text is rendered in telegraphic message style in between longer commentary by Doolittle. I do not think this is a dramatically viable play, but it is interesting for the poetry and poetic insights. I do not know if it has ever been produced.

Doolittle gives elaborate stage directions and a description of the temple of Apollo: "a row of Doric pillars, set on a raised dais approached by four or five steps" (p. 134). Kreousa should be in blue: "the blue of stones, lapis-blue, the blue of the fire in the earth, a blue that seems to symbolize not only her pride and her power but also her passion and her loss" (p. 148). Doolittle is a philhellene much like Eva Palmer, and both adored Delphi. This would have been a good play to initiate the first festival at Delphi to revive ancient Greek drama, but it was written ten years after the Palmer-Sikelianos opening.

T. S. Eliot has a version called *The Confidential Clerk* (1953). A light play of mistaken identities, without any of Euripides' darkness, it was performed at the Edinburgh Festival. A lord has an illegitimate daughter and has raised a child (Colby) he thinks is his illegitimate son. This boy turns out to be the son of the woman who was the sister of the supposed mother of the child. His father was an organist, and he is happy when he discovers his origin to indulge in his love for music and becomes an organist himself, with prospects for entering the ministry. The lord in this play (Sir Claude Mulhammer) has always been a frustrated potter. Both Sir Claude and Colby find that through art they have access to the Platonic form, an "escape from a sordid world to a pure one. . . . a world where the form is the reality, of which the substantial is only a shadow" (p. 47). One is reminded of Eliot's poetry: "to apprehend / The point of intersection of the timeless / With time" ("The Dry Salvages," in *Complete Poems and Plays*, p. 136).

Lady Mulhammer discovers her lost son from a former marriage in the fiancé of Lord Mulhammer's daughter (with the suggestive name of Lucasta Angel). This play resembles more *The Importance of Being Earnest* than *Ion*, and Greek New Comedy more than Greek tragedy, although *Ion* was a direct predecessor to the plays of Menander, which led to Plautus, Terence, and finally to the Shakespearean comedies that deal with discoveries of long-lost children such as *Comedy of Errors*, based on Plautus's *Menaechmi*.

In 1999 JoAnne Akalaitis performed *The Iphigenia Cycle* in New York, at the Theatre for a New Audience (American Place). This combined Euripides' *Iphigenia at Aulis* and *Iphigenia among the Taurians*. It was set in a TV studio where a talk show is taking place. The action unfolds with this narrative commentary in the background.

Akalaitis shows Orestes as intermittently mad, and this is an effective rendition of his being chased by the Furies. She uses many devices which were used earlier, such as Peter Stein's dramatic use of the stairs as an important acting space in his *Oresteia;* Akalaitis also uses the drums that Ariane Mnouchkine did in her *Les Atrides* as the audience entered the theater. The black actress who plays Clytemnestra also plays Athena: a black Athena, as Peter Sellars also used in his version of *Ajax*. Cacoyannis had Iphigenia crowned with a floral wreath before her sacrifice, and Akalaitis took this over (and Fugard used a similar wreath of fresh flowers to crown Antigone in my translation performed in Cork in 1999). Akalaitis added red ribbons tied around Iphigenia's arms, suggestive of the blood soon to flow. There was a lot of pop music and gyrations by an active chorus. There were TV interviews of the characters (in character) in the lobby as one entered. One review said this "unilluminating, unmoving, and unentertaining travesty pleased or irritated audiences for a month" (Hischak, *American Theatre*, p. 432). This was more a monument to a director who used a lot of gimmicks than something concerned about original texts or characters that moved audiences.

Bacchae

Euripides' *Bacchae*, like *Antigone, Medea,* and *Trojan Women,* is often used as social and political protest. The Nigerian Nobel Prize winner Wole Soyinka wrote a *Bacchae* (1973) that celebrates freedom after slavery and tyranny. His drama taps into the ritualistic nature of song and dance. African music is used throughout: drums, pipes, and chanting. Dionysus is a source of wine, life, and freedom along with Demeter, who provides grain. It is as if Dionysus represents the spirit, and Demeter, matter. Soyinka explicitly links Dionysus with the ether and inspiration, and freedom is not far behind.

By the end of Soyinka's play the slaves are freed by Dionysus. The leader of the slaves links wine with this freedom: "A scent of freedom is not easily forgotten. Have you ever slept, dreamt, and woken up with the air still perfumed with the fragrance of grapes?" (p. 236). Soyinka uses African dance with its masks to enhance the scene in which the palace is destroyed by Dionysus's earthquake and the scene of Pentheus's *sparagmos,* or ritual rending. He aptly draws a parallel between the symbol of the seat of power, which acts as a prison (the palace), and human power (the king). Both will be shattered by the spirit of revolution inspired by Dionysus.

Soyinka's mother raised him as a Christian, but his grandfather initiated him into the Yoruba religion. He was fascinated by Ogun, a god of war, iron, and fire, with both creative and destructive sides. It is obvious how this god influenced Soyinka's conception of Dionysus. So did the image of the victim-

Bacchae of Euripides: A Communion Rite. Adapted by Wole Soyinka. Tiresias (Julian Curry, left) and Cadmus (Paul Curran) carry the thyrsus (a wand wreathed in ivy and vine-leaves with a pine-cone at the top) in honor of Dionysus as they go to the mountains to join in his rites. The National Theater at the Old Vic (1973). Photo: Anthony Crickmay. Courtesy of the Theatre Museum, Victoria & Albert Museum.

ized and creative Christ, who turned water to wine. Soyinka uses this well in one of the visions he has his Dionysus send Pentheus. The other vision is of a story from Herodotus about Hippoclides dancing away his bride and marriage. Both visions are associated with weddings and their attendant rituals and wine.

The distinction between divine law, or the law of nature, and human law is drawn, just as it is in *Antigone*. Pentheus wants to find out about the Dionysiac religion, and Dionysus mocks his legalistic language: "Will you reduce it all to a court of inquiry? A fact-finding commission such as one might set up to decide the cause of a revolt in your salt-mines, or a slave uprising? These matters are beyond the routine machinery of state" (p. 267).

Racism and the distinction between "civilized" and "barbarian" are stressed. The slaves are of mixed races, and their leader is "fully negroid." When they are ordered by Pentheus to brutalize Teiresias and to destroy his property, they say, "Age is holy / To hit an old man / Or demolish the roof of a sage? / Yet we are the barbarians / And Greece the boast of civilization. / We are slaves and have no souls" (p. 264). The Greeks are identified with "masters" or colonial oppressors who act more barbarically than their slaves. We can find seeds of these thoughts in Euripides' *Bacchae, Medea, Hecuba,* and *Trojan Women.* This Dionysus is more of a magician than in the original, and Pentheus is made to believe he is donning armor rather than the clothes of a bacchante. For Soyinka religion is ecstatic and resembles the mystery cults.

Euripides saw Pentheus as a repressed adolescent, ultimately torn apart by his own prurient desire to spy on the women's orgies. The legend of Actaeon and his *sparagmos*—"tearing apart"—for spying on a goddess and the palace's destruction are warnings that go unheeded. In the final moment before Pentheus is torn apart by his mother, Euripides has him pitifully cry out to her, "Mother spare me; I am / Pentheus, whom you bore in the house of Echion; / pity me and do not slay me for my errors" (lines 1118–20). Soyinka does not include this heartrending moment in his play: although he indicts Dionysus, he also worships him. Euripides experienced brutal irrationality in the Peloponnesian War, a type of civil war where Greek fought Greek. Perhaps his bloodthirsty Dionysus reflects this experience, but I think we have more sympathy for the victims in Euripides than we do in Soyinka's cruel universe. Dionysus also shares the features of Ogun.

There is a ritual use of the victim. Pentheus is sacrificed to the gods for the sake of crops and for human life to go on (for bread and wine). An old slave laments Dionysus's cruelty, "To make a mother rip her son like bread / Across a banqueting board!" (p. 300). At the beginning of the play, Teiresias is beaten, and we are told in the past there have been other human sacrifices. Pentheus also tries to sacrifice Dionysus, but the tables are turned and Pentheus is not only sacrificed but becomes the god.

At the end of Soyinka's play, blood spouts from the wounds in Pentheus's head, and it turns out that the blood is wine. Here we have communion, as Soyinka advertised; in the Christian rite it is explicitly said, "This is my body, and this is my blood," before bread and wine are distributed to the congregation. In the play, wine spurting from the victim's head creates a dual metaphor of blood and wine: "A powerful red glow shines suddenly as if from within the head of Pentheus, rendering it near-luminous. The stage is bathed in it and, instantly, from every orifice of the impaled head spring red jets, spurting in every direction" (p. 307). We think of the blood all too often necessary for revolution and freedom.

Instead of the epiphany of the actual god in Euripides' *Bacchae,* Soyinka leaves us with the final image of his gift, wine, which is also the wine of inspiration. Agave is not punished in the same way as she is in Euripides' play.

Bacchae of Euripides: A Communion Rite. Adapted by Wole Soyinka. Tiresias (Julian Curry) celebrates the communion rite as wine flows from the decapitated head of Pentheus. The National Theater at the Old Vic (1973). Photo: Anthony Crickmay. Courtesy of the Theatre Museum, Victoria & Albert Museum.

At the end she drinks wine rather than reject Dionysus; she accepts communion. This is a study of freedom and religion, different from the tribal warfare that Rotimi showed us in his version of Greek tragedy. Soyinka's poetry shapes much of his drama.

Suzuki's *Bacchae* (1977) also shows the dire effects of tyrannical oppression. *Bacchae* showed people oppressed by a tyrant. They enact *Bacchae* as a sort of catharsis. Pentheus the tyrant is killed and the people rejoice. But Pentheus comes back from the dead, and the cycle repeats itself. Again and again throughout history the tyrant returns.

The chorus of bacchantes (in this case both men and women) move in the way they have been trained, keeping the upper parts of their bodies motionless. Shiraishi's Dionysus here is almost too masculine. He or she confronts Pentheus like a samurai and wins the initial confrontation silently, simply by projecting *ki,* a type of grounded force, from the center of his or her body.

In the 1993 version renamed *Dionysus,* performed in Saratoga, Suzuki represents Dionysus by a group of priests who encircle Pentheus as they kill him. *Dionysus* makes organized religion and the state the villains. Pentheus becomes a victim of Dionysus. Shakespeare is added as a group of people in wheelchairs enters the stage and leaves it reciting the lines from *Macbeth* that begin, "Tomorrow and tomorrow and tomorrow." They are members of the "Farewell to History" cult. One cult replaces another, and we see the individual as victim. Dionysus as group and Pentheus as individual are both deadly. At the end of the play in some performances, the priests advance on the audience in a menacing way.

Michael Cacoyannis's filmed trilogy comprises *Electra* (1961), *Trojan Women* (1971), and *Iphigenia* (1976), all protesting in their own way unjust op-

The Bacchae. Adapted by Tadashi Suzuki. Agave (Shiraishi Kayoto) raises the severed head of her son in triumph; she believes it is the head of a young lion she has just killed. Photo: Furudate Katsuaki. Used by permission.

pression. Mikis Theodorakis composed the music for these films. He also staged his translation of *Bacchae* in New York in 1980. Irene Papas gave a memorable performance as Agave, delivering a bloodcurdling scream when, at the end of the play, she recognizes the head she is carrying as that of her son Pentheus.

Derek Mahon wrote *Bacchae, after Euripides* (1991). It is a shortened version of Euripides' *Bacchae*, from 1392 lines to 1221, written in modern popular language: for instance Dionysus claims, "I'm afraid I've driven those aunties round the bend" (p. 12), in referring to his mother Semele's sisters who were being punished for denying his divinity. When we first meet Pentheus he says, "Oh, for fuck's sake" (p. 17), as he goes on to complain about the orgies in the mountain, just when he'd been "abroad." Mahon uses rhymes, clearly for the god but also in other places, and there does not seem to be a definite rule. I see these rhymes as a type of mask which at times cut down on the directness of the dialogue. In antiquity, rhymes were not a poetic device used in tragedy. Comedy had scatological language, not tragedy, and I find it a bit jarring in some modern Irish reworkings of Greek tragedy. *Bacchae* is not *The Commitments*.

There are references to modern films: "It's still the same old story, / a fight for love and glory" comes from "As Time Goes By" and was used in *Casablanca*, as the song played when Bogart said, "Play it again, Sam" (pp. 41 and 62). The music is equally eclectic, going "from a reflective mood to hard rock, according to the mood of the moment" (p. 13).

The verse:

> What pleases best, what grand
> gift can the gods bestow
> more than the conquering hand
> over the fallen foe? (pp. 41 and 62)

occurs not only where Euripides placed it, but also at the end of Mahon's play. This verse extends the formulaic ending Euripides had (he used it also to end *Andromache, Alcestis, Helen,* and *Medea*)

> The gods have many shapes
> and they bring to pass much that is unhoped for,
> and what was expected did not happen
> but the god found a way for the unexpected.
> So has this thing turned out here. (lines 1388–92)

Mahon changes this to

> Gods come in various shapes
> and act in curious ways;
> neither our fears nor hopes
> work out as we suppose.
> Life is unfair, no doubt,
> and yet the gods demand
> our homage, which is what
> we've tried to demonstrate. (p. 62)

Irish music (céili) and Irish words are used. Agave is said "to keen" (p. 58). Mahon also prizes words, so he has the chorus deliver them speaking in turn and without music.

We have the Catholic God also, and Mahon speaks of "religious faith":

> Gods move at their own pace
> ignoring earthly hours,
> when proud minds race
> in search of godly powers

the gods provide correction
to the vain man who tries
to replace faith with action,
tradition with vanities. (p. 62)

Mahon's version shows the characteristics that distinguish Irish versions of the classics: an Irish use of English; allusions to Irish history; folk sayings; scatological language; humor; sexual explicitness; references to a Christian God; rituals; colloquialisms; a sense of mystery, the inexplicable, and the spiritual; literary allusions and wordplay; repetition of words; rhyme and rhythm; the use of music and song; and in modern versions, references to "ordinary" people and gravitation toward plays which deal with human rights.

I would say the reference to Irish history peeks through in the repetition of the verse about conquering an enemy and in the use of the line "the same old story, a fight for love and glory." These words resonate for a country that is still involved in a struggle, as is the North of Ireland. The "ordinary" people appear in the language which is that of the common man. The mystery is in Dionysus himself and his cult. One might say the human right being defended in this play is freedom to worship. It is not only defended but imposed on Pentheus's city.

It is difficult to reconcile Dionysus with the Christ of Catholicism, but they do have things in common. There was a medieval manuscript, *Christus Patiens* (from about the eleventh century), which mixed Christian texts with lines from *Bacchae*. Both Christ and Dionysus were victims and wanted worship from the common man. Dionysus simply is not as merciful as Christ. If rights are denied, violence can follow. I think Euripides abhorred this violence as much as Heaney did, and very possibly Mahon. But these playwrights know that the existence and power of Dionysus cannot be denied. Mahon gave a close rendering of the play, but I found that the language and pop elements interfered with the elegance of Euripides.

Brian Friel's *Wonderful Tennessee* (1993) is an example of a play loosely based on *Bacchae*. It tells of three couples who are related by birth or marriage who arrive at a dock, waiting for a boat to take them to an island named Oileán Draíochta, "Island of Otherness; Island of Mystery." As most of Friel's plays, this takes place in Ballybeg, Donegal. The ferryman, Carlin (a faintly concealed Charon), never appears. Given the identification, it is probably a good thing he never appears. It is gradually revealed that sometime ago a boy was sacrificed by a group of young people (which totals fourteen, like a Greek chorus without a leader) who had come from a local parish, "just returned from Dublin from the Eucharistic Congress" (p. 63). They dismembered the boy after drinking and dancing to fiddle music. The sacrifice-murder was covered up, and the bishop who had led the group each year organized a pilgrimage to the island. For expiation at the bishop's behest, the thirteen young people went into self-imposed exile in Australia.

In the course of the play various things are revealed about the lives of the people, those who felt useless (Trish's husband, Frank) and those who had succeeded (Angela, a teacher of classics). Frank is writing a book on the history of time. He is a bit like Sir in *Living Quarters,* adding a spiritual element and sense of time, a frequent subject in Friel's plays. Angela is not only an angel but also a type of messenger in this play, helping to define the others and coming to terms with her husband's dying. George, her husband the musician, has a progressive fatal disease, and at the last checkup he is given three months to live.

This was a place where Dionysus could come and bring out not only their spirituality, but also a sense of death and danger that could give more definition to the rest of their lives. Angela says, "Once when the Greek god Dionysus was going to the island of Naxos he was captured by pirates who took him to be a wealthy prince—But suddenly his chains fell away, and vines and ivy sprouted all over the pirate ship, and the sailors were so frightened they jumped into the sea and turned into dolphins" (p. 21). They wonder if they will see dolphins.

This play shows the influence of existentialism and resembles *Waiting for Godot:* they are here waiting for Charon, for death as much as God. They enact a ceremony at the end, which they hear resembles one of the ceremonies enacted on the island. They make a mound of pebbles, like the pebbles that construct so many sacred mounds in Ireland, such as Maeve's, or an ancient burial cairn. They each leave "sacrifices," objects that they owned, and perform a ritual. Terry, whose birthday it is, had put a down payment on the island. When they all leave on the bus that comes for them in the morning, everyone is relieved to hear that Terry says he will let his option expire. They had found what they had come for.

We are also relieved that it is the bus and its driver, Charlie, who comes to pick them up and take them back to familiar surroundings, rather than Carlin-Charon, who would have taken them into the unknown, a site of death. One associates the name Charlie with Charlemagne, a saint. He, and their faith, can drive them to everlasting life in paradise instead of the mysterious dark world of the dead. Throughout secular songs alternated with religious ones, and this plays shows a mixture of an old pagan world with a modern Christian one.

This island is truly a mysterious island, and there are legends about it appearing and disappearing in mist every seven years. Its memory haunted Terry, the man who brought them there. Frank experienced an epiphany. First the legend of Dionysus where he was taken prisoner and turned the sailors into dolphins is told. Dolphins are associated with this mysterious island, and a dolphin dances for Frank:

Just as the last wisp of the veil was melting away, suddenly—as if it had been waiting for a sign—suddenly a dolphin rose up out of the sea. And for thirty seconds, maybe a minute, it danced for me. Like a faun, a satyr; with its manic, leering face. Danced with a deliberate, controlled, exquisite abandon. Leaping, twisting, tumbling, gyrating in wild and intricate contortions. And for that thirty seconds, maybe a minute, I could swear it never once touched the water— was free of it—had nothing to do with water. A performance—that's what it was. A performance so considered, so aware, that you knew it knew it was being witnessed; wanted to be witnessed. Thrilling; and wonderful; and at the same time —I don't know why—at the same time . . . with that manic, leering face . . . somehow very disturbing. (p. 59)

Frank has just seen a performance by Dionysus, or at least by one of the pirates he turned into a dolphin.

The group speaks of monks, and monks were classicists, part of the Irish who saved civilization (see Thomas Cahill's *How the Irish Saved Civilization*). These monks "were always seeing apparitions." Frank told Terry, "Be careful at matins—that's just before dawn. That's when you're most susceptible." He spoke about the island, calling it "the wonderful, the mystery." He spoke of the people who saw it: "They had their own way of dealing with it: they embraced it all—everything. Yes, yes, yes, they said; why bloody not? A rage for the absolute . . . maybe they *were* put in touch—what do you think?—so intimately in touch that maybe, maybe they actually *did* see" (pp. 40–41).

This play has elements that we find in Friel's *Faith Healer* and *Dancing at Lughnasa* with its respect for the supernatural and rituals. One never knows what is real or what is imagined, but at times there is a sense of terror. What Friel does is put us in touch with a primitive past where everything can be a god and have a mystery. It is also, as Frank says, "disturbing" (p. 59). This is not a benign Christian theocracy but rather a pantheon of spirits, and some could kill, seemingly without reason. It touches on the haunting prospect that everyone has to face death. And death can come without warning. George is the Orpheus figure and likewise soon to die. Orpheus also suffered a *sparagmos,* "a rending," at the hands of women. A legend tells us that Dionysus (Zagreus) himself was torn apart by the Titans and revived only because his heart remained. Lycurgus suffered a *sparagmos* like Pentheus and Actaeon did; the message is clear: accept Dionysus or be torn apart.

Likewise Terry, who brought this party to this island because of his childhood memories, is rent apart by his wife Berna, who has bouts of mental illness. She dives into the water at the end of act 1, and we are at first in doubt as to whether she is committing suicide, but it turns out to be more of a baptism. Swimming, along with drink, and music are other methods for approaching the ineffable. Terry must always mix his drink with water, a dilution for sanity and perhaps the antidote of baptism and a sane Christianity, in contrast to the wild pagan world, full of gods and danger, full of Dionysus. He had the memory of his father "filling a bottle with holy water" from a holy well on the island (p. 19). Both use grass as a stopper for bottles. Dionysus is juxtaposed to Christ, and when the group speaks of Poitín being made on the island, they invoke St. Dionysus.

Dionysus is the god of theater and wine, and his followers join to form a *thiasos,* or sacred band. This group has done the same. They make a scarecrow with Terry's clothes, so in a sense a "dressing scene," comparable to Dionysus dressing Pentheus, occurs here. The group forcibly tears the shirt off Terry in a ritual *sparagmos.* The scarecrow is a type of scapegoat, another offering in lieu of the humans. They leave the island with more insights, with both the anagnorisis and the catharsis offered by Greek drama. There was a spiritual acknowledgment of the mystery, and we can call their passing the night on the shore a ritual. They are mentally and spiritually renewed, as is the audience by seeing the play.

George has come to terms with his death and asks Angela to return one day, "in memory of me." She is truly his angel, his guide through his difficult passage from life to death.

On February 6, 1993, in Los Angeles, the Taper Lab presented Charles L. Mee's adaptation of Euripides' *Bacchae.* This ancient Greek masterpiece has been reshaped as a Freudian nightmare, but the result is still true to Euripides' fundamental questions about identity: the opposition between male and female is not resolved and therefore leads to tragedy. Dionysus in this play represents the ambiguous: the female in every male and the male in every female. If any part of one's nature is repressed, it will break free as easily as Dionysus breaks out of the prison where Pentheus, the king of Thebes, tries to contain him. Somehow male must be reconciled with female, rational with irrational, or chaos will ensue. As Mee's Teiresias puts it:

> There is a gentler way
> to come by the truth of life;
> but having resisted that
> we've had it brought home to us
> with a vengeance.
> (http://www.panix.com/~meejr/html/bacchae2.1.html)

Mee has made many changes which still underline some of the original themes. He has Dionysus as clearly feminine at the beginning, but then he changes his flowing clothing for black pants and a leather jacket at the same time as Pentheus puts on the white robe of a woman. Mee also has replaced the messenger speech about Pentheus's death by showing Pentheus join the women in the mountains and speak with them before he is discovered. The women are not simply Euripides' Asian bacchants and women of the city; rather, they represent the cultures of the world—Asian, black, and Hispanic as well as Caucasian. The women are inclusive, whereas the men are seen to be exclusive. Both groups express their violence toward each other and toward themselves. This is a play of suffering and created pain. Part of the pain is the lack of communication and the misunderstanding between the two groups. The men and women misunderstand each other as much as Pentheus misunderstands Dionysus. The audience shares in the tragic recognition: both seeming opposites are so very similar.

One difference mars the production. Agave and her followers are shown as man-hating, vicious women, and killing Pentheus is what one would expect from them. One has no sympathy for Agave. Mee arouses sympathy for Pentheus, one key message from the original, but none for the bereaved mother.

Orestes

"It's a nightmare, really." Characters intone this phrase several times during Charles L. Mee's reenactment of Euripides' *Orestes*. Mee's version illustrates the chaos of modern times by way of the ancient Greek myth.

Anne Bogart's direction of Charles Mee's *Orestes* in Saratoga, fall 1992, breaks the barriers between stage and audience: actors and actresses freely walk in the audience area. Past violence mingles with present violence, and the stage shows us victims of the Persian Gulf War in a hospital set in front of the White House. Orestes is one of the victims, and we see how suffering brutalizes. He victimizes others by the end of the play, and we see that such role reversals are merely based on opportunity. Iraq, Bosnia, Somalia, and Los Angeles come to mind, and the generalizations of Greek tragedy are often more revealing than the particulars from the six o'clock news.

Mee vividly replicates the chaos of the ancient world by drawing parallels with the modern world. He also speaks in brutally explicit language, the language of *The Godfather* and *The Terminator* rather than media-speak. He has made Euripides into Seneca, a drama which shocks, criticizes, and rehearses trauma in a cathartic way and keeps one riveted to the seat while delivering savage and yet satisfying blows. The nightmare is made flesh.

His drama has had two stagings before Bogart's, one by Tina Landau and another by Robert Woodruff, both early in 1992. Woodruff replicated the chaos manifested by the words and the audience had to follow multiple actions at once. The rain scene from Götz Friedrich's production of Richard Strauss's

Elektra, in which Elektra danced herself to death, was seen at the back of the stage while other actions were going on in at least four different places onstage. The violently explicit text was expanded by the visual to include an anal violation of Pylades by Electra wearing a dildo. The whole work concluded with Apollo talking from multiple TV screens. People enter and leave and then repeat their actions, and loud noises punctuate the action. This production was a symphony of chaos, comparable to Schoenberg's twelve-tone system playing itself out and repeating itself. No eighteenth-century harmony here. The audience was assaulted by images and sound; nothing resembled a linear plot or even Mee's play. By eliminating most of the text, Woodruff made violence boring.

Anne Bogart's production is very different. It allows chaos to appear in a more controlled setting and performance, which makes it even more terrifying by implicating the audience in the brutal message. The audience is rarely required to sort out multiple texts, except in the trial scene, which because of its rigid formalism shows the failure of the legal process to produce justice. The suggestion seems to be that he who shouts loudest carries the day. This was what probably happened during meetings in the Athens of Euripides' time. The democratic restoration, following the oligarchic takeover in 411 B.C., was filled with abuses. Orestes also represents the nobility, so there is a fitting parallel in that it is a man of the people who secures his condemnation. Orestes in the play shows that mob violence can be practiced on the aristocratic scale: all he needed was a few friends to wreak havoc. We hear about Orestes' careless brutalities and rapes, and one easily sees the modern parallels.

The set in the Saratoga production (fall 1992) is simple, suggesting a hospital, with a long diagonal pipe set against a rather dismal green wall. Beds are swung around the stage, and props are provided as necessary (e.g., a large pan to bathe Orestes, a long table for the trial scene, a table for the nurses as they play cards). The items on the set seem as disposable as the human beings.

Mee has brought the ancient myth into modern times against a backdrop of war and its idiocies. The characters are seen as patients, interacting with a staff of nurses. Some characters are added, and we are jarred by their modern names. A general comes and goes (Menelaus); we are told he is seeking a political position (to rule in Sparta) which he will hardly compromise by defending his unpopular nephew. We also see Electra, Helen, and a literal doll of Hermione. Electra and Helen are dressed in Armani and Chanel, and Helen speaks of her cosmetic preparations for the day. Pylades joins this yuppie crowd in dress and morality. He is definitely upwardly mobile, willing to do anything, including murder, to get what he wants. Mee allows for the possibility that all the characters coming and going are hallucinations.

Mee has Pylades, instead of Electra, come up with the suggestion of taking Hermione hostage. Euripides gives a simple twist to the basic story of Electra and Orestes killing their mother in retribution for Clytemnestra's killing her husband and their father by their taking Hermione prisoner; now Mee shows Orestes, Electra, and Pylades all prepared to kill gratuitously, simply so that Menelaus will suffer the way they are suffering. After they have decided to act, they become hyped by the realization that they have reached the point of no return; like Thelma and Louise, they relish their extraordinary power and freedom even more because they cannot retreat.

Mee adds various characters to the play. John and William are both war victims who are haunted by the violence of their past, and Nod is one who still revels in it. There is a man whose mouth is taped but untaped at intervals. He goes into the history of violence, beginning with Homer and ending with the messages of war written into the bodies of moderns. This character is eliminated: killed onstage, typically by Nod. Nod is associated with violence: "And Cain went out from the presence of the Lord, and dwelt in the land of Nod, on the east of Eden" (*Gen.* 4.16, King James Version)

Tape-mouth man functions rather like Teiresias, a prophet who not only tells of the disasters of the future, but who also shows their intimate connection with the past. He has the only poetic and hopeful lines in the text:

> The imagination
> is less a separate faculty
> than a quality of all our mental faculties . . .
>
> It sees the residues,
> the memories, and the reports of past or faraway social worlds and of
>   neglected or
>   obscure perceptions
> as the main stuff with which we remake our contexts.
> It explains the operation of a social order
> by representing our ideas.
> It generalizes our ideas
> by tracing a penumbra of remembered of intimated possibility around
>   present or past
>   settlements.
> By all these means
> it undermines
> the identification of the actual
> with the possible. (http://www.panix.com/~meejr/html/orestes.html)

He speaks of a way of making a better future, an ethical revolution. He must be silenced. By untaping and taping his mouth he is like Lucky in *Waiting for Godot*, called to perform on command.

Orestes and Pylades are clearly yuppies. Orestes' vulnerability is conveyed not only through the ancient text, which showed him as a haunted neurotic, too willing to follow his criminal friends, but also by costuming and actions. Orestes is bathed onstage, which can remind one of rituals to prepare a victim. Then his hospital gown is exchanged for a suit (from Agnès B. conservative), which functions as a double type of costume (in the play we are watching, and for Orestes as he goes to the "play" of his trial). When he hears the verdict he urinates on the stage, flooding it with his fear. Bogart has him assume a fetal position and suck his thumb. His hallucinations range from killing a date to killing his mother.

Electra's only saving grace is her loyalty to Orestes; she also discourses on the advantages of euthanasia, prostitution, and terrorism with a frightening detachment. Her social ideology is typical of the armchair liberal. Although one might agree with her arguments, we have to see her comments in the context of her final actions (attempted murder, arson, kidnapping, etc.). Helen is the vain and silly creature she was in Euripides. Hermione in this production is even without life (she first appears as a doll on a tricycle), like the daughter, Victoria, in the first act of Caryl Churchill's *Cloud Nine:* she also appears as a doll.

Tyndareus is the legalistic pedant as in Euripides. He discourses further on language, so the letter of the law is seen as merely letter in this drama. We agree with what Tyndareus says, "And yet, one can commit murder and find the words to justify it. This is your sort of civilization, then, it speaks nicely and behaves barbarously." It is a telling commentary on our times. Tyndareus is another prophet who comes and goes and affects nothing. The guilty verdict merely coincides with his wishes; it is not based on the points he made. This is now a world of chance and Tyndareus is an anachronism (the *Oresteia* has become *Orestes,* as the general becomes all too particular).

The Phrygian slave is still here, to allow Orestes a moment of brutal mental torture such as he displayed in the original. Now, as then, Orestes is the imperialist master, taunting the slave with the servility that functions only as his means for his survival.

In addition to the other characters who have been added, there is Farley the astrologer, the nurses, a radio voice (that announces the arrival of Menelaus), and a doctor who begins the play with a recitation of facts from an autopsy on a murdered woman. Clytemnestra has been reduced to a body with "no abdominal abnormalities or complications of the genito-urinary system."

Nurses, dressed in black, are benign Furies. They discuss their love life as Orestes' trial is going on. The personal is played against the public, and neither is given priority. This seems to be a world without values and without emotion. Bogart was influenced by Ken Kesey's depiction of Nurse Ratched, the big nurse in *One Flew over the Cuckoo's Nest.* Bogart duplicates the underlying current of sadism in the actions of the nurses. In both the novel and this play the nurses' reaction to minor infractions of their rules is to administer a sedative. Control is more important than cure, something our society learned early on.

The other stand-ins for the Furies are Orestes' companions in the hospital:

NOD: Sluts
MENELAUS: What's this?
JOHN: The sluts!
MENELAUS: Who are these people?
ORESTES: These are my fellows. You may speak in front of them just as you would speak to me in private.
MENELAUS: So these Furies pursue you.

These Furies have their own nightmares from the tortures they have inflicted and the tortures they have suffered. There are not only the public pains they have inflicted and suffered in the context of war and politics, but also the personal ones from madness and vengeance. John killed his sister, her husband, and his nephew. Orestes killed his date. Nod tells us of the serial murderer who collected various female parts, including peeled skin that he could wear. We are back in modern times with memories of Jeffrey Dahmer and *The Silence of the Lambs* (1990), another topical drama of modern violence.

From the horror of pain, we fly into the narcotic illusion of the gods: the television talk show. Apollo comes on with a microphone like a game show host to sort out who wins what. The prizes are as hollow and ephemeral as his own appearance. Bogart shows him as an electric robot whose batteries run down. He is carried offstage. Mee gives the following stage instructions: "Apollo's voice continues to be miked so that he can speak very quietly, Reagan-like, and his voice still fills the theatre." The artifice that controls our life is revealed to be as hollow as the blustering Wizard of Oz. The difference is that nightmare ended; ours does not.

We see we are still in the hospital and what we have just seen was merely an interlude. Perhaps the whole play was a TV sitcom by Euripides. Bogart has done comparable framings, such as *On the Town* being staged as a diversion for sailors on an aircraft carrier to allay their fears as they sail to war, or *South Pacific* staged in a rehabilitation clinic.

The play ends with William musing, "Every man must shout: 'There's a great destructive work to be done. We're doing it.'" The brutalized have learned the lesson: "What we need now are some strong, straightforward actions that you'd have to be a fool not to learn the wrong lessons from it." This is nightmare and criminal mania urged as sane practice. The nurse urges sleep, claiming, "We're finished." William says, "Thank you." This is the sleep of death, and at this point we can be thankful for death, if life is really like what we have just seen. Euripides ended this play with a prayer to Nike, victory, an ostensible plea for his play to win a prize. Yet his victory is as ironic as William's sleep. It anticipates the hollow victory of the Peloponnesian War and all the victories that Euripides had witnessed, victories that are generally indictments of the victors. We are the hollow men.

All of Mee's plays speak of pain and suffering. This play seems to make a fetish of violence, both mental and physical. It speaks of the violence that has engraved its message on the mind. We feel brutalized after seeing this and being assaulted by the language. But how can we be less assaulted by the daily news? The exponential damage our technology can effect in modern times is translated into this drama of modern victims turning victimizers. Mee also captures the fragmentation of modern life well. Mee has taken the domestic violence of Greek myth and tragedy and put it in a context of collective, political atrocities, so that matricide, which traditionally has shocked us, seems tame by comparison. This shows us how far we have come.

Euripides takes a giant step away from the other playwrights with his making the idea of neurosis explicit. The squalor of domestic crime is another theme in this work. Then there are the mass murders and political crimes that his various characters commit. The final theme is murder for the sake of murder, on both the individual and mass basis. Our categories proceed from the particular to the general, and from ethical to random killings. Perhaps we can see ethical killing as divinely inspired and random killing as all too human. Or perhaps we can see ethical killing as an oxymoron. I would hope this is Mee's intent. He shows that institutionalized violence and the torture of political prisoners worldwide are also not to be explained away with a simple, "My superiors made me do it." Does man like to torture, maim, and rape? I think Mee confronts us and urges us to raise these questions.

The parallel between our modern "authorized" terrorists (soldiers) and Orestes is made problematic; both have committed crimes on orders, and both will be rehabilitated. I claim that Euripides and Mee are showing us a nightmare that will haunt us, not an action-packed thriller to entertain us for a moment and to be forgotten tomorrow.

Anne Bogart's rendering of both the ancient and the modern text directly implicates us, the audience. She trains her actors and actresses with a rigorous physical program that makes them acutely aware of space, the movement of their bodies and their relation to each other and the audience. As the characters wander in and out of our space we see ourselves as victims like them. We feel that we are in a hospital in front of the White House, listening to our nurses gossip. Are the mouths of Plato and Aristotle bandaged? Perverted mania can only be hospitalized, and it is only a matter of time until the inmates burn the hospital, as Orestes burned Menelaus's palace. This is a parable for our times.

Both *Medea* and *Bacchae* provide popular themes for twentieth-century opera and even musicals: *Dionysus in 69* (with strong erotic and political themes, directed by Richard Shechner and made into a film by Brian De Palma, Robert Fiore, and Bruce Rubin); John Fisher's *Medea, the Musical* (1995); and Michael John LaChiusa's *Marie Christine* (1999).

Conclusion

We learn more about daily events from these classics than we do from any news broadcast. This is also theater that makes us think and use our minds as they should be used.

> What is a man,
> If his chief good and market of his time
> Be but to sleep and feed? A beast, no more.
> Sure, he that made us with such large discourse,
> Looking before and after, gave us not
> That capability and god-like reason
> To fust in us unused. (*Hamlet* 4.4.33–39)

Greek tragedy engages our intellect and tells us about the world we live in. We see vengeance that succeeds and the suffering of the victims. Then one must live with the knowledge of what one has done. Some call this conscience. Human beings are shown as capable of the greatest good and the greatest evil. Greek tragedy asks us what kind of a life we want to live.

Greek tragedy gives us tools for living. It shows us how the unexamined life is not worth living. Friedrich Hölderlin said that many try to express happiness in terms of happiness, but he has found that it is expressed best in tragedy. Greek tragedy offers us the keys to a better life. That is why we need it now more than ever.

The most open-ended source for music is the score; multiple performances are only limited by the human imagination. So also the text of a play is primary, but it is lifeless without performance.

Performance is the key. A Greek tragedy only begins to live once it has left the page. The characters walk on the stage before us, and their words are unforgettable. They weave the spell that all great dramatic poetry does. We are better and happier because of it.

SUGGESTED READING AND REFERENCES

The standard Greek texts in Greek are

Aeschylus
Page, Denys, ed. *Aeschyli septem quae supersunt tragoediae.* Oxford: Clarendon Press, 1972.

Sophocles
Lloyd-Jones, H., and N. G. Wilson, eds. *Sophoclis Fabulae.* 1990. Reprint with corrections, Oxford: Clarendon Press, 1992.

Euripides
Diggle, James, ed. *Euripidis Fabulae.* 3 vols. Oxford: Clarendon Press, 1984–94.

The standard edition of the fragments of Greek Tragedy is
Snell, B., R. Kannicht, and S. Radt, eds. *Tragicorum Graecorum Fragmenta.* Göttingen: Vandenhoeck u. Ruprecht, 1971–.

The main fragments are collected in
Diggle, James, ed. *Tragicorum Graecorum Fragmenta Selecta.* Oxford: Clarendon Press, 1998.

A Selection of Translations of the Extant Tragedies
Everyman Series (Dent): selected volumes of tragedies. http://www.everymanbooks.com/
Grene, D., and R. Lattimore. *The Complete Greek Tragedies.* Chicago: University of Chicago Press, 1942–68. http://www.press.uchicago.edu

Nick Hern Books, Drama Classics, London. http://www.nickhernbooks.co.uk
Penguin Classics: selected volumes of tragedies and comedies by all five Greek play-
    wrights. http://www.penguinclassics.com
Walton, J. Michael, ed. *Classical Greek Dramatists.* All forty-six Greek tragedies and come-
    dies in 13 volumes. London: Methuen, 1988–2000. http://www.methuen.co.uk

A Brief Selection of Suggested Reading besides References
The Agamemnon of Aeschylus. Translated by Louis MacNeice. London: Faber and Faber,
    1936.
Anouilh, Jean. *Five Plays: Antigone, Eurydice, The Ermine, The Rehearsal, Romeo and
    Jeannette.* New York: Hill and Wang, 1958.
———. *Medea,* in *Five Plays: The Modern Theatre.* Edited by Eric Bentley and trans-
    lated by Luce Klein and Arthur Klein. 1957. Reprint, Gloucester, Mass.: Peter
    Smith, 1978.
———. *Médée.* Paris: La Table Ronde, 1946.
———. *Oedipe, ou Le roi boiteux, d'après Sophocle.* Paris: La Table Ronde, 1986.
———. *Pièces secrètes.* Paris: La Table Ronde, 1977.
———. *Tu étais si gentil quand tu étais petit.* Paris: La Table Ronde, 1972.
Aristophanes. *The Comedies of Aristophanes: Frogs.* Edited, translated, and annotated
    by Alan H. Sommerstein. Vol. 9. Warminster, England: Aris and Phillips, 1996.
Aristotle. *The Complete Works of Aristotle:* Revised Oxford Translation. Edited by
    Jonathan Barnes. Vols. 1 and 2. Bollingen Series 71.2. 1984. Reprint, Princeton:
    Princeton University Press, 1985.
Arnott, P. D. *Public and Performance in Ancient Greece.* London: Routledge, 1989.
Athenaeus. *The Deipnosophists.* Vol. 4. Translated by Charles Burton Gulick. Loeb Clas-
    sical Library. Cambridge: Harvard University Press, 1969.
Auletta, Robert. *Aeschylus, The Persians: A Modern Version.* Introduction by Peter Sel-
    lars. Los Angeles: Sun and Moon Press, 1993.
Berkoff, Steven. *Agamemnon and The Fall of the House of Usher.* 1977. Reprint, Oxford:
    Amber Lane, 1996.
———. *Decadence and Greek.* London: John Calder, 1982.
———. *Free Association: An Autobiography.* London and Boston: Faber and Faber, 1996.
———. *The Theatre of Steven Berkoff.* London: Methuen, 1992.
Bond, Edward. *The Woman.* Woodstock, Ill.: Dramatic Publishing Company, 1981.
Brathwaite, Kamau. *Odale's Choice.* 1967. Reprint, London: Evans Brothers, 1993.
Brecht, Bertolt. *Antigone: A Version.* Based on the German translation by Friedrich
    Hölderlin. Translated by Judith Malina. New York: Applause, 1984.
———. *Brecht on Theatre: The Development of an Aesthetic.* Edited and translated by
    John Willett. 1957. Reprint, New York: Hill and Wang, 1992.
Breuer, Lee. *The Gospel at Colonus: An Adaptation.* 1983. Reprint, New York: Theatre
    Communications Group, 1989.
Butler, Guy. *Demea.* Cape Town and Johannesburg: David Philip, 1990.
Cahill, Thomas. *How the Irish Saved Civilization: The Untold Story of Ireland's Heroic
    Role from the Fall of Rome to the Rise of Medieval Europe.* New York, London,
    Toronto, Sydney: Doubleday, 1995.
Carr, Marina. *Plays: Low in the Dark, The Mai, Portia Coughlan, By the Bog of Cats. . . .*
    Vol. 1. London: Faber and Faber, 1991.
Cocteau, Jean. *Antigone, suivi de les mariés de la Tour Eiffel.* Paris: Gallimard, 1948.
———. *The Infernal Machine and Other Plays.* 1963. Reprint, New York: New Direc-
    tions, 1967.

Conacher, D. J. *Euripidean Drama, Myth, Theme and Structure*. London: Oxford University Press, 1967.

Corneille, Pierre. *Oedipe, Andromède, La conquête de la toison d'or*, in *Corneille Théâtre*. Text established and annotated by Pierre Lièvre. Vol 2. Paris: La Pléiade, 1934.

——. *Théâtre*. Vol. 2, *Clitandre, Médée, Le Cid, Horace, Cinna, Polyeucte, La mort de Pompée*. Edited by Jacques Maurens. Paris: Flammarion, 1980.

Corneille, Thomas. *Médée* (1693). Libretto for Marc-Antoine Charpentier's *Médée*. Directed by William Christie. Paris: Les Arts Florissants, 1983.

Doolittle, Hilda (H. D.). *Collected Poems, 1912–1944*. 1983. Reprint, New York: New Directions, 1986.

——. *Hippolytus Temporizes*. Boston and New York: Houghton Mifflin Co., 1927.

——. *Ion, A Play after Euripides*. 1937. Reprint with unpublished additions, Redding Ridge, Conn.: Black Swan Books, 1986.

Dove, Rita. *The Darker Face of the Earth*. 1994. Reprint, London: Oberon, 1996.

Easterling, P. E., ed. *The Cambridge Companion to Greek Tragedy*. Cambridge: Cambridge University Press, 1997.

Eliot, T. S. *The Complete Poems and Plays, 1909–1950*. 1950. Reprint, San Diego, New York, London: Harcourt Brace Jovanovich, 1967.

——. *The Confidential Clerk*. 1952. Reprint, San Diego, New York, London: Harcourt Brace Jovanovich, 1982

——. *The Elder Statesman*. New York: Farrar, Straus and Cudahy, 1959.

Euripides. *Andromache*. Translated and introduction by Marianne McDonald and J. Michael Walton. London: Nick Hern Books, 2001. http://www.nickhernbooks.co.uk

——. *Euripides, Trojan Women*. Translated by Marianne McDonald. *Six Greek Tragedies by Aeschylus/Sophocles/Euripides*. Edited and with an introduction by Marianne McDonald and Michael Walton. London: Methuen, 2002.

——. *Medea*. Translated by Alistair Elliot. 1993. Reprint, London: Oberon, 1997.

——. *The Plays of Euripides*. Vol. 2. Translated and introduction by Gilbert Murray. London: George Allen, 1914.

Falb, Lewis W. *Jean Anouilh*. New York: Frederick Ungar, 1977.

Fanon, Frantz. *The Wretched of the Earth*. Translated by Constance Farrington, with an introduction by Jean-Paul Sartre. New York: Grove Press, 1963.

Friel, Brian. *Selected Plays: Philadelphia, Here I Come! The Freedom of the City, Living Quarters, Aristocrats, Faith Healer, Translations*. Introduction by Seamus Deane. London: Faber and Faber, 1984.

——. *Wonderful Tennessee*. London: Faber and Faber, 1993.

Fugard, Athol. *Notebooks, 1960–1977*. New York: Theatre Communications Group, 1984.

——. *The Township Plays: No-Good Friday, Nongogo, The Coat, Sizwe Bansi Is Dead, The Island*. Oxford: Oxford University Press, 1993.

Gide, Andre. *Two Legends: Oedipus and Theseus*. Translated by John Russell. New York: Vintage, 1958.

Gilbert, Helen, and Joanne Tompkins. *Post-colonial Drama: Theory, Practice, Politics*. London and New York: Routledge, 1996.

Giraudoux, Jean. *Électre*. Paris: Bernard Grasset, 1937.

——. *Tiger at the Gates, Duel of Angels, Judith*. Translated by Christopher Fry. New York: Oxford University Press, 1963.

Goethe, Johann Wolfgang von. *Iphigenia in Tauris*. Translated by Charles E. Passage. 1963. Reprint, Prospect Heights, Ill. Waveland Press, 1991.

——. *Iphigenia in Tauris*. In *The Collected Works: Verse Plays and Epic*. Vol. 8. Edited by Cyrus Hamlin and Frank Ryder and translated by David Luke. Princeton: Princeton University Press, 1995.

———. *Prometheus.* In *The Collected Works: Verse Plays and Epic.* Vol. 7. Edited by Cyrus Hamlin and Frank Ryder and translated by David Luke. Princeton: Princeton University Press, 1995.

Green, J. R. *Theatre in Ancient Greek Society.* London: Routledge, 1994.

Grillparzer, Franz. *Medea, The Golden Fieece.* Translated by Arthur Burkhard. Yarmouthport, Mass.: Register Press, 1941.

Gurney, A. R. *The Cocktail Hour, and Two Other Plays: Another Antigone, and The Perfect Party.* New York: New American Library, 1989.

Halleran, M. R., *Stagecraft in Euripides.* London: Croom Helm, 1985.

Harrington, John. *Aeschylus.* New Haven, London: Yale University Press, 1986. Harrison, Tony. *Dramatic Verse, 1973–1985.* Newcastle upon Tyne, England: Bloodaxe, 1985.

———. *The Trackers of Oxyrhynchus.* London, Boston: Faber and Faber, 1990.

Heaney, Seamus. *The Cure at Troy, after Philoctetes by Sophocles.* Derry: Field Day, 1990.

Hegel, Georg. *Hegel on Tragedy.* Edited, translated, and introduced by Anne and Henry Paolucci. Westport, Conn.: Greenwood Press, 1962.

Hischak, Thomas S. *American Theatre: A Chronicle of Comedy and Drama, 1969–2000.* Oxford: Oxford University Press, 2001.

Hofmannsthal, Hugo von. *Electra.* Translated by Arthur Symons. New York: Brentano's, 1908.

Hölderlin, Friedrich. *Antigonae/Antigone.* Steinbach, Giessen: Günter Kämpf, 1969.

Homer. *Homer, The Odyssey.* Translated by Robert Fagles and introduced by Bernard Knox. New York: Viking Penguin, 1996.

———. *The Iliad of Homer.* Translated and with an introduction by Richmond Lattimore. Chicago: University of Chicago Press, 1951.

Hughes, Ted. *Aeschylus, The Oresteia: A New Translation.* New York: Farrar, Straus and Giroux, 1999.

———. *Euripides Alcestis: A Version.* London: Faber and Faber, 1999.

———. *Jean Racine. Phèdre: A New Version.* London: Faber and Faber, 1998.

———. *Seneca's Oedipus* (adapted). 1969. Reprint, London: Faber and Faber, 1983.

Jeffers, Robinson. *Cawdor and Medea.* 1928. Reprint, New York: New Directions, 1970.

Kallich, Martin, Andrew MacLeish, and Gertrude Schoenbohm, eds. and trans. *Oedipus: Myth and Drama: Oedipus the King,* by Sophocles, *Oedipus,* by John Dryden and Nathaniel Lee, and *Oedipus and the Sphinx,* by Hugo von Hofmannsthal. New York: Odyssey Press, 1968.

Kane, Sarah. *Compete Plays: Blasted, Phaedra's Love, Cleansed, Crave, 4.48 Psychosis, Skin.* Introduction by David Greig. London: Methuen, 1996.

Kennelly, Brendan. *Euripides' Medea: A New Version.* 1988. Reprint, Newcastle upon Tyne, England: Bloodaxe, 1991.

———. *Sophocles' Antigone: A New Version.* 1986. Reprint, Newcastle upon Tyne, England: Bloodaxe, 1996.

———. *The Trojan Women: A New Version.* Newcastle upon Tyne, England: Bloodaxe, 1993.

Knox, Bernard M. W. *The Heroic Temper: Studies in Sophoclean Tragedy.* Sather Classical Lectures. Berkeley and Los Angeles: University of California Press, 1966.

———. *Word and Action: Essays on Ancient Theater.* Baltimore: Johns Hopkins University Press, 1979.

Longinus. *On the Sublime.* Translated and with an introduction by A. O. Prickard. Oxford: Clarendon Press, 1906.

——. *On the Sublime.* Translated by W. Rhys Roberts. Cambridge: Cambridge University Press, 1899. Scanned and edited by Agathon for Peitho's web: http://classicpersuasion.org/pw/longinus/desub001.htm

Mahon, Derek. *The Bacchae, after Euripides.* Loughcrew, Oldcastle, County Meath, Ireland: Gallery Press, 1991.

——. *Racine's Phaedra.* Oldcastle, County Meath: Gallery Press, 1996.

Mandel, Oscar. *Philoctetes and The Fall of Troy: Plays, Documents, Iconography, Interpretations, Including Versions by Sophocles, André Gide, Oscar Mandel, and Heiner Müller.* Lincoln: University of Nebraska Press, 1981.

McDonald, Marianne. *Ancient Sun, Modern Light: Greek Drama on the Modern Stage.* New York: Columbia University Press, 1992.

——. *Euripides in Cinema: The Heart Made Visible.* Philadelphia: Centrum, 1983.

——. *Sing Sorrow: Classics, History and Heroines in Opera.* Westport, Conn.: Greenwood, 2001.

McDonald, Marianne, and J. Michael Walton, eds. *Amid Our Troubles: Irish Versions of Greek Tragedy.* London: Methuen, 2002.

McGuinness, Frank. *Sophocles' Electra: A New Version.* London, Boston: Faber and Faber, 1997.

Mee, Charles L., Jr. http://www.panix.com/~meejr/html/agamemnon.html

——. http://www.panix.com/~meejr/html/orestes.html

——. http://www.panix.com/~meejr/html/bacchae2.1.html

——. http://www.panix.com/~meejr/html/trojan.html

——. http://www.panix.com/~meejr/html/big_love.html

——. http://www.panix.com/~meejr/html/truelove.html

Müller, Heiner. *Hamlet-Machine and Other Texts for the Stage.* Edited and translated by Carl Weber. New York: Performing Arts Journal, 1984.

——. *Heiner Müller Reader: Plays/Poetry/Prose.* Edited and translated by Carl Weber, with a foreword by Tony Kushner. Baltimore and London: Johns Hopkins University Press, 2001.

——. *La mission, Prométhée, Vie de Grundling, Quartett.* Paris: Les éditions de minuit, 1982.

Murray, T. C. *Selected Plays: Sovereign Love, Birthright, Maurice Harte, The Briery Gap, Autumn Fire, The Pipe in the Fields.* Irish Drama Selections 10. Introduction and selections made by Richard Allen Cave. Gerrards Cross, Bucks., Ireland: Colin Smyth, 1998.

O'Neill, Eugene. *Complete Plays.* 3 vols., *1913–1920, 1920–1931, 1932–1942.* 1984. Reprint, New York: Library of America, 1988.

——. *Three Plays: Desire under the Elms, Strange Interlude, Mourning Becomes Electra.* New York: Vintage, Random House, 1924, 1928, and 1931.

Paulin, Tom. *The Riot Act, A Version of Antigone by Sophocles.* London, Boston: Faber and Faber, 1985.

——. *Seize the Fire: A Version of Aeschylus's Prometheus Bound.* London, Boston: Faber and Faber, 1990.

Pound, Ezra. *Sophokles, Women of Trachis.* New York: New Directions, 1957.

Racine, Jean Baptiste. *Oeuvres completes: La Thébaide, ou les frères ennemis, Alexandre le Grand, Andromaque, Les plaideurs, Britannicus, Bérénice, Bajazet, Mithridate, Iphigénie en Aulides, Phèdres, Esther, Athalie.* Paris: Éditions du Seuil, 1962.

——. *Racine: Phaedra, Andromache, Berenice, Athaliah, Brittanicus.* Translated by Kenneth Muir. New York: Hill and Wang, 1960.

Reinhardt, Karl. *Sophocles.* Translated by Hazel Harvey and David Harvey. New York: Barnes and Noble, 1979.

Rosenmeyer, Thomas. *The Art of Aeschylus*. Berkeley and Los Angeles: University of California Press, 1982.

———. *The Masks of Tragedy: Essays on Six Greek Dramas*. New York: Gordian Press, 1971.

Rotimi, Ola. *The Gods Are Not to Blame*. 1971. Reprint, Oxford: Oxford University Press, 1996.

Said, Edward. *Culture and Imperialism*. New York, Knopf, 1993.

Sappho. *Poetarum Lesbiorum Fragmenta*. Edited by Edgar Lobel and Denys Page. 1955. Reprint, Oxford: Clarendon Press, 1968.

Sartre, Jean-Paul. *Sartre on Theatre*. Edited, introduced, and annotated by Michel Contat and Michel Rybalka and translated by Frank Jellinek. New York: Pantheon 1976.

———. *Les Troyennes: Adaptation de Jean-Paul Sartre*. Paris, Gallimard, 1965.

———. *Two Plays by Jean-Paul Sartre: No Exit and The Flies*. Translated by Stuart Gilbert. New York: Knopf, 1948.

Segal, Charles. *Sophocles' Tragic World: Divinity, Nature, Society*. Cambridge: Harvard University Press, 1995.

———. *Tragedy and Civilization: An Interpretation of Sophocles*. Cambridge: Harvard University Press, 1981.

Seneca. *Seneca, the Tragedies*. Edited by David R. Slavitt and Palmer Bovie. Vols. 1 and 2. Baltimore and London: Johns Hopkins University Press, 1992.

———. *Tragedies*. Vol. 8 and 9. Edited and translated by Frank Justus Miller. Loeb Classical Library. 1917. Reprint, Cambridge, London: Harvard University Press, 1987, 1998.

Shakespeare, William. *The Plays and Sonnets of William Shakespeare*. Edited by William George Clarke and William Aldis Wright. Vols. 1 and 2. Great Books of the Western World. Mortimer J. Adler, associate editor. Chicago, London, Toronto: Encyclopaedia Britannica, 1952.

Shechner, Richard, ed. *Dionysus in 69*. New York: Farrar, Straus and Giroux, 1970.

Shelley, Percy Bysshe. *The Poetical Works of Shelley*. Edited by Newell F. Ford. Boston: Houghton Mifflin, 1974.

Sophocles. *Antigone*. Edited, translated, and introduced by Marianne McDonald. London: Nick Hern Books, 2000. http://www.nickhern books.co.uk

———. *Oedipus Tyrannos, Oedipus at Kolonos, Antigone*. Translated by Timberlake Wertenbaker. First published in 1992 as *The Thebans*. Reprint, London: Faber and Faber, 1997.

———. *Plays and Fragments*. Edited and translated by Hugh Lloyd-Jones. 3 vols. Loeb Classical Series. 1994, 1996. Reprint, Cambridge, London: Harvard University Press, 1998.

Sorgenfrei, Carol. *Medea: A Noh Cycle Based on the Greek Myth*. New York: Samuel French, 1975.

Soyinka, Wole. *Collected Plays: A Dance of the Forests, The Swamp Dwellers, The Strong Breed, The Road, The Bacchae of Euripides: A Communion Rite*. Oxford: Oxford University Press, 1973.

Spender, Stephen. *Oedipus Trilogy: The Oedipus Trilogy of Sophocles, A Version*. New York: Random House, 1985.

Stanford, W. B. *Tragedy and the Emotions: An Introductory Study*. New York: Routledge and Kegan Paul, 1983.

Steiner, George. *Antigones: How the Antigone Legend Has Endured in Western Literature, Art, and Thought*. 1984. Reprint, New Haven: Yale University Press, 1996.

Tacitus. *Agricola*. Vol. 5. Loeb Series. Translated by M. Hutton and revised by R. M. Ogilvie. Cambridge: Harvard University Press, 1980.

Thucydides. *History of the Peloponnesian War.* Translated by Rex Warner, with an introduction and notes by M. I. Finley. New York: Penguin Books, 1972.

Triana, José. *Medea en el espejo (Medea in the Mirror); La noche de los asesinos; Palabras communes.* 2d ed. Madrid: Editorial Verbum, 1998.

Walton, J. Michael. *The Greek Sense of Theatre: Tragedy Reviewed.* 2d ed. Amsterdam: Harwood Academic Publishers, 1996.

———. *Greek Theatre Practice.* Westport, Conn.: Greenwood Press, 1980.

———. *Living Greek Theatre: A Handbook of Classical Performance and Modern Production.* New York: Greenwood Press, 1987.

Wilde, Oscar. *The Complete Works of Oscar Wilde: Stories, Plays, Poems and Essays.* Introduction by Vyvyan Holland. New York: Harper and Row, 1966.

Wilder, Thornton. *The Alcestiad, or A Life in the Sun.* New York: Samuel French, 1955.

Wiles, David. *Greek Theatre Performance: An Introduction.* Cambridge: Cambridge University Press, 2000.

Winnington-Ingram, R. P. *Sophocles: An Interpretation.* Cambridge: Cambridge University Press, 1980.

———. *Studies in Aeschylus.* Cambridge: Cambridge University Press, 1983.

Yeats, William Butler. *The Collected Plays of W. B. Yeats.* London: Macmillan, 1914.

———. *The Collected Works of W. B. Yeats, The Poems.* Vol. 1. Edited by Richard J. Finnernan. 2d ed. New York: Scribner, 1997.

———. *The Letters of W. B. Yeats.* Edited by A. Wade. London: Macmillan, 1954.

Zimmermann, B. *Greek Tragedy: An Introduction.* Translation by T. Marier. Baltimore: Johns Hopkins University, 1991.

It is recommended that http://www.amazon.com, http://www.annee-philologique. com/aph/ (*L'Année Philologique*), and http://homepage.mac.com/mariannemcdonald be consulted for references and book titles. For reviews and updates on productions, see http://www.didaskalia.net.

INDEX

Page numbers in italics refer to illustrations.

Marianne McDonald is Professor of Classics and Theatre at the University of California, San Diego, and a member of the Royal Irish Academy. With over 170 publications, she pioneered modern versions of the classics. Many of her translations and versions have been staged. Her books include *Euripides in Cinema: The Heart Made Visible; Ancient Sun, Modern Light: Greek Drama on the Modern Stage; Sing Sorrow: Classics, History, and Heroines in Opera;* and the forthcoming *Space, Time, and Silence: The Craft of Athol Fugard.* She has six children, five grandchildren, and a black belt in karate.
http://homepage.mac.com/mariannemcdonald